Study Guide

to accompany

Life-Span Development

Eighth Edition

John W. Santrock
University of Texas at Dallas

Prepared by
Anita Rosenfield
The DeVry Institute of Technology, Southern California

Boston   Burr Ridge, IL   Dubuque, IA   Madison, WI   New York   San Francisco   St. Louis
Bangkok   Bogotá   Caracas   Lisbon   London   Madrid
Mexico City   Milan   New Delhi   Seoul   Singapore   Sydney   Taipei   Toronto

McGraw-Hill Higher Education

A Division of The McGraw-Hill Companies

Study Guide to accompany
LIFE-SPAN DEVELOPMENT, EIGHTH EDITION
JOHN W. SANTROCK

Published by McGraw-Hill Higher Education, an imprint of The McGraw-Hill Companies, Inc.,
1221 Avenue of the Americas, New York, NY 10020. Copyright © The McGraw-Hill Companies,
Inc., 2002, 1999, 1997. All rights reserved.

This book is printed on acid-free paper.

1 2 3 4 5 6 7 8 9 0 QPD QPD 0 3 2 1

ISBN 0-07-241435-9

www.mhhe.com

Contents

A Letter to You, the Student

Dear Student,

I am writing this letter to you to offer some thoughts on how you can use this Study Guide to help you learn the material contained in *Life-Span Development, Eighth Edition*, by John W. Santrock. Although these ideas come from many years of being a student (**many years**) and a psychology professor, they are not particularly new, and you may already know many of them—but sometimes we need to be reminded about how helpful these tips can be. I hope you will find this Study Guide and my suggestions to be useful.

First and foremost, let me tell you that **the most effective way to use this material is to apply it to your life!** What my students tell me at the end of the semester are things like: "This course really helped me to understand the things I did as a teenager—now I have better insight about how to live a more productive life as an adult"; "By taking this class, I have come to terms with some things in my life. I am getting divorced and am now better able to prepare for this stage in my life. . . . I have also seen what went wrong in my marriage. . . . I can see where things went wrong and I can now try to work them out"; "Now, when I think about middle age and late adulthood, I feel I have something to look forward to rather than be afraid. I can go through these stages with open arms now"; "The most important thing I learned in this class is a better understanding of people of all ages. I understand my son's feisty temperament and deal with him much more effectively"; "I thought that some of the things my 2-year-old was doing were problem behaviors; now I see how they are typical of 2-year-olds and I can work with her more effectively. It's amazing how this has improved our relationship and **her** behavior."

This is just a sampling, but you can get the idea of how you, as a consumer of information, can use the information in the text and your class for your own life, whatever your major in college.

Now, let me tell you how the Study Guide is set up. The first section is **Learning Objectives**, a set of approximately ten to twelve statements of the ideas and material you should be able to understand after having read the chapter. You may wish to read the learning objectives **before** you read the chapter, so you can have an idea of what you're trying to learn as you read; then again, after having read the chapter, by going through the learning objectives you can see if you did, indeed, "get it all."

The second section is a **Chapter Outline**. This is intended to help you organize your thoughts and your reading and be able to anticipate what you will encounter in the corresponding chapter of the text, and to use the various sections of this Study Guide to be sure you have understood the material in each section of the chapter.

The third section is included so you can **self-test** to be sure you are understanding the material. This includes three relatively formal subsections for testing: multiple choice, matching, and essays. There is also a less traditional section (word scramblers) that is designed to provide you with a fun and helpful memory strategy for retaining information about important people and terms. **Self-Test A: Multiple Choice** is a set of approximately 35 multiple-choice questions covering the material in each chapter so you can be sure you are not only memorizing terms (Heaven forbid!), but are actually understanding the concepts contained in the text. There are many "applied" questions that require you to think about how these ideas would work if you were looking at real people (well, okay, in this case they are hypothetical, but use your imagination). In the answer key, you will discover that each question is keyed to one of the learning objectives. This allows you to pinpoint particular concepts you may find difficult to understand. **Self-Test B** contains a **Matching** set where you are asked to identify the perspective of important researchers.

The **Essay Questions** are designed to help you crystallize the many concepts contained in the chapter so that you can explain and apply what you have learned. In two or three questions, I tried to tie the material from the entire chapter together so you can see how all of the research, ideas, facts, and theories fit together. My answers to these questions are merely skeletal; should you choose to answer them, you will have to expand on what is there by drawing on the material in the chapter. To be honest with you, when I give essay questions in my own classes, I want my students to be able to put together information from more than one chapter to answer the questions fully—so you may want to think about how you could do that.

The **Word Scramblers** are designed to challenge you intellectually and encourage you to use a variety of cognitive modalities in deciphering key terms and people and providing either their definition or their area of expertise. The answers to all four of these self-test methods are included at the end of the self-test section.

In the next two sections, **Research Projects** and **Personal Application,** you will find suggested activities that will require you to search out more information about the material in the chapter, either by reviewing the literature, or through your own empirical investigations (i.e., doing research), or by actively applying what you have learned to your own life. The best way to learn the course material of any class is to use it, to think about its application to your own life. These activities will force you to do just that. You may ask your professor if you may choose one of these as a class project, or for extra credit, or just do them for the fun of it to see how they work. Go through all of the activities, from Chapter 1 through Chapter 21, in the beginning of the term because you may see one in later chapters that you might have wanted to work on through the term, and if you wait until the last week or two you may not have enough time to get it done.

The final group of sections may be new to some of you and part of your everyday life for others (or anything in between). These are the **Internet Projects.** Note that the introductory section refers you to the McGraw-Hill website for some great activities (http://www.mhhe.com/santrockld8). In addition to elements from this Study Guide, you will find **Flash Cards** for each chapter. Throughout my undergraduate, graduate, and doctoral studies my friends and I made our own flash cards because we found them to be so helpful. All key terms in the chapters are contained on the flash cards. Another interesting feature on the site is the **Crossword Puzzles**. Also to be found on the web site are a substantial amount of suggested journal articles, exercises from the text, and other **visual aids**.

In addition to the Santrock website, I have included two projects for each chapter that ask you to go beyond what is covered in our text. Finally, the **Internet Section** concludes with a compilation of many relevant web sites for each chapter. Please note that all website addresses in this Study Guide have been checked and are correct at the time of publication, however, websites may be discontinued or addresses may change so when you search a given site it may no longer be viable. If that occurs, I apologize for the inconvenience, and would appreciate you notifying me so I could make appropriate revisions in future editions of this Study Guide. We try to ensure that they are up-to-date, however, as technology and businesses are constantly changing, this is not always possible.

Okay, so that's the structure of the chapters in the Study Guide. Now, let's talk about effective ways to study. As I mentioned earlier, you may already know some of these ideas, but oftentimes they can bear repeating because you say to yourself, "Oh, yeah, I knew that. I tried it before and it worked, but then for some reason I stopped. I think I'll try it again." Other ideas may be new to you, so you may want to give them a try. Remember that we are all unique, so some strategies work better for some people than for others—try out a suggestion for a fair period of time (only you can decide what "fair" is), and if it works, great—if it doesn't, try something else.

BEING AN EXCELLENT STUDENT[1]

Most students who are in college want to be good students, and most students have some particular goal in mind, which is probably why they chose the particular college or university they are attending. As you chose your college or university, and perhaps even an area of major interest or concentration, you had certain goals in mind, which likely included doing well in school, earning good grades, and graduating.

Unfortunately, many students do not do as well in college as they had hoped and expected. Let's examine some of the reasons for this disappointing outcome to see how to avoid it and to learn, instead, how to be a good student and guide your behavior to improve your chances of achieving your goals.

A common definition of education is that it is "how people learn stuff." For most of our history, educators have focused on the "stuff." Teachers were required to be masters of their respective academic fields. Even today, some states have requirements that speak only to the need to be qualified in the subject matter one teaches, not in the teaching methods themselves.

In the 1960s, we became more interested in the "people" part of the definition, which was evidenced by moving to strategies like open classrooms and free universities. The idea was that, given the opportunity to do so, people will naturally learn. Although these experiments were dismal failures, they taught us something.

The key to the definition of education is the word "how." Today, thanks to a wealth of research on the principles that guide the phenomenon of learning, and on the nature of learning and memory, we know much more about **how** learning occurs and **how** we can make it better. By using these principles, we can become better students.

Formulating the Plan

Anything worth having is worth planning for. Whether you hope to learn to teach, to fly, to write for profit, or to change diapers correctly, you have in mind a goal. An everyday question from the first days in elementary school is, "What do you want to be when you grow up?" The answer to this question is one way of formulating a goal. Now that you are a college student, many people will expect you to know what you want to do for a profession or career. Yet you may not have the foggiest notion, or you might have an idea that is still slightly unclear. That is okay. What is clear, however, is that you want to succeed in your college courses. This is a relatively long-range goal, and as such can serve a purpose in keeping you on track.

But our day-to-day behavior is often hard to connect to our long-range goals. We need short-term goals to keep us organized and to be sure that the flow of our activities is in the direction we want to be going. To accomplish our long-range goals, we need to focus on three types of short-term goals. First, we need goals for the day; second, we need goals for the week; and third, we need goals for the semester or term. Let's look at each of these separately.

---

[1]Much of the information on "Being an Excellent Student," including formulating the plan, establishing goals, attending classes, benefitting from lectures, reading for learning, taking tests, and parts of the section on dealing with test anxiety have been adapted from the 6th edition of the Student Study Guide to accompany *Life Span Development* by John Santrock, which was prepared by Blaine Peden, John W. Santrock, and Allen Keniston. I would like to thank them for sharing those ideas with me for incorporation into this 8th edition of the Study Guide.

Goals for Today

It is helpful to keep a daily checklist, diary, or schedule as a reminder of what must be done each day. Check off the things as you accomplish them. A pocket calendar is particularly helpful for this task. After you complete your list, use numbers, asterisks (*), or letters to prioritize each item on the list and be sure that you put most of your effort into completing those that have the highest priority.

Goals for the Week

Students who are successful in college also schedule their time weekly. Sometime during the course of registration, you made up a schedule showing your classes for the whole week. If you have a job, you must allow time for that, too. Also, many college or university students have family obligations that need to be considered as well. Finally, everyone needs some time for relaxing, eating, sleeping, and playing (even in graduate school we were advised that we needed to find some time to have fun in order to keep our balance). With all these things in mind, it is no wonder many students find little time to study.

But good students do all these things, too, yet they study. Do they have more time? No, we all have the same amount of time. But successful students schedule their time carefully. So, make up a weekly schedule and block off time for all these necessary events: classes, work, relaxation, eating, sleeping, playing, family, errands, and studying. Students who actually schedule their time and keep to their schedules are amazed at how much time they find they have! Be sure to leave some blocks (10 to 20 minutes) that are **unscheduled** just to maintain some flexibility—sometimes emergencies arise and you need some slack in your schedule "just in case."

As you make up your weekly schedule, you may find your study time fits into a large block. If this is the case, please remember to take short breaks every 20 to 30 minutes. This is called distributed practice and is far more efficient than studying for hours on end. After the first 20 or 30 minutes, most of us become much less efficient anyway. When you take that break, reward yourself somehow, then go back to your studying. Something I always tell my students is never to try to read a whole chapter in one sitting–in fact, when I am preparing for a new class or have changed texts in a class I have been teaching, I take that advice myself!

By the way, a word many of us feel uncomfortable using is "No." Oftentimes when friends or family ask for help students give up important study time to accommodate the friend or family member (or feel so guilty about **not** doing so that their guilt interferes with concentration as they try to study). Most of the time when people ask for our help they could either get help from someone else (or become independent and do it themselves) or work with you to accomplish the activity during one of your free periods. Of course, if it's really an emergency, such as someone needs hospitalization, then by all means help; if it's not, you need to consider yourself and your education as high priorities. Some of us really need to feel we have "permission" to say "no" —so, I am giving you that permission!

Goals for the Semester

At the beginning of each semester, we find ourselves immersed in many new courses. Often, you will be confronted by several new professors with whom you have never worked before. It is difficult to sort out the expectations and demands of these several courses. However, it is important to organize the information that will be needed for completing all of the course requirements in order to be successful in the courses.

If you can, obtain a large wall calendar (available in any stationery store), and mark on it the dates of tests and exams, and term paper due dates, being sure to indicate the course for which each date applies. Now, estimate how long it will take you to make final preparations for those exams, and mark those dates as warning or alert dates. Look over the dates on which papers are due, and see if they are bunched together. If your college is typical, they will probably be close. You can help yourself to avoid the last-minute all-nighters if you simply determine a spread of due dates for yourself and mark those on the calendar, too. As you do this step, please be sure to avoid any days that have personal significance for you, such as birthdays, anniversaries, upcoming weddings you'll be attending, and so on. This calendar gives you an overview of major dates in your semester.

If you have followed this carefully, you now have a large semester calendar plastered on your wall, a weekly schedule of major life events, classes, and study times taped over your desk, and a daily checklist of must-do items in your pocket or purse. **So, your scheduling is on its way. Let's look now at other important strategies**.

Attending Classes

Many students believe that, because they are in college, they can decide whether to go to class at all. This is true. Some students also believe that attendance in class is not important to their grade. This is not true! Some colleges or universities have attendance requirements, so that if students miss a given number of classes it will either lower their grade a full letter grade, or the instructor may drop the student from the course; some instructors have in-class activities that count toward students' grades, so if students are not in class they do not get credit for participating. Even without such strategies, students who do not attend class sessions almost always do more poorly on the tests, quizzes, and exams. Perhaps they were absent when a crucial item was discussed, or when the instructor lectured over the material this examination required. Remember that more often than not, instructors will include information in their lectures that is not in your textbook, and the information (whether from class lecture, videos shown in class, guest lectures, and so on) is fair game for tests. Moreover, if you are not there, the instructor cannot get to know you, and therefore cannot give you the benefit of the doubt on your answers. It should come as no surprise that in study after research study, the data clearly show that those students who attend class regularly receive the highest grades and actually learn more, too! So, the first rule of being an effective student is to attend classes. Besides, how else can you get your money's worth?

Now that you've determined you will go to class, what else will you do?

Benefitting from Lectures

Sometimes students think that if they come to class and "pay attention" they will remember what the instructor talked about; they think that if they take notes, they will miss much of what the instructor says. But sitting and paying attention is difficult. For one thing, most people can think much faster than they can speak. While the instructor lectures at 80 words per minute, the student thinks at about 350 words per minute. If the student is using this extra "thinking capacity" to focus on what the instructor is saying, it is fine. This rarely lasts more than 5 minutes at a time, however. Most of the time, this extra "thinking capacity" is used in daydreaming.

Daydreaming can be helpful in resolving our emotional problems, planning the course of our lives, and avoiding work. Often, in fact, it is motivated by the desire to avoid work. For whatever motive, however, daydreaming is not compatible with attending a lecture. Human beings simply cannot attend to more than one stimulus at a time. And you have to admit that oftentimes your daydreams can be ever so much more interesting than your professor's lectures.

Benefitting from lectures is best achieved by taking notes. Use plenty of paper and leave blank lines at regular intervals, or leave wide side margins. You will use these spaces later (they are not wasted!). If the instructor permits it, be brave and interrupt with questions if you do not understand what is being said. One thing I try to stress to my students is that I may know what I am talking about, but it may be unclear to them—and if it's unclear to one student, it may well be unclear to other students. So, for the sake of the other students who didn't understand what I was talking about, each student should take on the responsibility of asking me to clarify what I said, or to expand in a way that will help them understand. Remember that lectures have a way of progressing and building on earlier information. It is important to understand each point, or later points will be lost. (But please, DO NOT ask the person sitting next to you what the professor said—it disrupts the class, disturbs the professor, and you are likely NOT to get an accurate response!)

When you take notes, write out the major points and try to make simple notations for the supporting minor points. If you miss something and you cannot ask a question about it, approach the instructor immediately afterward when it is still likely to be fresh in both your minds. DO NOT try to write down every word, and DO try to use abbreviations or symbols (the Greek symbols Ψ and Φ are a lot shorter to write than the words "psychology" and "physiology"; using typographic symbols, such as $<$ and $>$ are much shorter than writing out "less than" and "greater than"); or, you could do what I did––learn shorthand (or make up your own).

Often my students will ask if they may tape my lectures. Personally, I have no objection to this practice, although some professors do. Having returned to college after a 16-year break, I taped my psychology classes (somehow German didn't seem conducive to being tape recorded). It was so tedious transcribing the tapes, though, that I didn't do it after that first quarter. The students for whom taping may be particularly helpful are those who have visual, auditory, or motor impairments. However, do not ever tape record a lecture without first asking for and obtaining the professor's permission.

Within 1 or 2 hours after the lecture, on the same day, go back over your notes and do two things. First, fill in the rest of the minor points. This often amounts to completing the sentence or other element. Second, write brief summaries and any questions that you now have in the blank spaces (lines or margins) you left earlier (clever of you to leave those spaces). These few minutes spent reviewing and organizing your notes will pay off in greatly improved memory. The questions you have you can ask in class, or during the instructor's office hours, and reap two benefits. First, you will get the answers; second, you will demonstrate that you are a serious student, which will impress your instructor.

One other thing about going to class. While this is not always true, I have found that typically my best students sit in front. And most students seem to have a need to have "their seat," while a few students have a need to move around, sitting in one seat one day and a different seat the next. It wasn't until my graduate school days that I realized why I needed "my seat"—as a student, we are constantly being overwhelmed with new information, a stressful experience; we need some structure we can count on to reduce that stress. So, if you are one of those who likes to wander, be considerate of your classmates' needs for stress reduction.

By the way, to get the most out of the lectures, do complete the assigned reading BEFORE the class begins so you are familiar with the material. This will help you keep up with what the instructor is talking about, will reduce the amount of information you do not understand, but may also bring up important questions for you to ask in class if the instructor does not talk about them.

Reading for Learning

We all know **how** to read. You are proving it by reading these words. Hopefully, you are also realizing some ideas as a result of reading. If you are only reading words, please WAKE UP! STOP DAYDREAMING!

We can read a variety of things: newspapers, movie reviews, novels, magazines, and textbooks. Textbooks are unlike all the others and must be read with a strategy all their own.

There are many reading and studying strategies, and all of them work to an extent. Perhaps you learned one or more in the course of going to high school. Perhaps you even took a how-to-study course when you entered college. If so, you probably learned one or two of these systems. If you have one you like that works for you, keep it. If you are interested in learning a new one, read on.

The PQ4R Method

One of the most successful and most widely used methods of studying written material was the SQ3R method, which was first developed at the Ohio State University. Researchers had noted that students who were more successful were more active readers. More recently, this method has been updated to the PQ4R method, which adds an additional step. This method teaches you the same skills that have made many thousands of students successful. If you use this method when you read and study, you will be more successful, too. I have outlined the steps below.

The P stands for PREVIEW. After you have read the overview or chapter outline and the list of learning objectives, you should survey (preview) the chapter in the text. This is also called skimming. Look at the headings and subheadings, and get the gist of the major points in the chapter. Check off each point in the outline of this Study Guide as you pass it in the pages of the text.

The Q stands for QUESTION. Reading is greatly enhanced if you are searching for the answers to questions. For this text, the Study Guide provides learning objectives that can serve as questions. For other texts, make up questions for yourself that are based on the chapter overview or on your own survey of the chapter. Be sure that you have at least one question for each major unit in the chapter; you will be less efficient at studying those units for which you do not have questions.

The first of the four Rs is for READ. As you read, look for the answers to the questions you posed, or to the study or learning objectives furnished for you. When you find material that answers these questions, put a mark (X) or a "post-it" note in the margin next to that material. This will help now, as you are actively involved, and later, when you review. It is a good idea to wait to underline or highlight lines of text until after you have read the entire chapter at least once, so you will know what is and what is not most important. (In fact, while some "authorities" suggest you underline or highlight no more than 10 percent of what you are reading, I find that when most of us begin to underline or highlight, we wind up doing it to most of the chapter–I suggest not doing it at all because it becomes too passive, which counteracts your attempts to read actively.)

The second R stands for REFLECT. As you are reading, stop every so often and reflect on the material to increase its meaningfulness. This includes analyzing the material, thinking about how to apply it to your own life, interpreting the information, and connecting it with information you already have in your long-term memory.

The third R is for RECITE. One of the oldest classroom techniques in the world (Aristotle used it) is recitation. In the classroom version, the teacher asks the questions and the students answer them. Unless you can get your instructor to study with you regularly, you'll have to play both roles. Periodically, stop in your reading and say aloud (if possible) what the author is telling you. Try to put it in your own words, but be sure to use technical terms as you learn them. If you are not in a situation where you can recite out loud, do it in writing. Just thinking it is not enough. When should you pause to recite? A good rule of thumb is that each time you come to the end of a major subheading, you should recite. One professor encourages his students to recite at least one sentence at the end of each paragraph, and two or three or more sentences at the end of each subunit (when you come to a new heading).

People who do not use recitation usually forget half of what they read after 1 hour, and another half of the half they remembered by the end of the day. People who use recitation often remember from 75 to 90 percent of what they studied. This technique pays off. By the way, if anyone questions why you are talking to yourself, tell them that a psychologist recommended it.

The fourth R is for REVIEW. You should review a chapter soon after you have studied it (using the PQ and the first 3 Rs). You should review it again the day or evening before the test. It is not usually helpful to cram the night before a test, and particularly not the day of the test. That type of studying does not produce good memory and is likely to make you more anxious during the test itself, which brings us to our next topic.

Taking Tests

One of the things students fear most is failure. Failure signifies that things are not going well and alerts us to the possibility that we may not achieve our goals. Unfortunately, many students see tests and exams as opportunities to fail, rather than as opportunities to shine. They prepare by becoming anxious and fearful, and by trying to cram as much as possible right before the exam. These students rarely do well on the exam. They often fail, thus accomplishing just what they feared.

Taking tests requires strategy and planning. First, it is helpful to know what type of test you will have. Your instructor probably told you during the first class meeting, or it may be in the class syllabus or course outline. If you do not know, ask.

If you are going to be taking essay exams, the best way to prepare is by writing essays. Before you do this, it is a good idea to find out what types of questions the instructor asks and what is expected in a response. Again, it is helpful to ask the instructor for this information. Perhaps you can even see some examples of essay questions from previous years—some instructors at some colleges have copies of their exams on file in the department office or in the library. By finding out what is expected, you can formulate a model against which you can evaluate your answers.

Now, using the learning objectives, or some essay questions you wrote, actually sit down and write out the answers. I have prepared at least two essay questions for each chapter in this Study Guide. HINT: If you usually feel more anxious during a test, it may help you to practice writing your essays in the room in which the test will be given. Simply find a time when the room is vacant, then make yourself at home.

If your instructor gives multiple-choice tests, then you should practice taking multiple choice tests. For each chapter, either use questions provided in the Study Guide, or make up your own. You may find it helpful to work out an arrangement to pool questions with other students, thereby reducing the amount of work you have to do, and developing a network of friends. Or, you may ask your professor if he or she would entertain the idea of having students write some of the exam questions—some of my professors did that in my undergraduate classes, and it is something I sometimes have my students do.

Whichever way you do it, the important thing is to prepare for tests and exams. Preparation is about 95 percent of the secret to getting a good grade. (Yes, there is some actual luck or chance involved in test scores, as even your instructor will admit!). Preparation is not only a good study and review technique, but also helps to reduce anxiety.

Dealing with Test Anxiety

Anxiety can be a helpful response when it occurs at low levels. In 1908, Yerkes and Dodson showed that the amount of anxiety that could benefit performance was a function of the difficulty and complexity of the task. As the difficulty of the task rose, anxiety became less helpful and more likely to interfere with performance.

If you have ever been so anxious in a test situation that you were unable to do well, even though you knew the information, you have test anxiety. If you get your exams back and are surprised that you marked wrong answers when you knew the correct answers, or if you can only remember the correct answers after you leave the examination room, you, too, may have test anxiety.

Strategy Number 1: Effective Study

Use study habits that promote learning and make the best use of time. Strategies, such as scheduling your time and using the PQ4R method, reduce anxiety by increasing confidence. As you come to realize that you know the material, your confidence rises and anxiety retreats.

Strategy Number 2: Relaxation

Each of us develops a unique pattern of relaxation. Some people relax by going to a specific place, either in person or mentally. Others relax by playing music, by being with friends, by using autogenic relaxation phrases, or by meditating. Whatever you do, be aware of it and try to practice relaxation techniques. If you are good at relaxing, try thinking about those situations that make you anxious, and relax while you think of them. To do this, allow yourself to think only briefly (15 to 30 seconds at a time) of the situation that makes you anxious, and then relax again. After a number of such pairings, you will find that thinking about that situation no longer makes you anxious. At this point, you may be surprised to find that the situation itself also no longer produces anxiety. You may find that it is helpful to think about these anxiety-provoking situations in a sequence from those that produce very little anxiety to those that are more anxiety-evoking. Such a list, from low to high anxiety, might look something like this:

1. Your instructor announces that there will be a test in 4 weeks.
2. Your instructor reminds you of the test next week.
3. As you study, you see on the course outline the word "test," and remember next week's test.
4. One of your friends asks you if you want to study together for the test, which is the day after tomorrow.
5. You choose not to go out with your friends because of the test tomorrow.
6. As you get up in the morning, you remember that today is the day of the test.
7. You are walking down the hall toward the classroom, thinking about what questions might be on the test.
8. The instructor enters the classroom carrying a sheaf of papers in hand.
9. The instructor distributes the papers and you see the word "test" or "exam" at the top.
10. After reading the first five questions, you have not been able to think of the answer to any of them.

If you work at it gradually and consistently, pairing these types of thoughts (briefly) with relaxation and remembering to let go and relax after each one, this will dispel test anxiety and make test taking a more productive and successful experience.

Strategy Number 3: Thinking Clearly

Most students who have test anxiety think in unclear and unproductive ways. They say to themselves things like: "I can't get these answers correct . . . . I don't know this stuff. . . . I don't know anything at all. . . . I'm going to fail this test. . . . I'm probably going to flunk out of school. . . . I'm just a dumb nerd." These thoughts share two unfortunate characteristics: they are negative and they are absolute. They should be replaced.

When we tell ourselves negative and absolute thoughts, we find it impossible to focus on the test material. The result is that we miss questions even when we know the answers. Our thinking prevents us from doing well.

A good strategy for replacing these negative and absolute thoughts is to practice thinking positive and honest thoughts, such as, "I may not know all of the answers, but I know some of them. . . . I don't know the answer to that right now, so I will go on to the next one and come back to that. . . . I don't have to get them all right. . . . I studied hard and carefully, and I can get some of them correct. . . . I am a serious student and have some abilities. . . . Hmm. This is a hard question, so I'll skip it, come back, and look for any clues in other questions that might help me answer this one. . . . I am prepared for this test and know many of the answers. . . . This test is important, but it is not going to determine the course of my entire life, and if I don't do well it doesn't mean I'm a horrible person or a dummy."

By thinking clearly, honestly, and positively, we quiet the flood of anxiety and focus on the task at hand. Students who use this technique invariably do better on the tests. It takes practice to think clearly, but it is worth the effort. After a while, you will find that it becomes natural and does not take any noticeable effort. And as anxiety is reduced, more energy is available for studying and doing well on examinations. The eventual outcome is more enjoyment with learning, better learning, more success in college, and the achievement of your goals.

Strategy Number 4: Guided Imagery

Something I often do with my students before a test is to have them relax (see Strategy 2), close their eyes, and visualize themselves walking into a tall building. They go into the elevator in the building and take it to the top floor, which is 56 stories up. They walk out of the elevator and go to the stairwell, then climb to the top of the building. There is no railing on top of the building. I direct them to walk over to the very edge of the building and put their toes at the very edge, then look down. I ask them to pay attention to how they are feeling—physically and emotionally—as they are looking down onto the street from the top of this building. I then instruct them to back up away from the edge, take a deep breath, and have the realization that they can fly–just spread out their arms and they can fly. Then they are directed back to the edge of the building, knowing that they can fly. Again they put their toes on the edge, look down, then spread their arms and fly, eventually floating down to land safely on the ground below. Next I have them visualize themselves in the classroom; on the desk before them is their test. They look at the test and see themselves reading the questions, saying, "I know the answer. Yes, I remember learning that." They visualize themselves being successful, answering all the questions correctly, feeling good about themselves. Then I have them visualize getting their tests back with a big "A" staring them in the face.

Some students are much better able to visualize than others. You can try combining strategy 2 with this strategy to help you improve your visualization, as it can be an effective success strategy.

As an aside, after the guided relaxation, I remind my students they really **can't** fly, so please don't try!

Strategy Number 5: Do the Easy Ones First

One technique I learned while studying for the GRE (Graduate Record Exam) was to read each question, answer the ones I knew, then go back to the harder ones. Two things to watch out for on this: first, be sure you get the answers in the right place—sometimes when we skip a question or two, we wind up marking the wrong space, so check that your answer to question 10 is in space 10; second, you may find you're stumped by the first several questions—don't let that throw you, just keep going because there is bound to be one you jump on and say, "Yes! I know that one!" Answer the easy ones first, then go back to the others after you've built up your confidence seeing you DO know "stuff." Then, always go back over the whole test to be sure you answered every question (the exception here is if you have a professor who takes more than one point off for wrong answers—in that case, it's better not to answer than to answer wrong, but I don't know anyone who does that).

Strategy Number 6: State Dependent Learning

Research has found that we remember information best when we are in the same "state" we were in when we first learned the information. So, for example, you might remember a certain song when prompted by a specific stimulus (seeing someone who reminds you of your "first true love"); or, we will remember things we learned when we were particularly happy if we are again in that mood. This goes for physical contexts as well—so that we have an advantage if we take an exam in the same room where we learned the information in the first place (though we have little control over this because exams may be scheduled in a room that was not our classroom). This also goes to physical context in terms of our bodies—if you drink coffee or caffeine-laden sodas when you study, try to do the same before your exam. On the other hand, if you don't consume caffeine when you study, by all means, DO NOT suddenly have a cup of coffee before your exam. Because of the power of this phenomenon, you may want to create a particular mental context for yourself when you study so that you can put yourself into the same mental context when you take your exams.

Strategy Number 7: Take a Break

If you find yourself getting stressed out during the test, take a break. Put your pencil down, breathe deeply, you may even want to put your head down on the desk (please, do not fall asleep). Use the relaxation techniques or the guided imagery strategy; visualize yourself looking at the test and suddenly realizing that you DO know the answers to at least most of the questions. Then go back to taking the test.

Remember that with all of these test taking strategies, if you don't do the first one, none of the others will help. Passing the course requires that you actively study the material!

Memory Techniques

No matter how much you read, it won't help you if you don't remember **what** you read. The most critical factor in remembering is being able to apply what you have learned. Of course, some things, such as people's names or certain dates or statistical information, are not easily applied to your life, so you'll have to use other techniques for that information. But first, let's talk about the "easy way."

Apply It to Your Life

If you can take the material you are learning and use it in your everyday life, you will remember it without any problem. If you have a 2-year-old child, then you read what Piaget said about how 2-year-olds think, or what Erikson said about the need for children to gain a sense of autonomy over their bodies, or what the information processing theorists say about how much a 2-year-old can remember, you can see how (and if) these theories apply to your child. Of course, not everyone has a 2-year-old child, but we all were 2 years old at some point in our lives, or we may know children who are that age. Watch children, see how the theories work by observing what these children do. The same goes for observing infants, teenagers, adults—and particularly yourself!

Another method of applying the material to your life is to connect it with what you already know, either from life experience or other courses you have taken. Sometimes what you are learning fits nicely with what you already know, sometimes it will contradict what you learned before, and sometimes it appears to be brand new. This is an opportunity for you to look at how the new information fits in with the old—were there new research findings? or, is it merely a difference of opinion? Make these associations—don't keep the information for any class neatly compartmentalized—if you do, you'll have a hard time trying to find it when you need it.

Teach It to Someone Else

When we start teaching something to someone else, we find we HAVE TO learn it, and by trying to explain the material to another person, we examine it and think about it differently. So, take the material you are learning in this class (or any class) and teach it to someone else. When they ask you questions, you can look them up and find the answers, or think them out together, or ask someone else. As you explain these concepts to someone else (your children, your friends, or even your dog or cat), you will suddenly see them in a totally different light.

Mnemonic Techniques

Some things are just really difficult to apply to your own life. Dates, names, places, statistics, and such may not have a great deal of meaning for you. In that event, use the tricks that memory specialists use—mnemonics. There are many different types. For example, one famous mnemonic is an acronym for remembering the Great Lakes: HOMES=Huron, Ontario, Michigan, Erie, and Superior; the colors of the spectrum is someone's name: ROY G. BIV=red, orange, yellow, green, blue, indigo, and violet (if not for this fictitious man I'd never remember indigo). You can make up your own acronyms by taking the first initial of any term, person, etc. It's easiest, though, if it's something that makes sense to you.

Another mnemonic technique is called the "method of loci," and I've been told it's the method medical students use to remember body parts. You list the things you need to remember, then visualize yourself walking around a familiar place (like your living room), putting one item on a particular piece of furniture, another item on the next piece, etc. Then when you need to remember those items, you go through your "living room" to see where each one is. Say, for example, you need to remember the theorists in Chapter 2 of this text. You might put Piaget on the piano, Freud on the sofa, Skinner in the television (i.e., a "box"), and so on. (They don't have to be on the object that starts with their name, although that might be an additional mnemonic technique; or you might put them on objects that you associate with their work.) Since you also need to associate the theorists with their theories, you might imagine Piaget is thinking about how to play the piano; Freud has hidden unacceptable thoughts under the sofa; Skinner has been reinforced for sitting so nicely in front of the television, etc.

One other mnemonic technique is the story method. Take the information you need to remember and put it into a story. So, you may make up a story about how Piaget came up with his four stages of development (because he relied so heavily on his own three children, you might want to incorporate them into the story, but it's your story—do it the way you want).

There are many other mnemonic techniques—you might want to check out a book on memory strategies from the library to find some that will work well for you.

Be an "Information Dropper"

This is similar to the suggestion to teach, but less formal. Ask your friends to "indulge" you by listening to what you learned in your life-span development class (or any other class). Then **tell** them what you are learning. You may, in fact, find that you have managed to help one of your friends by sharing this information —wouldn't that be a nice feeling!

Rote Memory

If you can remember back to grade school, when you learned to multiply, somehow the only way that seems to happen is by repeating the multiplication tables over and over and over again. Personally, I think this is about the worst way to learn most anything, but for some things (like multiplication tables) it works. The Flash Cards that are available on the McGraw-Hill website for the text (http://www.mhhe.com/santrock ld8) are a way to help you learn through repeating the material you don't know. Hopefully you will then go further and apply the information to other areas of your life.

Most Important

Remember this: professors don't actually "teach" their students. Rather, they facilitate learning so students end up teaching themselves. While we try really hard to motivate our students, keep them interested, and present information in a way that helps students to understand, the ultimate responsibility for learning rests with the student. Some students have learned **despite** their professors, others don't learn even with the very best of professors. So, keep your goals in mind, study hard, ask questions, and aim for success.

If you have thoughts you'd like to share with me—or other ideas for how to study and learn, things that worked for you or didn't work for you—you may reach me through my e-mail address: arosenfield@eee.org.

With good thoughts for your continued success,

Anita Rosenfield, Ph.D.

Two Important Notes About Getting Permission

In each chapter of this Study Guide you will find suggested Research Activities. Some of these involve working with children, many involve requesting participation by persons (children, adolescents, and/or adults) who are not members of your Life-Span Development class. Whenever you work with persons under the age of 18, you should obtain written permission from a parent or guardian (even if that is not specifically mentioned in the particular Research Activity); also, **always** ask the person assisting you if he or she is willing to help you with your project, despite that person's age. (A sample form is included below.) If the parent, guardian, or participant indicates a reluctance to participate, thank them anyway and move on to someone else. If, at any point during the project, participants indicate a desire to discontinue participation, stop immediately and thank them for their help up to that point. Participation in research is **always** voluntary; no one should ever be coerced into involvement and, once having begun, participants **always** have the right to discontinue their participation should they so desire.

Further, each institution (college, university, etc.) has its own standards for conducting research. Before engaging in any of the suggested Research Activities, check with your instructor to determine whether you need to obtain approval from your school's Institutional Review Board (IRB). If approval is necessary, be sure to plan sufficient time for completing your project that includes time for getting your proposal reviewed.

SAMPLE CONSENT FORM

Life-Span Development - Psychology _____

In partial fulfillment of the requirements of this course, I will need to [**fill in what you will need to do, for example**: *observe a child who is between five and ten years of age. I will need to have this child perform three tasks and answer questions about_____. During the observations I will assess the child's ability to complete various tasks, including:*
- *Discussing whether various items (such as a car or an egg) are alive*
- *Telling me if the child thinks certain shapes look like boys or girls]*

I will compile a summary report based on these observations, and I will submit this report to my Psychology Professor, _____. In my report, I will include information about the child's age and gender, but I will not disclose the child's identity. The child' performance on these tasks cannot be used to speculate about the child's potential, and I will make no speculations about the child based on these observations. I will read the above statements to the parents of the child I will observe.

_____   _____
Date   Student's Signature

The above statements were read to me. I understand   _____ / _____
that my child will be observed in the manner described.   Child's Name   Age
I agree to allow my child to participate in these
observations. I understand that I can withdraw this   _____
agreement at any time. If I have any further questions,   Parent's Name Printed
I understand that I may contact _____,
Professor of Psychology at _____   _____ _____
(Phone #: _____).   Parent's Signature   Date

Chapter 1: Introduction

Learning Objectives

1. Explain the importance of studying life-span development.
2. Describe the history of interest in children and adolescents and indicate how contemporary concerns have arisen from previous views.
3. Describe the seven basic characteristics of the life-span perspective.
4. List and describe the three interacting systems of contextualism.
5. Describe the role that experts in developmental psychology have regarding health and well-being, parenting and education, sociocultural contexts, and social policy.
6. Define and distinguish between biological processes, cognitive processes, and socioemotional processes.
7. Understand the major developmental periods from conception to death.
8. Define and distinguish between chronological age, biological age, psychological age, and social age.
9. Understand the three major developmental issues (nature and nurture, continuity and discontinuity, stability and change).
10. Identify several options that are available to individuals who are interested in careers in life-span development.

Chapter Outline

THE LIFE-SPAN PERSPECTIVE
    Why Study Life-Span Development?
    The Historical Perspective
        Child Development
        Life-Span Development
        The Twentieth Century
    Characteristics of the Life-Span Perspective
        Development Is Lifelong
        Development Is Multidimensional
        Development Is Multidirectional
        Development Is Plastic
        Development Is Contextual
        Development Is Studied by a Number of Disciplines
        Development Involves Growth, Maintenance, and Regulation
    Some Contemporary Concerns
        Health and Well-Being
        Parenting and Education
        Sociocultural Contexts
        Social Policy
THE NATURE OF DEVELOPMENT
    Biological, Cognitive, and Socioemotional Processes
    Periods of Development
        Prenatal Period
        Infancy
        Early Childhood
        Middle and Late Childhood
        Adolescence

Self-Test A: Multiple Choice

1. Which of the following is NOT a reason the text gave to study life-span development?
   a. The more you learn about children, the better you can deal with them.
   b. You may gain insight into your own history.
   c. It is a requirement for such fields as nursing, psychology, and child development.
   d. As a parent or teacher, you may have responsibility for children.

2. In thinking about the importance of studying life-span development, research has found:
   a. massage therapy decreases the immune system functioning of preterm infants.
   b. secure attachment to parents in adolescence is linked with a host of negative outcomes.
   c. researchers have been able to extend the life span of human cells in human subjects.
   d. extending the life span of human cells in a test tube has implications for expanding human life.

3. Parents who believe their children are basically good and need little discipline have adopted which philosophical view?
   a. original sin
   b. *tabula rasa*
   c. innate goodness
   d. experiential

4. Parents adhering to the fundamental premise of Jean-Jacques Rousseau's "innate goodness" argument would:
   a. reject the need to "teach" language since speech is inherited.
   b. provide their children with little monitoring or constraints.
   c. view their child as intellectually indistinguishable from themselves.
   d. argue that their newborn's brain is like a "blank slate."

2

5. Today, childhood is conceived of as:
   a. a unique period of life that lays an important foundation for the adult years and is highly differentiated from them.
   b. a period when children are like balls of clay ready to be molded.
   c. an inconvenient waiting period during which adults must suffer the incompetencies of their young.
   d. a unique period of life when adults must use caution to be sure they elicit the good from their children and suppress the evil.

6. The traditional approach to development emphasizes:
   a. little change from birth through old age.
   b. extensive change from birth to adolescence, adulthood, and old age.
   c. extensive change from birth to adulthood, then little change for the rest of the life span.
   d. extensive change from birth to adolescence, little or no change in adulthood, then decline in late old age.

7. In the twentieth century:
   a. life expectancy has increased by 30 years.
   b. life expectancy has increased by 25 years.
   c. life span has increased by 30 years.
   d. life span has increased by 25 years.

8. The maximum life span of humans since the beginning of recorded history has:
   a. increased.
   b. almost caught up with that of the Galapagos turtles.
   c. decreased.
   d. remained the same.

9. As the older population continues to increase in the twenty-first century, concerns are raised about the number of older adults who will be:
   a. living in poverty.
   b. a financial drain on society.
   c. able to care for themselves.
   d. without either a spouse or children.

10. According to Baltes (1987), the life-span perspective has the following characteristics EXCEPT being:
    a. lifelong.
    b. unidirectional.
    c. multidimensional.
    d. plastic.

11. Many older persons become wiser with age, yet perform more poorly on cognitive speed tests. This supports the life-span perspective notion that development is:
    a. multidirectional.
    b. multidimensional.
    c. lifelong.
    d. plastic.

12. In the _____ view, individuals are thought of as changing beings in a changing world.
    a. plastic
    b. sociocultural
    c. contextual
    d. cognitive

13. The onset of puberty is an example of:
    a. normative age-graded influences.
    b. normative history-graded influences.
    c. nonnormative life events.
    d. storm-and-stress events.

14. The AIDS epidemic in the United States would be an example of a:
    a. normative age-graded influence.
    b. normative history-graded influence.
    c. nonnormative life event.
    d. storm-and-stress event.

15. Concerns for health and well-being have:
    a. been important goals for most of human history.
    b. become important goals since the great advances in medicine in the nineteenth century.
    c. become important goals with the discovery of penicillin.
    d. yet to become goals of major importance.

16. The main interests of Luis Varga are:
    a. gerontology and development of the life-span perspective.
    b. cultural issues and the assessment and treatment of children, adolescents, and families.
    c. ending spousal abuse and establishing shelters for abused women and children.
    d. age and happiness in adolescence and adulthood.

17. The behavior patterns, beliefs, and all other products of a particular group that are passed on from generation to generation are called:
    a. nationality.
    b. religion.
    c. culture.
    d. ethnicity.

18. A national government's course of action designed to influence the welfare of its citizens is called:
    a. social policy.
    b. social slate.
    c. national policy.
    d. policy agenda.

19. Marian Wright Edelman, president of the Children's Defense Fund, states that with respect to how well children are treated in industrialized nations, the United States:
    a. is the highest ranking.
    b. ranks among the highest.
    c. ranks around the middle.
    d. is at or near the lowest ranking.

20. With respect to women's experience of violence it occurs:
    a. around the world.
    b. most frequently in industrialized countries.
    c. most often in third world countries.
    d. least often in technologically advanced countries.

21. The concept of generational inequity describes:
    a. the situation in which older individuals receive more of the resources than younger individuals.
    b. differences in values, and is commonly called the "generation gap."
    c. differences in years of education between older, less educated individuals and younger, better educated individuals.
    d. family power patterns in which older individuals typically have more decision-making power.

22. Development is defined as the pattern of movement or _____ across the life span.
    a. growth
    b. change
    c. decline
    d. stability

23. Which of the following would involve a cognitive process?
    a. hormonal changes at puberty
    b. an infant responding to her mother's touch with a smile
    c. an elderly couple's affection for each other
    d. putting together a two-word sentence

24. What is true concerning the biological, cognitive, and socioemotional processes?
    a. Each is distinct from the others.
    b. The cognitive and socioemotional are more closely related than the cognitive and biological.
    c. They are intricately interwoven.
    d. They are more obvious in the early years of life.

25. Penny is just beginning to use language and other symbols. If she is developing normally, we would expect her to be in which developmental period?
    a. perinatal
    b. prenatal
    c. infancy
    d. early childhood

26. _____ typically marks the end of the early childhood period of development.
    a. Walking without assistance
    b. The emergence of the first word
    c. First grade
    d. The onset of puberty

27. Which period of development is characterized by establishing independence, developing an identity, and thinking more abstractly?
    a. middle childhood
    b. late childhood
    c. adolescence
    d. early adulthood

28. Bernice Neugarten has emphasized reemerging life themes in development. Her observations have led her to conclude that:
    a. life stages are important for understanding development.
    b. each person relives his or her childhood during later development.
    c. we must focus on the later developmental periods.
    d. age is becoming less important for understanding development.

29. Rozee is 86 years young. She continues to learn phrases in new languages, she writes poetry, and she enjoys going to museums to see the latest up-and-coming artists. These examples of her adaptive capacities demonstrate:
    a. chronological age.
    b. biological age.
    c. psychological age.
    d. social age.

30. Researchers who are proponents of the nurture perspective would argue that:
    a. genetics determines all behavior.
    b. the environment a person is raised in determines that individual's longevity.
    c. how long an individual's parents lived is the best predictor of that individual's longevity.
    d. genetics and the environment in which an individual is raised will jointly determine that person's longevity.

31. In studying changes in the way we think as we age, Dr. Long notes a child moves from not being able to think abstractly about the world to being able to, which is a qualitative change in processing information. Dr. Long emphasizes:
    a. continuity.
    b. discontinuity.
    c. stability.
    d. maturation.

32. An important dimension of the _____ issue is the extent to which early experiences or later experiences are the key determinants of a person's development.
    a. stability-change
    b. nature-nurture
    c. continuity-discontinuity
    d. multidimensional

33. Most life-span developmentalists recognize that:
    a. nature, continuity, and stability are the primary determinants of behavior.
    b. nurture, discontinuity, and change are the primary determinants of behavior.
    c. the key to development is in the interaction of nature and nurture, continuity and discontinuity, and stability and change.
    d. while nurture (the environment) is important, nature (heredity) plays the stronger role.

34. The answers to questions about the issues of nature-nurture, continuity-discontinuity, and stability-change:
   a. influence public policy decisions and how people live their lives.
   b. have little influence on public policy decisions, but do influence how people live their lives.
   c. influence public policy decisions, but have little influence on how people live their lives.
   d. are primarily concerns for psychologists, but end up having little impact in policy or people's lifestyle choices.

35. Jennifer has been working with the elderly for many years diagnosing their medical problems, evaluating treatment options, and making recommendations for nursing care or other arrangements. Jennifer is most likely a:
   a. gerontologist.
   b. geriatric physician.
   c. geriatric nurse.
   d. geropsychologist.

Self-Test B: Matching

Match the following persons with the statement or theory that most closely reflects their perspective:

1. Marian Wright Edelman
2. John Locke
3. Jean-Jacques Rousseau
4. Bernice Neugarten
5. Paul Baltes
6. Jerome Kagan
7. K. Warner Schaie

a. The life-span perspective has seven fundamental contentions
b. Children are innately good
c. Suggests both early and later life experiences contribute to development
d. Children are like blank slates and grow through experience
e. Helped create the life-span perspective
f. The U.S. ranks very low in the treatment of children
g. Our society is increasingly age-irrelevant

Essay Questions

1. At a family gathering one evening, one of your uncles says he has heard you are taking a course in life-span development. He scoffs at this course saying, "What a waste of time! Everyone knows that children are basically mindless creatures until they get to be around six years old. Then they change into monsters as they become teenagers, but once they're adults they become human and nothing changes until they get old and senile. So, why bother studying life-span development?" Bring your uncle up to date on today's life-span perspective, being sure to include in your response Baltes' seven factors of development (and any others you consider relevant).

2. The "nature-nurture controversy" has been around for a long time. At coffee in the cafeteria, you get into a discussion about this with two of your friends. One of them stubbornly states that nature is the only thing that matters; the other one just as stubbornly argues that nurture is the only thing that is important in terms of who we are, how we develop, and what our lives will be like. Knowing you are taking this class in life-span development, they turn to you to tell them who is right. Discuss this issue with them, being sure to incorporate into your answer all you know about the biological, cognitive, and socioemotional processes.

Scramblers

Unscramble the following people or terms, then describe what they are known for (people) or define them (terms):

1. **IIGLNROA NIS**

   ORiGinal SiN - advocated during middle ages - children perceived as being basically bad

2. **FEIL-NASP CEEVPRESTIP**

   Life-span Perspective - Development is lifelong, multidemensional, multidirectional, plastic, contextual, multidisciplinary, and involves growth, maintenance + regulation.

3. **YEICTHTNI**

   Ethnicity- Based on cultural heritage, nationality characterities, race, religion + language

4. **DRENEG**

   Gender- The socioculture dimension of being female or male

5. **VICGOINTE ESCRPOSSE**

   Cognitive processes - Changes in the individual's thoughts, intelligence + language

6. **ISCOLA GEA**

   Social Age - Social roles and expectations related to a person's age

7. **LGITANNERAOE QYNEIUTI**

   Generationa Inequity - The concern that an aging society is being unfair to its younger members

8. **RUEANT-RUERNTU SUSIE**

   Nature-Nurture Issue - Debate about whether development is heredity or influence

9. **LUAP TSLABE**

   Paul Baltes - The life-span perspective has 7 fundamental contentions

10. **NARMIA HGTRIW LDEMENA**

    Marian Wright Edelman - Believes the b.s. U.S ranks very low in how we care for our children

7

Key to Self-Test A

1.	c	LO 1		13.	a	LO 4		25.	c	LO 7
2.	d	LO 1		14.	b	LO 4		26.	c	LO 7
3.	c	LO 2		15.	a	LO 5		27.	c	LO 7
4.	b	LO 2		16.	b	LO 5		28.	d	LO 8
5.	a	LO 2		17.	c	LO 5		29.	c	LO 8
6.	d	LO 2		18.	a	LO 5		30.	b	LO 9
7.	a	LO 2		19.	d	LO 5		31.	b	LO 9
8.	d	LO 2		20.	a	LO 5		32.	a	LO 9
9.	d	LO 2		21.	a	LO 5		33.	c	LO 9
10.	b	LO 3		22.	b	LO 6		34.	a	LO 9
11.	a	LO 3		23.	d	LO 6		35.	b	LO 10
12.	c	LO 3		24.	c	LO 6				

Key to Self-Test B

1.	f		4.	g		7.	e
2.	d		5.	a			
3.	b		6.	c			

Key to Essay Questions

1. A proper answer should describe the seven factors that Baltes states are important to understanding life-span development, that development is: lifelong, multidimensional, multidirectional, plastic, contextual, multidisciplinary, and involves growth, maintenance, and regulation. (Be sure to discuss what each of these elements means.) You would also want to mention the different periods of development (e.g., prenatal, infancy, etc.), and the general changes that occur in each period, as well as making some reference to the work of Bernice Neugarten, who raises issues concerning how age should be conceptualized (i.e., chronological, biological, psychological, and social).

2. A proper answer should first explain what "nature" and "nurture" are in terms of biological predisposition and environmental influence, then look at the interaction between the two, discussing the ideas of Jerome Kagan with respect to how each might influence the other.

Key to Scramblers

1. Original sin: Children are born into the world as evil beings
2. Life-span perspective: Development is lifelong, multidimensional, multidirectional, plastic, contextual, multidisciplinary, and involves growth, maintenance, and regulation
3. Ethnicity: Based on cultural heritage, nationality characteristics, race, religion, and language
4. Gender: The sociocultural dimension of being female or male
5. Cognitive processes: Changes in the individual's thought, intelligence, and language
6. Social age: Social roles and expectations related to a person's age
7. Generational inequity: The concern that an aging society is being unfair to its younger members
8. Nature-nurture issue: Debate about whether development is primarily influenced by heredity or experience
9. Paul Baltes: The life-span perspective has 7 fundamental contentions
10. Marian Wright Edelman: Believes the United States ranks very low in how we care for our children

Research Project 1: Observing Developmental Periods

This project is designed to help you hone your skills for observing behavior and become aware of what abilities are generally apparent in different periods of early development. Go to a place where you will be able to find children of different ages, such as a park, your institute's day care center, a local child care facility, etc. Select two children of the same sex, between the ages of 3 and 10, but at least four years apart in age. For ease of recording, you may wish to go with another classmate. Carefully observe each child's behavior for approximately 15 to 30 minutes, recording the activities in which each child participates as well as the types of social interactions in which each engages. Using the chart below, describe each child's activity, the type of social interaction (whether none [N], with another child [C], or with an adult [A]), and how long the activity and the social interaction took place.

Child 1: Sex____ Age_____			Child 2: Sex____ Age_____		
Activity	Time	Type of Interaction (N,C,A)	Activity	Time	Type of Interaction (N,C,A)

1. What types of activities did each child engage in? How were they similar? How were they different?
2. How did the amount of time for each activity differ for each child?
3. How were the social interactions similar for each child and how were they different?
4. Based on each child's age, what developmental period would each be in? Did their behavior fit the descriptions given in Chapter 1 for those developmental periods? Describe how the behaviors did fit and how they did not fit.
5. Why do you think you were instructed to observe two children of the same sex?
6. What other observations did you make that would be relevant to this course in life-span development?

Research Project 2: Issues in the Media

Review the learning objectives for this chapter and notice the issues that Santrock discusses. Then monitor the media (newspapers, talk/news radio, television) for a week and keep track of when and in what context these issues are raised. Calculate how often each specific issue is discussed and note which issue was raised most often, how it was presented (did you notice biased reporting, was it presented in terms of the life-span perspective, was it fully covered, etc.), and what additional information you would need to understand the issue (or story presented in the media) better. Discuss your findings in class.

Personal Application Project 1: Reflecting on What You Learned

Consider what you read in Chapter 1, then answer the following questions:

1. What information in this chapter did you already know?
2. How can/do you use that information in your own life?
3. What information in this chapter was totally new to you?
4. How can you use that new information in your own life?
5. What information in this chapter was different from what you previously believed?
6. How was this information different?
7. How do you account for the differences between what you believed and what you learned in the chapter?
8. What is the most important thing you learned from reading this chapter?

Personal Application Project 2: Consider Your Own Development

Looking at your life, using your own reflections and input from family members, reconstruct your development from as early as you can remember up to who you are today. Consider the developmental issues of nature-nurture, continuity-discontinuity, and stability-change discussed in the chapter. Describe which parts of you (e.g., aspects of your personality, your intellect, your values and beliefs, your basic behavior patterns) you believe result from each of these six elements. You may use the chart below, or create a pie chart, or come up with some other graphic aid to help you visualize which elements have played the strongest role in shaping you into the person you are now. How would you explain your findings?

Aspect of Your Self	Nature-Nurture	Continuity-Discontinuity	Stability-Change
Personality traits (describe)			
Intellect (describe)			
Values & beliefs (describe)			
Behavior patterns (describe)			
Other (describe)			

Internet Projects

Check out the McGraw-Hill web site for this text (http://www.mhhe.com/santrockld8). You'll find numerous activities there, in particular various quizzes, flash cards of key terms, and a challenging and fun crossword puzzle. Please note that all website addresses in this Study Guide have been checked and are correct at the time of publication, however, websites may be discontinued or addresses may change so when you search a given site it may no longer be viable. If that occurs, I apologize for the inconvenience, and would appreciate you notifying me so I could make appropriate revisions in future editions of this Study Guide.

Internet Project 1: Beginning to Search On-Line

Go to http://www.search4science.com and do an on-line search for any of the terms in the Key Terms section of the text. How many links[1] did you find? How many of those links referred you to professional journal articles? How many were someone's personal opinion? Compare the information you got from these different sources of information. What other types of links came up on the screen? How helpful was the information you found?

---

[1]For those of you who are not familiar with the Internet, a link is either a topic or a web address (such as the one given here: http://www.search4science.com) and will be a color such as blue or purple. If you point the screen cursor on the link and click the left side of the mouse, you will go to the website for that link. If you want to get back to where you were before, **usually** left clicking the "back" key at the top left of the screen will do it.

Internet Project 2: Careers in Life-Span Development

There are several sections in Chapter 1 where the author talks about careers in life-span development, including Table 1.8. The Internet offers many job sites, some more general and others more specific. The two sites that are particularly geared toward psychologists are sponsored by the American Psychological Association (APA) and the American Psychological Society (APS). A third site belongs to *The Chronicle of Higher Education*, a publication that is widely read by college faculty and administrators. All three of these sites (and their print publications) have excellent articles on relevant topics for anyone interested in the social sciences and higher education; they also have job postings. Go to each of these sites and check out the positions they list that are relevant to life-span development. Then answer the following questions:

1. Which site is easiest to navigate?
2. Which site offers the most positions generally?
3. Which site offers the most positions in life-span development?
4. How many positions did each site have that related to life-span development?
5. Which site offers positions that are most relevant to your interests?
6. How would you go about applying for a job that you found on each of these sites?
7. Did you learn anything about life-span development from exploring these sites?
8. What else did you learn from exploring these sites?

APA site:
http://www.apa.org   (note there is a special "classified ads" link in the student section, and if you check out their books, you'll find one titled *Career Paths in Psychology: Where Your Degree Can Take You*)

APS site:
http://www.psychologicalscience.org/   (note that if you add "apssc" after the "org/" you will get to the student section)

Chronicle of Higher Education site:
http://chronicle.merit.edu/

Other Relevant Sites on the Internet

American Association for Retired Persons (AARP)
http://www.aarp.org is the web site for AARP, an especially powerful organization that educates, lobbies, and provides services about and for persons age 50 and above.

Children's Defense Fund (CDF)
http://www.childrensdefense.org is the web site for CDF, the organization headed by Marian Wright Edelman to promote child welfare (discussed in Chapter 1 of the text).

Society for Research in Child Development (SRCD)
http://srcd.org is the web site for SRCD, an organization whose purposes are to promote multidisciplinary research in the field of human development, to foster the exchange of information among scientists and other professionals of various disciplines, and to encourage applications of research findings.

Chapter 2: The Science of Life-Span Development

Learning Objectives

1. Define and distinguish between theory, hypotheses, and the scientific method.
2. Compare and contrast Freud's psychoanalytic theory with Erikson's psychoanalytic theory.
3. Describe Piaget's theory of cognitive development and explain how it differs from Vygotsky's sociocultural cognitive theory and the information-processing approach.
4. Understand the basic principles underlying the behavioral theories.
5. Understand how social cognitive theory has been modified in recent years.
6. Describe the basic concepts from ethological theories.
7. Consider how Bronfenbrenner's ecological theory is similar to and different from social cognitive theory.
8. Describe what is meant by an eclectic theoretical orientation.
9. Describe the different research measures used by developmental psychologists.
10. Compare and contrast the correlational and experimental strategies for collecting information scientifically.
11. Define independent variable, dependent variable, and random assignment, and explain why causal conclusions cannot be made from correlational studies.
12. Describe cross-sectional, longitudinal, and sequential approaches to research, then define cohort effects and their role in each type of study.
13. Grasp the basics of understanding professional journal articles.
14. Understand the standard ethics of developmental research.

Chapter Outline

THEORIES OF DEVELOPMENT
    Psychoanalytic Theories
        Freud's Theory
        Erikson's Theory
        Evaluating the Psychoanalytic Theories
    Cognitive Theories
        Piaget's Cognitive Developmental Theory
        Vygotsky's Sociocultural Cognitive Theory
        The Information-Processing Approach
        Evaluating the Cognitive Theories
    Behavioral and Social Cognitive Theories
        Pavlov's Classical Conditioning
        Skinner's Operant Conditioning
        Social Cognitive Theory
        Evaluating the Behavioral and Social Cognitive Theories
    Ethological Theory
        Evaluating Ethological Theory
    Ecological Theory
        Evaluating Ecological Theory
    An Eclectic Theoretical Orientation
RESEARCH METHODS
    Observation
    Interviews and Questionnaires
    Case Studies

Self-Test A: Multiple Choice

1. As he was studying life-span development, Tyrell had to learn several interrelated, coherent sets of ideas that would help him explain and make predictions about development. Tyrell had to learn:
    a. theories.
    b. hypotheses.
    c. models.
    d. scientific methods.

2. An assumption or prediction that can be tested to determine its accuracy is a:
    a. theory.
    b. hypothesis.
    c. model.
    d. scientific method.

3. Socioemotional processes are important in all of the following theories EXCEPT:
    a. ethological.
    b. Freud's.
    c. Vygotsky's.
    d. ecological.

4. Tyisha will not take illegal drugs because she believes that any law breaking is immoral. She is relying on her _____ the decision-making process.
    a. id
    b. superid
    c. ego
    d. superego

5. Freud believed defense mechanisms reduce:
    a. anxiety.
    b. dependence on others.
    c. pleasure.
    d. schizophrenia.

6. During the _____ stage, Freud believed that pleasure centers on the genital area and resolution of the Oedipus complex occurs.
    a. oral
    b. anal
    c. phallic
    d. genital

14

7. Erik Erikson's theory emphasized:
    a. repeated resolutions of unconscious conflicts about sexual energy.
    b. success in confronting specific conflicts at particular ages in life.
    c. changes in children's thinking as they mature.
    d. the influence of sensitive periods in the various stages of biological maturation.

8. Issa is interested in school. He reads a lot and likes to do experiments. Assuming normal development, according to Erik Erikson's theory Issa is in which stage?
    a. autonomy versus shame and doubt
    b. initiative versus guilt
    c. industry versus inferiority
    d. identity versus identify confusion

9. The first feminist-based criticism of Freud's theory was proposed by psychoanalytic theorist Karen Horney, who:
    a. asserted that women find meaning in their emotions.
    b. believed that women are more likely than men to define themselves in terms of relationships.
    c. agreed with Malinowski's observations that the Oedipus complex is not universal.
    d. developed a model of women with positive feminine qualities and self-evaluation.

10. Within the framework of Piaget's cognitive theory, _____ occurs when a person is able to fit new information into an existing schema.
    a. assimilation
    b. accommodation
    c. organization
    d. disequilibrium

11. The key to formal operational thinking is the ability to think about _____ concepts.
    a. concrete
    b. sensory
    c. symbolic
    d. abstract

12. All of the following statements represent Vygotsky's views of development EXCEPT:
    a. the child's way of knowing is best advanced through internal mechanisms, which are separate from the social environment.
    b. the child's cognitive skills can be understood only when they are developmentally analyzed and interpreted.
    c. cognitive skills are mediated by words, language, and forms of discourse, which serve as psychological tools for facilitating and transforming mental activity.
    d. cognitive skills have their origins in social relations and are embedded in a sociocultural backdrop.

13. The information-processing approach to development emphasizes:
    a. the quality of thinking among children of different ages.
    b. overcoming certain age-related problems or crises.
    c. age appropriate expressions of sexual energy.
    d. perception, memory, reasoning ability, and problem solving.

14. From B. F. Skinner's point of view, behavior is explained by paying attention to:
    a. external consequences of that behavior.
    b. the self-produced consequences of that behavior.
    c. individuals' cognitive interpretations of their environmental experiences.
    d. the biological processes that determine maturation.

15. B. F. Skinner raised his daughter Deborah in an Air Crib, a sound-proofed, temperature controlled environment. What effect has this had on Deborah in her adult life?
    a. It has caused her to become claustrophobic.
    b. It eliminated severe allergies that she had as a child.
    c. It resulted in her total alienation from her father.
    d. It seems to have had no noticeable harmful effects.

16. According to Albert Bandura's social cognitive theory, the three factors that reciprocally influence development involve:
    a. behavior, the person, and the environment.
    b. punishment, reward, and reinforcement.
    c. memory, problem solving, and reasoning.
    d. cognition, reward, and observation.

17. Konrad Lorenz discovered that baby geese imprint to:
    a. their mother only.
    b. any adult female bird.
    c. any adult bird.
    d. any large moving object.

18. One of the most important applications of ethological theory to human development involves:
    a. John Bowlby's research demonstrating that critical periods are evident in birds, but do not occur in humans.
    b. John Bowlby's research demonstrating that attachment to a caregiver in the first year of life has important consequences throughout the life span.
    c. John Bowlby's research demonstrating that despite negative or insecure attachment in the first year, the individual is still likely to develop into a healthy adult.
    d. Mary Salter Ainsworth's research demonstrating a lack of connection between attachment early in life and later life adjustment.

19. According to Bronfenbrenner's ecological theory, growing up in a particular culture would be a part of an individual's:
    a. microsystem.
    b. exosystem.
    c. macrosystem.
    d. chronosystem.

20. A major strength of ecological theory is its framework for explaining:
    a. environmental influences on development.
    b. biological influences on development.
    c. cognitive development.
    d. affective processes in development.

21. Growing up as a "Baby Boomer" would be part of a person's:
    a. microsystem.
    b. mesosystem.
    c. exosystem.
    d. chronosystem.

22. An approach that simultaneously consists of several different theoretical perspectives is referred to as:
    a. nondescript.
    b. eclectic.
    c. quasi-experimental.
    d. pseudoscientific.

23. One difficulty of conducting research in the laboratory setting is that:
    a. it is artificial, thus difficult to generalize findings to the real world.
    b. random assignment is impossible.
    c. extraneous factors are difficult to control.
    d. participants tend to be unaware that they are in an experiment.

24. The main advantage of the naturalistic observation technique involves:
    a. real world validity.
    b. great control over extraneous variables.
    c. the ability to utilize inferential statistics.
    d. a lack of ethical controls.

25. Dr. Somberg is using a method of gathering information that gives an in-depth look at one individual. She is using the:
   a. interview.
   b. emic approach.
   c. participant observation.
   d. case study.

26. An advantage of using multiple materials in the life-history records approach is that:
   a. comparing sources and resolving discrepancies provides greater accuracy.
   b. archival data are easier to understand.
   c. it avoids the subjectivity of interviews.
   d. it avoids the subjectivity from a subject's written and oral reports.

27. Standardized tests are:
   a. difficult to administer and to interpret.
   b. considered less accurate than individualized assessments.
   c. commercially prepared tests that assess individuals' performance in different domains.
   d. used so often that they have begun to lose their meaning.

28. Animal studies permit researchers to do all of the following EXCEPT to:
   a. control their subjects' genetic background.
   b. make accurate assumptions about human behavioral responses.
   c. investigate the effects of treatments that would be unethical with humans.
   d. track the entire life span over a relatively short period of time.

29. Which of the following questions would best be answered using a correlational study?
   a. Does depression increase with age?
   b. Are people more depressed before or after retirement?
   c. Does exercise decrease depression?
   d. How depressed are 14-year-olds?

30. A common caution for correlational research is:
   a. they are difficult to administer.
   b. correlation does not equal causation.
   c. correlations do not tell direction of relationship.
   d. correlations do not indicate the strength of a relationship.

31. Which type of research allows researchers to determine the causes of behavior?
   a. correlational
   b. archival
   c. experimental
   d. case study

32. Experimental designs are superior to correlational approaches when dealing with:
   a. concepts that have not been studied in any great detail (e.g., dating behaviors among the elderly)
   b. variables that are difficult to manipulate (e.g., factors that lead to suicide).
   c. variables that are unethical to manipulate (e.g., the relationship between alcohol consumption and birth defects).
   d. variables that can be controlled easily (e.g., the relationship between stimulus presentation time and item recall).

33. An experiment involves the effects of aerobic exercise by pregnant women on their newborns' breathing and sleeping patterns. In this experiment, the newborns' breathing and sleeping patterns are the _____ variable.
   a. random
   b. dependent
   c. independent
   d. confounding

34. A _____ design compares individuals of different ages (e.g., 30-year-olds, 40-year-olds, and 50-year-olds) at one testing time.
    a. cross-sectional
    b. longitudinal
    c. Latin squares
    d. correlational

35. Effects due to a participant's time of birth or generation, but not to actual age are referred to as _____ effects.
    a. subjective
    b. cohort
    c. confounding
    d. historical

36. Most journal articles in the field of life-span development:
    a. refer to archival studies.
    b. address issues of either the very young or the very old.
    c. are reports of original research.
    d. use more rigorous methods than articles in other fields.

37. When psychologists are conducting research with children, once the parents have provided consent:
    a. the psychologist may continue to the end of the study unless the child becomes ill.
    b. if the child does not want to participate, the psychologist must not continue testing the child.
    c. if the child does not want to participate, the psychologist must stop long enough to talk to the parents and calm the child down before proceeding.
    d. if the child does not want to participate, the psychologist will ask the parents to calm the child down so the testing may continue.

38. When researchers use an ethnic label, such as African American or Latino, in a superficial way that makes an ethnic group look more homogeneous than it really is, this is referred to as:
    a. ethnic gloss.
    b. ethnic bias.
    c. stereotyping.
    d. xenophobia.

Self-Test B: Matching

Match the following persons with the statement or theory that most closely reflects their perspective:

1. Sigmund Freud   a. Presented the first feminist-based criticism of Freud's theory
2. Erik Erikson   b. Children actively construct their understanding of the world in four stages
3. Jean Piaget   c. Perceiving, encoding, representing, storing, retrieving information is thinking
4. Lev Vygotsky   d. Behavior is strongly influenced by biology
5. Robert Siegler   e. A neurologist who believed personality has three structures: id, ego, superego
6. Karen Horney   f. People cognitively represent others' behavior and sometimes adopt it themselves
7. Ivan Pavlov   g. Believed rewards and punishments shape individuals' development
8. B. F. Skinner   h. Suggested that humans develop in psychosocial stages
9. Albert Bandura   i. Russian physiologist who discovered the principle of classical conditioning
10. Konrad Lorenz   j. Language is used as a tool that helps children plan activities and solve problems

Essay Questions

1. One of your good friends works at a day care center and, knowing you are taking a class in life-span development, he has asked you to talk to the parents about the types of behaviors they might expect from their children as they develop. He told you the parents have many questions and concerns about Sigmund Freud's theories and his emphasis on sexuality, but they have heard good things about Jean Piaget's theories. Your friend has also recently learned about the Russian educator, Lev Vygotsky, and would like

you to cover all three of these, plus any others you think are important. How would you inform these parents about these theories and what they can expect from their children?

2. Your roommate's mother works at a Youth Center that offers after-school activities for school-aged children (kindergarten through 12th grade). She has noticed that while some older children have been teasing the younger children, other older children have been quite nurturing. She asks you to come to the Center to assess the situation, then to design some type of intervention so children of all ages would have mutually beneficial experiences. What research methods would you employ to accomplish these goals?

Scramblers

Unscramble the following people or terms, then describe what they are known for (people) or define them (terms):

1. VLE YYKVOGTS

_____

2. EBTRLA UDNRAAB

_____

3. NTISCIFECI DHMETO

_____

4. SHPYTHOEES

_____

5. MSINSALAITOI

_____

6. CMOCMOAADNOIT

_____

7. AMTIROONFNI-ECSOSRIPGN ORAPCPAH

_____

8. TYEHOOLG

_____

9. ARLUITSATNCI AVTRIEOSNBO

_____

Key to Self-Test A

1.	a	LO 1	14.	a	LO 4	27.	c	LO 9
2.	b	LO 1	15.	d	LO 4	28.	b	LO 9
3.	a	LO 1	16.	a	LO 5	29.	a	LO 10
4.	d	LO 2	17.	d	LO 6	30.	b	LO 10
5.	a	LO 2	18.	b	LO 6	31.	c	LO 10
6.	c	LO 2	19.	c	LO 7	32.	d	LO 10
7.	b	LO 2	20.	a	LO 7	33.	b	LO 11
8.	c	LO 2	21.	d	LO 7	34.	a	LO 12
9.	d	LO 2	22.	b	LO 8	35.	b	LO 12
10.	a	LO 3	23.	a	LO 9	36.	c	LO 13
11.	d	LO 3	24.	a	LO 9	37.	b	LO 14
12.	a	LO 3	25.	d	LO 9	38.	a	LO 14
13.	d	LO 3	26.	a	LO 9			

Key to Self-Test B

1.	e	5.	c	9.	f
2.	h	6.	a	10.	d
3.	b	7.	i		
4.	j	8.	g		

Key to Essay Questions

1. A proper answer describes the basic elements of Freud's, Piaget's, and Vygotsky's respective theories. With regard to Freud, include the importance of unconscious motives to behavior, development of the three parts of the personality (id, ego, superego), and the five developmental stages, noting what types of behavior one might expect in each (e.g., toilet training would take place most easily in the anal stage when the child is focusing on the anal region as a source of pleasure). Note that Piaget was interested in the process of **how** children think, and saw children as little scientists who need a sufficiently simulating environment to develop their cognitive abilities. Discuss his four stages of development and his concepts of assimilation, accommodation, and schemas. While Vygotsky (like Piaget) believed children actively construct their knowledge, he emphasized the importance of social relations in the child's development, and he said that to understand a child's cognitive skills they must be analyzed and interpreted developmentally (they build on each other); he also believed that cognitive skills are mediated by language. Suggest how parents could see evidence of these theories (e.g., when a child begins to "identify" with the same sex parent by imitating that parent's behaviors) and how they can use the information for their child's healthy development (e.g., don't expect a child to be toilet trained until the child is ready). Then select one of the other theories to discuss that you think would be particularly helpful for parents in providing a healthy environment for their children.

2. The first thing to discuss is naturalistic observation and how you would do that. You might try a correlational strategy to explore relationships among certain variables that currently exist, particularly for

what behaviors seem to go along with either teasing or nurturing young children. You would then need to design an experimental intervention, being careful to discuss your independent and dependent variables, as well as random assignment to experimental and control groups.

Key to Scramblers

1. Lev Vygotsky: Emphasized developmental analysis, the role of language, and social relations
2. Albert Bandura: People cognitively represent others' behavior and sometimes adopt it themselves
3. Scientific method: An approach that can be used to discover accurate information
4. Hypotheses: Specific assumptions and predictions that can be tested to determine their accuracy
5. Assimilation: In Piaget's theory, incorporation of new information into existing knowledge
6. Accommodation: In Piaget's theory, adjustment to new information
7. Information-processing approach: Individuals manipulate information, monitor it, strategize about it
8. Ethology: An approach that stresses that behavior is strongly influenced by biology, tied to evolution, and characterized by critical or sensitive periods
9. Naturalistic observation: Observations that take place out in the real world instead of in a laboratory
10. Sequential approach: A combined cross-sectional, longitudinal approach to research

Research Project 1: How Well Do the Theories Fit?

Note that some of the theories in Chapter 2 pertain primarily to child development (e.g., Freud, Piaget), while others take more of a life-span perspective (e.g., Erikson, information processing). Note, too, that later in the text you will encounter theories that are more keyed toward adult development. For this project, you will need to observe a young child, somewhere between the ages of 2 and 6, and also an adult. You may wish to do your observations in a public place, such as a school, a park, or the mall, or you may observe people you know in their own homes (or your home). Each observation should take half an hour, and you should accurately record what you observe, being careful merely to record behaviors, oral communications, and interactions with others rather than your own inferences or interpretations. (Oral communications and interactions with others should **not** be with you because your job here is to observe and record, not to interact.) On the basis of these observations, indicate the following:

1. What theory do you think best explains development of the child? Explain your reasons for choosing this theory.
2. What hypothesis would you make that could help you test development at this level? How would you go about testing that hypothesis?
3. What other theories do you think fit the behaviors you observed? Explain how these fit.
4. What theory do you think best explains adult development? Explain your reasons for choosing this theory.
5. What hypothesis would you make that could help you test development at this level? How would you go about testing that hypothesis?
6. What other theories do you think fit the behaviors you observed? Explain how these fit.
7. Are the theories you believe best explain child development also the best explanation of adult development? Explain your response.
8. Did any of the theories completely explain both child and adult development? Explain how they did fit and how they did not fit.
9. Describe how you would design your own theory to describe development over the lifespan.

Research Project 2: Exploring Professional Journals

Professional journals are an integral component of every field in psychology. They are one of the primary means psychologists (and other social scientists) have of staying current on all of the research that is being done. Chapter 2 outlines some important aspects of professional journals, such as the rigorous nature of research for most journal articles (although not all journal articles are about the authors' research) and the peer review process to ensure the high quality of research content and methodology, analysis, writing, and ethical standards. Professor Santrock also outlines the various components of professional journal articles in psychology (and most social sciences), from the abstract in the beginning to the reference section in the end. Select a topic of your choice that is related to life-span development, then locate an article in one of the professional journals (e.g., *Child Development, Developmental Psychology, Gerontology*) and consider what you learned and how you reacted to that research. Consider the following:

1. As you read about the research, could you easily determine both the independent and the dependent variable? (Note that there may be more than one of each.)
2. What theories were emphasized in the introduction? What hypotheses were tested by the research?
3. What did you learn from reading the methods section? Describe the participants and the procedures that were used.
4. What did you learn from reading the results section of this article? What statistical methods were used? Did you understand why those methods were chosen? Which results, if any, did the researchers state were statistically significant? How were (or weren't) the graphs, figures, tables, or charts helpful?
5. What did you learn from reading the discussion section of this article? How did the authors interpret the results? Did the authors discuss any limitations of the research? Did they suggest any further study based on their findings?
6. What stumbling blocks, if any, did you encounter in reading and understanding this article? How might the authors have made their paper more clear? If you did have any problems understanding sections of the article, which sections were they? What was the problem with understanding these sections?
7. As you consider the research reported in this article, were there any ethical issues that were raised for you? What were they? How were they (or how could they be) handled?
8. Did this article suggest a research area you might be interested in pursuing? How would you design that research?

Personal Application Project 1: Reflecting on What You Learned

Consider what you read in Chapter 2, then answer the following questions:

1. What information in this chapter did you already know?
2. How can/do you use that information in your own life?
3. What information in this chapter was totally new to you?
4. How can you use that new information in your own life?
5. What information in this chapter was different from what you previously believed?
6. How was this information different?
7. How do you account for the differences between what you believed and what you learned in the chapter?
8. What is the most important thing you learned from reading this chapter?

Personal Application Project 2: How Are the Theories Reflected through Your Own Development?

Reflect on your own development and, using your own reflections and input from family members, reconstruct your development from as early as you can remember up to who you are today. Consider the developmental theories discussed in the chapter and decide which best applies to your own experiences. Feel free to use more than one theory to describe different aspects of your development, or as overlapping explanations.

Aspect of Your Self	Theory (or Theories) and Explanation of How It Applies (or They Apply)
Personality traits (describe)	
Intellect (describe)	
Values & beliefs (describe)	
Behavior patterns (describe)	
Other (describe)	

1. When looking at this chart, what patterns do you see?
2. What theory or theories best describe how you came to be the person you are today?
3. Which theories don't fit your own development?
4. From looking at how the theories do or do not apply to your own development, how do they help you (or not help you) understand development generally?
5. How would you describe your own theory of development if you were to create one?
6. In what ways do you think theories are useful? In what ways might they limit how we view development or any other issue?

Internet Projects

Check out the McGraw-Hill web site for this text (http://www.mhhe.com/santrockld8). You'll find numerous activities there, in particular various quizzes, flash cards of key terms, and a challenging and fun crossword puzzle. Please note that all website addresses in this Study Guide have been checked and are correct at the time of publication, however, websites may be discontinued or addresses may change so when you search a given site it may no longer be viable. If that occurs, I apologize for the inconvenience, and would appreciate you notifying me so I could make appropriate revisions in future editions of this Study Guide.

Internet Project 1: Psychological Theories

Go to http://www.search4science.com and search for "psychological theories." What types of links did you find? How does the information you found at these links compare with the information in your text? Was there additional information that was not in the text? Were there additional theories or theories that related to different topics? How much of what you found in the links appeared to be someone's personal opinion as opposed to researched information? How do you judge the credibility of what you found? How helpful was the search?

Internet Project 2: Child Advocacy

There are many different web sources that deal with the welfare of children. Some are based on empirical research, some are voices of advocacy, some are biased and others more balanced. Even on the same site you might find a mixture. Explore some of these sites and describe each of them in terms of the type of information provided, the source of the information, how useful it is, how emotionally laden it is, how balanced or biased the site appears to be, and any other comments you might have concerning each site. Try some of the following:

The Child Development Website
http://www.idealist.com/children provides information on children's topics.

ChildrenAtRisk-STREETKIDS
http://www.groups.com/group/ChildrenAtRisk-STREETKIDS offers a first-hand look of children's issues around the world, including photo galleries.

Children's Defense Fund
http://www.childrensdefense.org is the web site for CDF, the organization headed by Marian Wright Edelman to promote child welfare (discussed in Chapter 1 of the text).

National Coalition for the Homeless
http://nch.ari.net is a major resource on all aspects of homelessness, including homeless children.

Society for Research in Child Development (SRCD)
http://srcd.org is the web site for SRCD, an organization whose purposes are to promote multidisciplinary research in the field of human development, to foster the exchange of information among scientists and other professionals of various disciplines, and to encourage applications of research findings.

Other Relevant Sites on the Internet

American Association for Retired Persons (AARP)
http://www.aarp.org

American Psychological Association (APA)
http://www.apa.org

American Psychological Society (APS)
http://www.psychologicalscience.org/

Sigmund Freud
http://freud.t0.or.at/freud/index-e.htm discusses Freudian theories and explores the psychoanalytic paradigm.

Carl Jung
http://www.cgjungpage.org discusses Carl Jung, his writings, and his theories, including the collective unconscious.

Erik Erikson's Eight Stages of Psychosocial Development
http://snycorva.cortland.edu/~Andersmd/erik/ offers a web tutorial on Erikson's theory and his work.

Jean Piaget
http://www.piaget.org/ explores Piaget's theories as well as cognitive differences in children and adults.

Chapter 3: Biological Beginnings

Learning Objectives

1. Discuss natural selection and the evolutionary perspective of human development.
2. Understand the relationship between chromosomes, DNA, genes, and human reproduction cells.
3. Distinguish between mitosis and meiosis.
4. Discuss the genetic principles of dominant-recessive genes, sex-linked genes, polygenic inheritance, genotype and phenotype, reaction range, and canalization.
5. Discuss the goals of twin studies and adoption studies in behavior genetics, being sure to mention the difference between the two types of twins.
6. Discuss the disorders associated with abnormalities in genes and chromosomes.
7. Describe the method and purpose for tests such as amniocentesis, ultrasound sonography, chorionic villus sampling, and the maternal blood test.
8. Describe the five most common techniques for helping infertile couples.
9. Present the common explanations for why outcomes for adopted children may be problematic.
10. Discuss the controversy surrounding research on the heritability of intelligence.
11. Explain Sandra Scarr's views that genotypes drive experience and outline criticisms of Scarr's views.
12. Define and distinguish between passive, evocative, and active genotype-environment interactions.
13. Distinguish shared environmental experiences from nonshared environmental experiences.
14. Present some conclusions about the research on heredity-environment interaction.

Chapter Outline

THE EVOLUTIONARY PERSPECTIVE
    Natural Selection and Adaptive Behavior
    Evolutionary Psychology
        Evolution and Life-Span Development
        Evaluating Evolutionary Psychology
GENETIC FOUNDATIONS
    What Are Genes?
    Mitosis and Meiosis
    Genetic Principles
    Behavior Genetics
    Molecular Genetics
    Chromosome and Gene-Linked Abnormalities
REPRODUCTION CHALLENGES AND CHOICES
    Prenatal Diagnostic Tests
        Amniocentesis
        Ultrasound Sonography
        Chorionic Villi Sampling
        Maternal Blood Test
    Infertility
    Adoption
HEREDITY-ENVIRONMENT INTERACTION
    Intelligence
    Heredity-Environment Correlations

Passive
Evocative
Active
Shared and Nonshared Environmental Experiences
Conclusions about Heredity-Environment Interaction

Self-Test A: Multiple Choice

1. The key to survival in an environment based on natural selection involves:
   a. aggression.
   b. size.
   c. adaptation.
   d. mutation.

2. The emphasis of evolutionary psychology behavior is on:
   a. the importance of adaptation, reproduction, and "survival of the fittest" to explain behavior.
   b. cultural evolution as the dominant type of evolution among humans.
   c. genes as the most important determinant for survival.
   d. physical and psychological aspects of humans as different determinants of behavior.

3. David Buss believes that _____ not only shapes our physical features, but also influences our decision making, aggressive behavior, fears, and mating patterns.
   a. adaptation
   b. instinct
   c. evolution
   d. genetics

4. According to Baltes, the benefits of evolutionary selection:
   a. increase with age.
   b. decrease with age.
   c. remain the same over the life span.
   d. first increase in early adulthood, then decrease following the decline in reproductive capacity.

5. Albert Bandura criticizes evolutionary psychology because it:
   a. is "one-sided evolutionism."
   b. takes a bidirectional view of development.
   c. is too complex.
   d. fails to take account of biological processes.

6. The units of hereditary information that act as a blueprint for cells to reproduce themselves and manufacture the proteins that maintain life are:
   a. chromosomes.
   b. DNA.
   c. genes.
   d. ribosomes.

7. In the process of meiosis:
   a. the cells divide into gametes, which have half the genetic material of the parent cell.
   b. the focus is on cell growth and repair.
   c. the number of chromosomes present remains the same.
   d. two daughter cells are formed.

8. Each human gamete has:
   a. 46 paired chromosomes.
   b. 46 unpaired chromosomes.
   c. 23 paired chromosomes.
   d. 23 unpaired chromosomes.

9. The typical female chromosome pattern is:
   a. YY.
   b. XX.
   c. XY.
   d. XXY.

10. Traits that are produced by the interaction between two or more genes are called:
    a. dominant.
    b. recessive.
    c. monogenic.
    d. polygenic.

11. A person's genetic heritage is his or her:
    a. genotype.
    b. phenotype.
    c. dominant character.
    d. recessive character.

12. The way an individual's genetic heritage is expressed in observed and measurable characteristics is his or her:
    a. genotype.
    b. phenotype.
    c. dominant character.
    d. recessive character.

13. The basic premise of the reaction range model is that:
    a. genetic factors determine an infant's range of behavior and environmental factors determine an adult's behavior.
    b. genetic factors determine a possible range of expressions and environmental factors determine the ultimate expression achieved.
    c. most behaviors are determined by genetic factors and the environment contributes little to human reactions.
    d. most behaviors are determined by the environment and genetic factors contribute little to human reactions.

14. The narrow path marking the development of characteristics that appear immune to vast changes in environmental events is called:
    a. canalization.
    b. meiosis.
    c. phenotype.
    d. heredity.

15. Which of the following is the best example of canalization?
    a. Twins reared apart in very different environments have different temperaments.
    b. Two brown-eyed parents have a blue-eyed child.
    c. An extra X chromosome causes genetic abnormalities.
    d. Infants smile at exactly 40 weeks after conception, regardless of when they are born.

16. Behavioral geneticists believe that behaviors are determined by:
    a. only biological factors.
    b. only environmental factors.
    c. biological factors at birth and environmental factors throughout the rest of life.
    d. a continuous interaction between biological and environmental factors.

17. If heredity is an important determinant of a specific behavior, what prediction can we make about expression of the behavior in identical twins reared apart compared to its expression in fraternal twins reared apart?
    a. Fraternal twins will express the behavior more similarly than identical twins.
    b. There will be little similarity in the expression of the behavior in either set of twins.
    c. Identical twins will express the behavior more similarly than fraternal twins.
    d. The behavior will be expressed similarly by identical twins and fraternal twins.

18. In adoption studies, psychologists compare the behavior of:
    a. identical fraternal twins.
    b. family members with that of randomly selected others.
    c. fraternal twins with each other.
    d. children living with adoptive parents and children living with biological parents.

19. Down syndrome is caused by:
    a. an extra chromosome.
    b. alcohol consumption by the mother during pregnancy.
    c. the mother's poor nutrition.
    d. an extra X chromosome on the 23rd pair.

20. Which of these syndromes is NOT sex-linked?
    a. sickle-cell anemia
    b. Klinefelter syndrome
    c. Turner syndrome
    d. XYY syndrome

21. If amniocentesis is performed to determine if a woman's fetus is genetically normal, this will involve:
    a. taking a blood sample from the mother.
    b. drawing a sample of the fluid that surrounds the baby in the womb.
    c. taking a sample of the placenta between the 8th and 11th week of pregnancy.
    d. taking a blood sample from the fetus.

22. _____ involves removal of a small sample of the placenta.
    a. The alpha-fetoprotein test
    b. An ultrasound
    c. Amniocentesis
    d. Chorionic villi sampling

23. All of the following are common causes of male infertility EXCEPT:
    a. low sperm count.
    b. sperm lacking motility.
    c. a blocked passageway.
    d. superovulation.

24. Intrauterine insemination is a possible solution to infertility that involves:
    a. having sperm and egg unite outside of a woman's body.
    b. implanting a fertilized egg into a substitute mother's womb.
    c. enhancing the possibility of conception by taking fertility drugs.
    d. placing frozen sperm from a male donor directly into the uterus.

25. Which is a disadvantage of adoption in comparison to medical treatments for infertility?
   a. Adoptive parents tend not to try as hard as nonadoptive parents to care for their children.
   b. Adopted children are more likely than nonadopted children to have adjustment problems.
   c. Adoption is more likely to involve third parties than nonadoption.
   d. Biological parents find it easier to love their children than do adopting parents.

26. Arthur Jensen argues that heredity is a more important determinant of intelligence than environment because the:
   a. educational level of biological parents correlates more strongly with children's IQs than do IQs of adoptive parents.
   b. IQs of fraternal twins are as highly correlated as the IQs of identical twins.
   c. IQs of identical twins, whether reared together or apart, are more strongly correlated than IQs of fraternal twins or other siblings.
   d. correlations between fraternal twins' IQs are similar to correlations of siblings' IQs.

27. In Arthur Jensen's review of studies on intelligence, he discovered that _____ had the highest correlated IQ scores.
   a. identical twins reared together
   b. identical twins reared apart
   c. fraternal twins reared together
   d. fraternal twins reared apart

28. What do Arthur Jensen's views have in common with those of Richard Hernstein and Charles Murray?
   a. Their specific views illustrated the more general issue of heredity's influence on development.
   b. These individuals are on the same side with regard to the debate concerning shared and nonshared environmental influences.
   c. Their specific views illustrate the more general issue of an evolutionary perspective.
   d. These individuals are proponents of genetic counseling.

29. Most experts today agree that _____ plays an important role in intelligence.
   a. socioeconomic status
   b. health care
   c. environment
   d. creativity

30. Behavioral geneticist Sandra Scarr argues that:
   a. most aspects of family context are shared by all siblings within the family.
   b. the environment the parents select for their children is due, in part, to the parents' genotypes.
   c. only cross-cultural studies can be used to support the role of genetics in determining behavior.
   d. females are genetically superior to males in all aspects of development except physical strength.

31. Children who are highly active, easily distracted, and move very fast frequently elicit adult attempts to quiet them down, punishment for lack of concentration, and angry warnings to slow down. This describes an example of a(n) _____-environment interaction.
    a. passive genotype
    b. active genotype
    c. niche-picking genotype
    d. evocative genotype

32. Larry and Anita grew up in the same household, went to the same schools, participated in their family's social activities, and observed their parents' dedication to work and community. These experiences constitute Larry and Anita's:
    a. shared environmental influences.
    b. nonshared environmental influences.
    c. niche-picking experiences.
    d. heritability.

33. Behavioral geneticist Robert Plomin argues that differences between siblings' personalities are primarily a result of:
    a. genetics.
    b. nonshared environmental experiences.
    c. random variance.
    d. shared environmental experiences.

34. Craig Ramey and colleagues (1984, 1998) studied the effects of early intervention on intelligence. They found that _____ can significantly raise the intelligence of young children from impoverished environments.
    a. providing medical care and dietary supplements
    b. high-quality early educational day care
    c. teaching mothers parenting skills
    d. placing children into adoptive homes with highly intelligent parents

35. Judith Harris' (1998) book *The Nurture Assumption* has been:
    a. highly praised by developmentalists such as T. Berry Brazelton and Jerome Kagan.
    b. well received by developmentalists who believe that parents are a critical component of a child's healthy development.
    c. called "terrifying" by developmentalist T. Berry Brazelton.
    d. largely ignored by the psychological community.

Self-Test B: Matching

Match the following persons with the statement or theory that most closely reflects their perspective:

1.	David Buss	a.	The human species has been selected for learnability and plasticity
2.	Thomas Bouchard	b.	Intelligence is primarily inherited
3.	Charles Darwin	c.	High-quality early educational day care can raise intelligence
4.	Albert Bandura	d.	Children reared in the same environment often have different personalities
5.	Theodore Dobzhansky	e.	Minnesota Study of Twins Reared Apart
6.	Richard Hernstein	f.	Rejects the notion of social behavior as the product of evolved biology
7.	Judith Harris	g.	Natural selection; survival of the fittest
8.	Robert Plomin	h.	Co-author who said America is evolving an intellectually deprived underclass
9.	Arthur Jensen	i.	Each individual has a range of potential but won't exceed that range
10.	Craig Ramey	j.	Evolution pervasively influences how we make decisions, fears, & aggression
11.	Sandra Scarr	k.	What parents do does not make a difference in children's behavior

Essay Questions

1. Imagine that you are a genetic counselor and a couple has come to you because they are concerned about whether they should have children. The wife is 40 years old and comes from an Eastern European Jewish background. Her husband is a 42-year-old African American. What potential problems might this couple's children have? How would you counsel them?

2. Your roommate has been reading Arthur Jensen's claims about the relationship between heredity and intelligence, and has determined that you will never become a major success in life because your hereditary background will limit you to mediocrity. Consider what you know about Jensen's work and the later similar claims by Hernstein and Murray, then examine criticisms of this body of research and the various theories that address heredity and environment in an effort either to support or refute your roommate's assertions.

Scramblers

Unscramble the following people or terms, then describe what they are known for (people) or define them (terms):

1. LCAHRSE WNDRAI

   _____

2. HMOTSA DUBOHRAC

   _____

3. MMOOSSCRHEO

   _____

4. STOISIM

   _____

5. SEOISIM

   _____

6. TONEPEYHP

   _____

7. ZNCNALAIAOIT

   _____

8. NDOW DSEMYRON

   _____

9. RRNUTE SEMYNORD

_____

10. LIESKC-LECL EMANIA

_____

Key to Self-Test A

1.	c	LO 1	13.	b	LO 4	25.	b	LO 9
2.	a	LO 1	14.	a	LO 4	26.	c	LO 10
3.	c	LO 1	15.	d	LO 4	27.	a	LO 10
4.	b	LO 1	16.	d	LO 5	28.	a	LO 10
5.	a	LO 1	17.	c	LO 5	29.	c	LO 10
6.	c	LO 2	18.	d	LO 5	30.	b	LO 11
7.	a	LO 3	19.	a	LO 6	31.	d	LO 12
8.	d	LO 3	20.	a	LO 6	32.	a	LO 13
9.	b	LO 3	21.	b	LO 7	33.	b	LO 13
10.	d	LO 4	22.	d	LO 7	34.	b	LO 14
11.	a	LO 4	23.	d	LO 8	35.	c	LO 14
12.	b	LO 4	24.	d	LO 8			

Key to Self-Test B

1.	j	5.	a	9.	b		
2.	e	6.	h	10.	c		
3.	g	7.	k	11.	i		
4.	f	8.	d				

Key to Essay Questions

1. First of all you would need to look at the potential risk factors for Tay-Sachs (mother's background), Down syndrome (mother's age), and sickle-cell anemia (father's background). Discuss how you might do this (look at family history, genetic testing). In terms of counseling on how they should proceed, you would help them consider their own wishes and options (what kinds of tests would you suggest? what other options/ procedures might be available?). What personal issues (e.g., the couple's ethical and religious beliefs) might you consider?

2. Here you would need to discuss Jensen's (1969) research and the later concurring findings of Herrnstein and Murray (1994) in their book, _The Bell Curve: Intelligence and Class Structure in Modern Life,_ then explain the criticisms of this position. Present the notion of range of potential, but also look at the evidence suggesting that environmental factors are dominant in development. Discuss the various types of heredity-environment interactions (e.g., passive genotype-environment interactions), as well as the findings from twin studies and adoption studies. Based on your evaluation of this research, state which position you find most compelling.

Key to Scramblers

1. Charles Darwin: Natural selection; survival of the fittest
2. Thomas Bouchard: Directed the Minnesota Study of Twins Reared Apart
3. Chromosomes: Threadlike structures that contain the genetic substance DNA
4. Mitosis: The process by which each chromosome in the cell's nucleus duplicates itself
5. Meiosis: The process by which cells divide into gametes
6. Phenotype: The way in which an individual's genotype is expressed
7. Canalization: The process by which characteristics take a narrow path or developmental course
8. Down syndrome: A chromosomally transmitted form of mental retardation caused by an extra chromosome
9. Turner syndrome: A chromosome disorder in which females are missing an X chromosome
10. Sickle-cell anemia: A genetic disorder that affects the red blood cells; occurs most often in people of African descent

Research Project 1: Heritability of Eye Color

To help you understand the concept of heritability (and the dominant-recessive genes principle), collect data from your own family and from one other family that is willing to participate. (Look only at blood relatives, not relatives by marriage.) Record the eye color of all family members, using the tables provided below, then answer the following questions:

1. What patterns did you notice for members of each family in terms of eye color?
2. Which eye color seems most prominent for each family?
3. Describe how the dominant-recessive genes principle would explain the patterns you found.
4. Are your observations consistent with what this principle would predict? Explain.

(Note that if there are fewer of one category of siblings, aunts, uncles, and/or cousins, but more of another, feel free to change category names, e.g., from "siblings" to "cousins.")

	Family 1	Family 2
# with brown eyes		
# with blue eyes		
# with green eyes		
# with other color (describe)		

Family 1		Family 2	
Family Member	**Eye Color**	**Family Member**	**Eye Color**
Self			
Mother		Mother	
Father		Father	
Maternal Grandmother		Maternal Grandmother	
Maternal Grandfather		Maternal Grandfather	
Paternal Grandmother		Paternal Grandmother	
Paternal Grandfather		Paternal Grandfather	
Sibling		Sibling	
Sibling		Sibling	
Sibling		Sibling	
Maternal Aunt		Maternal Aunt	
Paternal Aunt		Paternal Aunt	
_____ Aunt		_____ Aunt	
Maternal Uncle		Maternal Uncle	
Paternal Uncle		Paternal Uncle	
_____ Uncle		_____ Uncle	
Maternal Cousin		Maternal Cousin	
Maternal Cousin		Maternal Cousin	
Paternal Cousin		Paternal Cousin	
Paternal Cousin		Paternal Cousin	

Research Project 2: Charting Chromosome and Gene-Linked Abnormalities

Referring back to the section on chromosome and gene-linked abnormalities, chart each of them, indicating the description, risk factors (e.g., mother's age, parents' ethnic background), treatment, incidence, and type (i.e., chromosome, sex-linked, gene-linked). Note that most, but not all, of this information is included in tables in the chapter. What other information would be helpful for you to know about each of these disorders? If you were counseling a couple who were planning to have a baby, what specific information would you need to elicit from them to ensure the best chances for a healthy child?

Disorder	Description	Risk Factors	Treatment	Incidence	Type
Down syndrome					
Klinefelter syndrome					
Fragile X syndrome					
Phenylketonuria					
Sickle-cell anemia					
Diabetes					
Hemophilia					
Huntington disease					
Tay-Sachs disease					
Cystic fibrosis					
Spina bifida					
Others _____ _____					

Personal Application Project 1: Reflecting on What You Learned

Consider what you read in Chapter 3, then answer the following questions:

1. What information in this chapter did you already know?
2. How can/do you use that information in your own life?
3. What information in this chapter was totally new to you?
4. How can you use that new information in your own life?
5. What information in this chapter was different from what you previously believed?
6. How was this information different?
7. How do you account for the differences between what you believed and what you learned in the chapter?
8. What is the most important thing you learned from reading this chapter?

Personal Application Project 2: How Can This Chapter Help You Understand Your Own Development?

Reflect on your own development and, using your own reflections and input from family members, reconstruct your development from as early as you can remember up to who you are today. Consider the developmental theories discussed in the chapter and decide which best applies to your own experiences. Feel free to use more than one theory to describe different aspects of your development, or as overlapping explanations.

Aspect of Your Self	Arguments Presented	Describe How the Information Applies to Your Life
Personality traits (describe)		
Intellect (describe)		
Physical characteristics (e.g., height, eye color) (describe)		
Physical disorders (e.g., diabetes, Klinefelter syndrome) (describe)		
Other (describe)		

From looking at your own chart, based on the information in the chapter (and any other you may have gathered), explain:

1. Does the information in the chapter and in your chart provide you with a better understanding of yourself? In what way?
2. How can you use this information in your own life?
3. In what way (if any) will this information affect your decisions concerning family planning?
4. Was any of this information frightening to you, or did it make you feel less fearful? Explain.
5. What other insights have you gained from preparing this chart?

Internet Projects

Check out the McGraw-Hill web site for this text (http://www.mhhe.com/santrockld8). You'll find numerous activities there, in particular various quizzes, flash cards of key terms, and a challenging and fun crossword puzzle. Please note that all website addresses in this Study Guide have been checked and are correct at the time of publication, however, websites may be discontinued or addresses may change so when you search a given site it may no longer be viable. If that occurs, I apologize for the inconvenience, and would appreciate you notifying me so I could make appropriate revisions in future editions of this Study Guide.

Internet Project 1: Biological Beginnings

Go to http://www.search4science.com and do an on-line search for any of the terms in the Key Terms section of the text. How many links did you find? How many of those links referred you to professional journal articles? How many were someone's personal opinion? Compare the information you got from these different sources of information. What other types of links came up on the screen? How helpful was the information you found?

Internet Project 2: Prenatal Testing

Go to www.howstuffworks.com/prenatal-testing-htm[1] and check out their whole section on how prenatal testing works. What different types of tests did you learn about? Which tests were discussed in the text? Were there tests that were not presented in the text? When would you use each of these tests, and why would each be used? Were there chromosome or gene-linked disorders that weren't in the text? Describe them. Select a link that interests you from the end of the article and summarize what you learned from that site.

Other Relevant Sites on the Internet

American Association for Retired Persons (AARP)
http://www.aarp.org

American Psychological Association (APA)
http://www.apa.org

American Psychological Society (APS)
http://www.psychologicalscience.org/

Human Genome Project Information
http://www.ornl.gov/hgmis provides the latest updates on the Human Genome Project and detailed explanations of this fascinating area of study.

National Down Syndrome Society
http://www.ndss.org/ provides comprehensive, on-line information about Down syndrome, including education, research, and advocacy.

---

[1]How Stuff Works is a wonderful site that gives clear explanations about how almost anything you can think of works. If something you're interested in is not on the site, suggest it and they will most likely research it and publish what they've learned on their site.

Nature Genome website
http://www.nature.com/genomics presents a variety of sources on genome projects—human and non-human —around the world.

Professor Lawrence M. Hinman of University of San Diego
http://ethics.acusd.edu/reproductive_technologies.html is another site that would provide good subject matter for discussion on the ethical and legal issues surrounding reproductive technology, including cloning.

Web MD
http://www.webmd.com offers a wide variety of information for the medical profession and for consumers.

Chapter 4:   Prenatal Development and Birth

Learning Objectives

1. Describe the germinal, embryonic, and fetal periods of prenatal development
2. Define placenta and umbilical cord, and describe how they prevent the transmission of harmful substances from mother to infant.
3. Define organogenesis and explain its importance.
4. Understand how cultural beliefs affect the experience of pregnancy.
5. Describe the effects that drugs can have on the unborn child.
6. Discuss maternal diseases and conditions that influence prenatal development such as rubella, syphilis, herpes, and HIV/AIDS.
7. Explain how maternal and paternal characteristics affect prenatal development.
8. Describe the three stages of birth.
9. State what researchers know and do not know about the effects of drugs administered during childbirth.
10. Contrast the different childbirth strategies, noting the pros and cons of each.
11. Define and distinguish between preterm infants and low-birthweight infants.
12. Describe the two most widely used measures of neonatal health and responsiveness.
13. Describe the physical, emotional, and psychological adjustments women have to make after pregnancy.

Chapter Outline

PRENATAL DEVELOPMENT
    The Course of Prenatal Development
        The Germinal Period
        The Embryonic Period
        The Fetal Period
    Cultural Beliefs About Pregnancy
TERATOLOGY AND HAZARDS TO PRENATAL DEVELOPMENT
    Exploring Teratology
    Prescription and Nonprescription Drugs
    Psychoactive Drugs
        Alcohol
        Nicotine
        Illegal Drugs
    Environmental Hazards
    Other Maternal Factors
        Infectious Diseases
        Nutrition
        Emotional States and Stress
        Maternal Age
    Paternal Factors
    Prenatal Care
    Positive Prenatal Development
BIRTH
    Exploring the Birth Process
        Stages of Birth
        The Fetus/Newborn Transition

Self-Test A: Multiple Choice

1. All of the following are periods of prenatal development EXCEPT:
   a. ovulation.
   b. germinal.
   c. embryonic.
   d. fetal.

2. Human fertilization typically takes place in the:
   a. ovary.
   b. fallopian tube.
   c. uterus.
   d. vaginal canal.

3. A fertilized ovum is called:
   a. a blastocyst.
   b. an egg.
   c. an embryo.
   d. a zygote.

4. The period of prenatal development that occurs in the first two weeks after conception is called the _____ period.
   a. fetal
   b. germinal
   c. embryonic
   d. blastocystic

5. A skin defect might be traced back to an initial problem with the embryo's _____ cells.
   a. mesoderm
   b. ectoderm
   c. microderm
   d. endoderm

6. How does the placenta/umbilical cord life-support system prevent harmful bacteria from invading a fetus?
   a. Bacteria are too large to pass through the placenta walls.
   b. The placenta generates antibodies that attack and destroy bacteria.
   c. Bacteria become trapped in the maze of blood vessels of the umbilical cord.
   d. No one understands how the placenta keeps bacteria out.

7. During the second trimester, the amniotic sac is filled mainly with:
   a. blood.
   b. mucus.
   c. urine.
   d. air.

8. The fetal period is best described as a time when:
   a. major organ systems emerge from the less differentiated endoderm and mesoderm.
   b. support systems that sustain the fetus become fully formed and functioning.
   c. fine details are added to systems that emerged during the embryonic period.
   d. teratogens are most likely to impair development.

9. Organogenesis takes place during which stage of development?
   a. germinal
   b. zygotic
   c. embryonic
   d. fetal

10. While looking over a newborn, a physician notes that the neonate's outer ears are severely deformed. Based on her knowledge of prenatal development, the physician would suspect the damage occurred during the _____ stage of development.
    a. germinal
    b. zygotic
    c. embryonic
    d. fetal

11. _____ are important dimensions for providing adequate health care for expectant mothers from various cultural groups.
    a. Cultural assessments
    b. Home care remedy evaluations
    c. Hospice care options
    d. Neonatal care units

12. A medicine woman or medicine man is an indigenous healer in which culture?
    a. Anglo American
    b. Asian American
    c. Mexican American
    d. Native American

13. Which phrase best defines a teratogen?
    a. a life-support system that protects the fetus
    b. an agent that stimulates the formation of organs
    c. an abnormality in infants of alcoholic mothers
    d. an environmental factor that produces birth defects

14. Which of the following statements about fetal alcohol syndrome is most accurate?
    a. The infant is often physically deformed and below average in intelligence.
    b. Fetal alcohol syndrome commonly results in miscarriages.
    c. Fetal alcohol syndrome causes ectopic pregnancies.
    d. Babies suffering from fetal alcohol syndrome are often born before term and with low birthweights.

15. A common characteristic of babies born to women who smoke during their pregnancies is:
    a. a missing arm or leg.
    b. facial deformities and below-average intelligence.
    c. restlessness and irritability.
    d. lower birthweights.

16. All of the following have been found to endanger the unborn child EXCEPT:
    a. saunas and hot tubs.
    b. PCB-polluted fish.
    c. carbon monoxide.
    d. computer monitors.

17. Researchers now believe that maternal stress may lead to birth defects by:
    a. reducing the amount of oxygen received by the embryo and fetus.
    b. increasing the mother's susceptibility to viruses.
    c. reducing the likelihood of a good placenta-to-uterus connection.
    d. increasing the likelihood of an unusual chromosome split during meiosis.

18. Which of the following statements about the relationship between age and pregnancy outcome is most accurate?
    a. Adolescent mothers are most likely to have retarded children.
    b. Artificially inseminated women in their thirties and forties are more likely to become pregnant than those in their twenties.
    c. Mothers over age thirty are most likely to have retarded babies.
    d. Adolescent mothers suffer the lowest infant mortality rates of any age group.

19. Now that Eric and Luz have established their careers and are in their mid-twenties, they are planning to have a baby. In terms of Eric's concerns about the paternal factors that may affect his child, he should be most concerned about:
    a. his high-stress job as an attorney.
    b. the second-hand smoke he encounters in his law office.
    c. his age.
    d. his low dietary intake of vitamin C.

20. With respect to prenatal care, which of the following countries has the lowest quality medical and educational services?
    a. Norway
    b. the United States
    c. Sweden
    d. France

21. Mrs. Peters is experiencing contractions every 2 to 5 minutes. She is in which stage of birth?
    a. first
    b. second
    c. third
    d. fourth

22. Which of the following can lead to anoxia during the birth process?
    a. having the umbilical cord tighten around the neck of the fetus
    b. use of forceps to help ease the infant from the birth canal
    c. an episiotomy (surgically widening the vaginal opening)
    d. Braxton-Hicks contractions

23. A physician might elect to give a pregnant mother an oxytocic if:
    a. her contractions have stopped.
    b. she is bleeding vaginally.
    c. she has stopped ovulating.
    d. her placenta has partially detached.

24. Which statement about the influence on newborns of drugs used during birth is the most accurate?
    a. Experiments on the effects of drugs on childbirth raise few ethical questions.
    b. Methodological problems complicate the results of studies of drug use during labor.
    c. Drugs affect all infants in almost the same way.
    d. Most mothers choose standard childbirth, so researchers are able to learn about how drugs affect labor.

25. Eleni is a doula. This means she is a:
    a. physician who specializes in obstetrics.
    b. nurse with a specialty in obstetrics.
    c. caregiver who provides support for the mother during birth.
    d. nurse-practitioner who is trained as a midwife to delivery babies.

26. The main premise of natural or prepared childbirth is summarized by the phrase:
    a. "knowledge is power."
    b. "always say 'no' to drugs."
    c. "it takes two to tango."
    d. "easy does it."

27. Aisha is using a childbirth strategy that includes a detailed anatomy and physiology course during pregnancy and a special breathing technique to control pushing in the final stages of labor. She is using which method?
   a. natural childbirth
   b. the Lamaze method
   c. cesarean delivery
   d. the Read method

28. During the 1980s, the rate of cesarean deliveries performed in the United States:
   a. increased dramatically.
   b. increased slightly.
   c. decreased slightly.
   d. decreased dramatically.

29. A "preterm" baby cannot have gestated for more than _____ weeks.
   a. 26
   b. 30
   c. 34
   d. 38

30. Which of the following statements about a shortened gestation period is most accurate?
   a. It is common for low-birthweight infants.
   b. It often leads to organ malformation.
   c. It is almost always devastating.
   d. It alone does not necessarily harm an infant.

31. Increases in survival rates for infants who are born very early and very small would predict:
   a. increases in severe brain damage.
   b. a more adaptable immune system.
   c. a tendency toward substance abuse later in life.
   d. higher levels of academic achievement than normal weight infants.

32. In contrast to the Brazelton scale, the Apgar primarily assesses a newborn's:
   a. psychological status.
   b. reflexes.
   c. physiological health.
   d. responsivity to people.

33. Two-day-old Terry's very low Brazelton Neonatal Behavioral Assessment Scale score is often a good indicator that:
   a. he has brain damage.
   b. his mother took heroin while she was pregnant.
   c. he will develop a "difficult" temperament.
   d. he is unlikely to bond with his primary caregiver.

34. Which of the following terms refers to a physical change that occurs to women after childbirth?
   a. decompression
   b. decompensation
   c. involution
   d. menarche

35. Marjorie has just had a healthy baby boy and a relatively easy birth. However, now that she is home with her baby, she is experiencing emotional fluctuations. Which of the following is most likely true?
   a. Marjorie should get professional counseling immediately.
   b. Marjorie needs to get more education about how to care for her baby and deal with her feelings.
   c. Marjorie's husband should stay home from work to help her care for the baby.
   d. Marjorie's emotional fluctuations may be due to hormonal changes, fatigue, or demands of having a new baby.

Self-Test B: Matching

Match the following persons with the statement or theory that most closely reflects their perspective:

1. Fernand Lamaze
2. Tiffany Field
3. T. Berry Brazelton
4. Ann Streissguth
5. Christine Dunkel-Schetter
6. Linda Pugh
7. Grantley Dick-Read

a. Researcher in the area of fetal alcohol syndrome
b. Women under stress are much more likely to have premature babies
c. English obstetrician who developed natural childbirth
d. Explored the role of touch and massage in development
e. French obstetrician who developed prepared childbirth
f. Developed a neonatal assessment of neurological development
g. Neonatal nurse who researches interventions with low-income women

Essay Questions

1. You are asked to talk to a high school class about potential hazards to prenatal development. The principal of the high school has suggested that you discuss not only alcohol and other drugs, but environmental hazards and maternal diseases as well. She has asked that you be honest about the different agents that can cause problems, the problems they may cause, and how these problems can be avoided. What would you tell these students about teratogens and prenatal care?

2. One of your friends has recently married and has now confided in you that she is pregnant. She knows you're taking this class in life-span development and asks for your input concerning what she can expect when giving birth, and she wants your suggestions concerning her childbirth options. What would you tell her about the three stages of birth, complications she might expect, options about the use of drugs, and the childbirth strategies that are available to her?

Scramblers

Unscramble the following people or terms, then describe what they are known for (people) or define them (terms):

1. LSYTBASOCT

_____

2. YROBNMIEC DIROEP

_____

3. ECNATLAP

_____

4. IBLMIUALC DROC

_____

5. OGNENASGIRSOE

_____

6. NTERGEOAT

_____

7. TAELF CLOLHAO ESMYONRD

_____

8. LUAOD

_____

9. LNTAERYG KIDC-DREA

_____

10. DNRINADEF MZAELA

_____

Key to Self-Test A

1.	a	LO 1	13.	d	LO 5	25.	c	LO 10
2.	b	LO 1	14.	a	LO 5	26.	a	LO 10
3.	d	LO 1	15.	d	LO 5	27.	b	LO 10
4.	b	LO 1	16.	d	LO 6	28.	a	LO 10
5.	b	LO 1	17.	a	LO 7	29.	d	LO 11
6.	a	LO 2	18.	c	LO 7	30.	d	LO 11
7.	c	LO 2	19.	d	LO 7	31.	a	LO 11
8.	c	LO 2	20.	b	LO 7	32.	c	LO 12
9.	c	LO 3	21.	a	LO 8	33.	a	LO 12
10.	c	LO 3	22.	a	LO 8	34.	c	LO 12
11.	a	LO 4	23.	a	LO 9	35.	d	LO 12
12.	d	LO 4	24.	b	LO 9			

Key to Self-Test B

1.	e		5.	b
2.	d		6.	g
3.	f		7.	c
4.	a			

Key to Essay Questions

1. An appropriate answer should include alcohol and other drugs, such as marijuana and cocaine, and their potential effects on the developing embryo/fetus, noting when during development the particular organs are most vulnerable (note that no amount of alcohol is considered safe at any point during pregnancy). You should also discuss what is known about the effects of certain diseases, such as rubella, syphilis, HIV/AIDS, etc., and about environmental hazards such as radiation, lead, etc. Explain how each of these problems can be avoided (e.g., do not consume alcohol or other drugs during pregnancy); and then describe the type of prenatal care that a pregnant woman should get to ensure the health of her child.

2. Describe the three stages of birth (e.g., first stage, the longest, lasts an average of 12 to 24 hours, with contractions first being 15 to 20 minutes apart); discuss possible complications (e.g., breech position); explain why your friend may or may not want to use drugs during childbirth, which drugs might be used, and potential consequences of using drugs for mother and child; and finally, describe the different childbirth strategies, such as standard childbirth, the Lamaze method, etc., and why "your friend" might prefer one over another. Be sure to discuss also the benefits of having her husband present during the birth process.

Key to Scramblers

1. Blastocyst: The inner layer of cells that develops in the germinal period; they provide nutrition and support for the embryo
2. Embryonic period: The period of prenatal development that occurs 2 to 8 weeks after conception
3. Placenta: A life-support system that consists of a disk-shaped group of tissues in which small blood vessels from the mother and offspring intertwine
4. Umbilical cord: A life-support system containing two arteries and one vein that connects the baby to the placenta
5. Organogenesis: Organ formation that takes place during the first 2 months of prenatal development
6. Teratogen: From the Greek word *tera*, meaning "monster," any agent that causes a birth defect
7. Fetal alcohol syndrome: A cluster of abnormalities that appears in the offspring of mothers who drink alcohol heavily during pregnancy
8. Doula: A caregiver who provides continuous physical, emotional, and educational support to the mother before, during, and just after birth
9. Grantley Dick-Read: English obstetrician who developed natural childbirth
10. Ferdinand Lamaze: French obstetrician who developed prepared childbirth

Research Project 1: Women's Health Practices

The text discusses certain behaviors that are potentially harmful to the unborn child, such as smoking or using alcohol and other drugs; it also discusses healthful practices, such as good nutrition, safe exercise, prenatal care, etc. Talk to women you know who are of childbearing age to see how much they know about what is both harmful and healthful for their unborn child; assess the behaviors in which they engage; and for those who smoke, drink, or use other drugs, have them tell you why they do so, whether they will continue to do so when they are pregnant, and what they expect the consequences might be for their child. If they are unaware of the potential harmful effects of teratogens, explain these to them, then ask if they would engage in these practices while pregnant. Compare the responses you get to see if you can draw any conclusions. What type of campaign do you think might be useful to have women discontinue unhealthy behaviors and engage in healthful ones instead?

Research Project 2: Understanding Teratogens

The chapter describes various teratogens, environmental agents that are harmful to the unborn child. There are other potentially dangerous elements not included due to space limitations. Consider the list of teratogens that were included, then check out others that were not (for example, did you know that the bacteria in cat litter can result in toxoplasmosis, which causes premature birth, as well as eye and brain defects?). Chart the teratogens described in the text, then add others from your own research. Indicate the period of development when each teratogen affects the unborn child, potential problems that may result, how (if at all) the problem can be treated, how to protect the pregnant mother and her child, and other information you think is important.

Teratogen & Its Source	Critical Period	Problems Caused	Treatment If Any	Protection	Other Relevant Information
Rubella (German Measles)					
Syphilis					
Alcohol					

1. Which of these teratogens are easily avoidable? How can they be avoided?
2. Which are difficult to avoid? What can be done to protect the mother and her unborn child?
3. What teratogens come from paternal factors?
4. Based on what you have learned, what is the best advice you can think of for a couple who are planning to have a child?

Personal Application Project 1: Reflecting on What You Learned

Consider what you read in Chapter 4, then answer the following questions:

1. What information in this chapter did you already know?
2. How can/do you use that information in your own life?
3. What information in this chapter was totally new to you?
4. How can you use that new information in your own life?
5. What information in this chapter was different from what you previously believed?
6. How was this information different?
7. How do you account for the differences between what you believed and what you learned in the chapter?
8. What is the most important thing you learned from reading this chapter?

Personal Application Project 2: Consider Your Choices

The chapter offers several different options for childbirth. Other options are also available. These may include natural or prepared childbirth, elective cesarean delivery, use of drugs (from local to general anesthetic), participation of fathers (and other family members), etc. In the chart below, describe the various options that are currently available (include those in the chapter as well as others that you can find), indicate the positive and negative aspects of each, then decide which would seem the best option for you if you were to have a child at this point in time. If you already have children, indicate which you used and why you chose that option (or, if you didn't choose the option yourself, who did?) and if you would choose a different one now that you have more information. What would be the major deciding factors for you in making this choice? This is **not** a women only—fathers are obviously a necessary part of procreation, so guys, think about this, too!

Type of Childbirth Option	Positive Aspects	Negative Aspects	Whose Choice Would This Option Be?	Deciding Factors for Choosing/Not Choosing
No. 1 Choice:				

Internet Projects

Check out the McGraw-Hill web site for this text (http://www.mhhe.com/santrockld8). You'll find numerous activities there, in particular various quizzes, flash cards of key terms, and a challenging and fun crossword puzzle. Please note that all website addresses in this Study Guide have been checked and are correct at the time of publication, however, websites may be discontinued or addresses may change so when you search a given site it may no longer be viable. If that occurs, I apologize for the inconvenience, and would appreciate you notifying me so I could make appropriate revisions in future editions of this Study Guide.

Internet Project 1: Predicting the Baby's Sex

This is a fun project for predicting whether a child will be a boy or a girl. If you/your spouse is currently pregnant, try this for predicting your own child's sex; otherwise, interview someone you know who is pregnant by asking the questions on this website: http://www.childbirth.org. If the parents-to-be already know the sex of the child, see if this prediction agrees with the doctor's prediction. Note that there is a lot of other information about pregnancy and childbirth on this site as well.

Internet Project 2: Preventing FAS

Fetal alcohol syndrome (FAS) is 100 percent preventable. How? By not consuming alcohol when the baby is being conceived or at any time during pregnancy. Once the damage is done, though, it can't be undone. There are, however, ways to work with children who have FAS (or the milder FAE). Go to the website for the National Organization for Fetal Alcohol Syndrome, http://www.nofas.org, and research this topic. Try to answer the following questions:

1. What is fetal alcohol syndrome?
2. What characteristics does an FAS child have, cognitively and physically?
3. What are the major problems encountered by someone with FAS?
4. How does FAS differ from FAE?
5. How does either FAS or FAE occur and how can it be prevented?

After clicking on the link that discusses how to work with children who have fetal alcohol syndrome, design a program that you think would help maximize the abilities (and minimize the challenges) of an FAS child. How long-lasting do you think this intervention would be? Explain your reasoning. What type of campaign would you suggest to eliminate FAS and FAE altogether?

Other Relevant Sites on the Internet

APA site
http://www.apa.org offers a multitude of options for learning about pregnancy, childbirth options, and other topics covered in this chapter.

Childbirth.org
http://www.childbirth.org offers information about all topics covered in the chapter, plus links to other sites.

Embryo Visualization
http://embryovis.com presents excellent graphics of the gestational period with links to other sites.

Family Web

http://www.familyweb.com/pregnancy/natal is another excellent site with good photographs that help the viewer understand fetal development.

Society for Research in Child Development (SRCD)

http://srcd.org is the web site for SRCD, an organization whose purposes are to promote multidisciplinary research in the field of human development, to foster the exchange of information among scientists and other professionals of various disciplines, and to encourage applications of research findings.

Ultrasound Pictures

http://www.ob-ultrasound.net/ may be a bit overwhelming for those not yet initiated into interpreting ultrasound radiographs, but it's an excellent introduction and many of the graphics have markers to help you understand what you are looking at.

Web MD

http://www.webmd.com offers a wide variety of information for the medical profession and for consumers.

Chapter 5: Physical Development in Infancy

Learning Objectives

1. Distinguish between cephalocaudal and proximodistal growth patterns.
2. Describe the physical changes during the first 2 years, including those in height and weight, and changes in brain organization and structure.
3. Describe each of the eight categories of infant states, then define REM sleep and explain its purpose.
4. Describe sudden infant death syndrome (SIDS), and list its risk factors.
5. Discuss the array of nutritional needs for the infant, including the pros and cons of breast- versus bottle-feeding and findings about infant malnutrition.
6. Summarize the arguments surrounding the question of when to toilet train.
7. Describe the various infant reflexes and explain their importance.
8. Explain how the development of gross motor skills and fine motor skills follow the principles of cephalocaudal and proximodistal sequences.
9. State how developmental biodynamics explains how motor behaviors are assembled for perceiving and acting.
10. Differentiate between sensation and perception.
11. Describe the infant's visual abilities, including visual acuity, color vision, visual preferences, depth perception, and visual expectations.
12. Describe the infant's senses in addition to vision, explaining how we know that infants can hear before birth and identifying odors and tastes that newborns can discriminate.
13. Define intermodal perception and the notion of perceptual-motor coupling and unification.

Chapter Outline

PHYSICAL GROWTH AND DEVELOPMENT IN INFANCY
    Cephalocaudal and Proximodistal Sequences
    Height and Weight
    The Brain
        The Brain's Development
        The Brain's Hemispheres
        Early Experience and the Brain
    Infant States
        REM Sleep
        Shared Sleeping
        SIDS
    Nutrition
        Nutritional Needs and Eating Behavior
        Brest-Versus Bottle-Feeding
        Infant Malnutrition
    Toilet Training
MOTOR DEVELOPMENT
    Reflexes
    Gross and Fine Motor Skills
    Developmental Biodynamics
SENSORY AND PERCEPTUAL DEVELOPMENT
    What Are Sensation and Perception?

Self-Test A: Multiple Choice

1. Which best demonstrates the basic principle of cephalocaudal development?
   a. an infant first producing an endogenous smile, then an exogenous smile, then a laugh
   b. an infant first being able to raise the head, then sit up, then stand up
   c. an infant obtaining visual skills, then olfactory skills, then auditory skills
   d. an infant cooing, then babbling, then the first word, then language

2. The proximodistal progression pattern is seen in children's:
   a. drawings, which are first done using the entire arm, and eventually using only the wrist and fingers.
   b. toileting behavior, which proceeds from urine control to bowel control.
   c. head size, which originally comprises about one-fourth of the body, and eventually only one-eighth of the body.
   d. memory, which proceeds from sensory store to short-term to long-term store.

3. Which statement most accurately describes height and weight changes during infancy?
   a. Both increase more rapidly during the second year than during the first year.
   b. Girls increase in height and weight faster than boys do during infancy.
   c. The sexes grow at the same rate during infancy.
   d. Both height and weight increase more rapidly during the first year than during the second year.

4. Which of the following is NOT one of the characteristics of the infant brain?
   a. Increasing experience increases the number of neurons.
   b. Increasing experience increases the number of connections between neurons.
   c. The dendrites branch out with increasing age.
   d. Neurotransmitters change with increasing age.

5. The process of encasing axons with fat cells, which protects nerve cells and helps nerve impulses travel faster, is referred to as:
   a. neuronal growth.
   b. myelination.
   c. lipidation.
   d. insulation.

6. Charles Nelson has made great strides in finding out about the brain's development in infancy by using:
   a. PET scans.
   b. MRIs.
   c. electrodes.
   d. CT scans.

7. The most extensive research on brain lateralization has focused on:
   a. language.
   b. visual coordination.
   c. olfaction.
   d. motor coordination.

8. Research on language processing in the brain has found that:
   a. virtually all language is carried out in the left hemisphere.
   b. virtually all language is carried out in the right hemisphere.
   c. in normal people, the complex thinking required to produce language results from communication between both hemispheres.
   d. in normal people, tasks involving logical thinking are carried out in the left hemisphere and those involving creative thinking occur in the right hemisphere.

9. Neuroscientists believe that what wires the brain is:
   a. genetic heritage.
   b. repeated experience.
   c. constant stimulation.
   d. a delicate balance of proteins and amino acids.

10. Before birth, it appears that:
    a. the brain is fully "wired" and ready for action.
    b. intrauterine experiences preprogram the brain's development.
    c. extrauterine experiences preprogram the brain's development.
    d. genes mainly direct how the brain establishes basic wiring patterns.

11. If an alien randomly dropped in on ten newborns, it might conclude that humans spend their entire first months of life:
    a. eating.
    b. crying.
    c. playing.
    d. sleeping.

12. Which statement most accurately portrays the sleep-wake cycle of infants?
    a. Infants sleep less as they grow older.
    b. Newborn sleep is reflexive, whereas infant sleep is intentional.
    c. Infants eventually sleep more during the day than they do at night.
    d. Infants spend less time sleeping than do adults.

13. Cross-cultural research demonstrates that infant sleep patterns around the world:
    a. are the same.
    b. differ for each culture.
    c. may relate to mother-child contact.
    d. have been steadily changing as humans evolve.

14. Sleep researchers have found that:
    a. infants and adults exhibit very similar patterns of REM sleep.
    b. infants engage in more REM sleep than adults.
    c. adults engage in more REM sleep than infants.
    d. adults enter REM sleep earlier in the sleep cycle than infants do.

15. Since 1992, when the American Academy of Pediatrics began recommending that infants _____, the frequency of SIDS has decreased.
    a. sleep on their stomachs
    b. sleep on their backs
    c. sleep on their sides
    d. do not sleep with their mothers

16. Juan was a low-birthweight infant, while Serge was a premature infant. Which statement applies to them?
    a. Neither is vulnerable to SIDS.
    b. Juan is less vulnerable to SIDS than Serge.
    c. Juan is more vulnerable to SIDS than Serge.
    d. Both are vulnerable to SIDS.

17. Infants require about _____ calories a day for each pound they weigh.
    a. 25
    b. 50
    c. 75
    d. 100

18. Breast-feeding is superior to bottle-feeding because:
    a. breast-feeding is more convenient and more adaptable to the time requirements of demand feeding.
    b. breast milk is a superior source of the nutrients babies need.
    c. bottle-fed infants suffer psychological damage because they become only weakly attached to their mothers.
    d. breast-feeding is not superior to bottle-feeding; this is a myth.

19. Which of the following conditions is NOT necessary for a young child to be toilet trained?
    a. adequate motivation
    b. muscular maturation
    c. muscular control
    d. a regulated toileting schedule

20. Which statement best characterizes infant reflexes?
    a. Reflexes are vestigial remnants of early evolutionary processes.
    b. Reflexes are genetically carried survival mechanisms.
    c. Modern infants rely more on learning than on reflexes.
    d. All reflexes disappear by the end of infancy.

21. The sucking style of an infant is dependent on all of the following EXCEPT:
    a. the way the milk is coming out of the bottle or breast.
    b. the infant's sucking speed and temperament.
    c. the way the infant is held.
    d. the nourishment being offered.

22. Charlie turns his head, opens his mouth, and begins sucking when his cheek is stroked. Charlie is demonstrating which reflex?
    a. rooting
    b. Babinski
    c. tonic neck
    d. Moro

23. Which infant motor event typically occurs first?
    a. stands with support
    b. cruises around furniture
    c. rolls over
    d. sits without support

24. The American Academy of Pediatrics recommends that parents:
    a. slowly ease their babies into structured exercise regimes.
    b. enroll their babies in exercise classes.
    c. use exercise sessions as a way to bond with their babies.
    d. avoid structured exercise classes for babies.

25. As a researcher who uses the developmental biodynamics perspective, Dr. Sandee would:
    a. describe the ages at which various motor achievements are reached.
    b. describe universal milestones (e.g., crawling, walking) as a process of adaptation.
    c. explain the ages at which various motor achievements are reached as a result of brain maturation.
    d. explain the ages at which various motor achievements are reached as a result of maturation of the central nervous system.

26. _____ occurs when information interacts with sensory receptors.
    a. Sensation
    b. Perception
    c. Intermodal perception
    d. Perceptual-motor coupling

27. Was William James right when he proclaimed that newborns experience a "blooming, buzzing" world of confusion?
    a. No, because infants display visual preferences.
    b. Yes, because infants' visual acuity is less than that of adults.
    c. Yes, because infants sense the world but do not perceive it.
    d. No, because infants' reflexes allow for organization into perceptual categories.

28. Robert Fantz (1963) found that infants as young as 2 days old:
    a. were able to focus on their mothers' eyes.
    b. were able to distinguish contour.
    c. showed a preference for patterned stimuli over plain stimuli.
    d. began to perceive the oval shape of the head.

29. In Gibson and Walk's (1960) experiment, infants placed on one side of a visual cliff refused to go to their mothers who were coaxing them from the other side. This result was cited as evidence for:
    a. depth perception.
    b. failure of visual acuity.
    c. inability to hear at a distance.
    d. inability to crawl.

30. What evidence indicates that a fetus can hear?
    a. A fetus moves when a loud noise occurs.
    b. Newborns prefer their mother's voice to strangers' voices.
    c. Hearing is more sensitive and better developed among newborns who have been experimentally stimulated before birth
    d. Newborns prefer to hear stories that were read to them in their mother's womb.

31. One current controversy concerning the medical treatment of infants involves:
    a. the use of small amounts of cocaine to stimulate the heart rate of sluggish neonates.
    b. the rule of now allowing mothers to hold their at-risk low-birthweight neonate immediately after birth.
    c. not using any anesthetics when performing surgery on young infants.
    d. the fact that a mother's opinion outweighs a father's when it comes to a decision of whether a child should be given a heart transplant.

32. Which of the following smells do infants like the LEAST?
    a. vanilla
    b. fish
    c. their mother's milk
    d. strawberries

33. Jessica turned her head when she heard footsteps in the hall, then she smiled when she saw her mother come into the room. This demonstrates _____ perception.
    a. depth
    b. intermodal
    c. auditory
    d. visual

Self-Test B: Matching

Match the following persons with the statement or theory that most closely reflects their perspective:

1. Charles Nelson
2. Ernesto Pollitt
3. T. Berry Brazelton
4. Rachel Clifton
5. Esther Thelen
6. William James
7. Robert Fantz
8. Eleanor Gibson
9. Elizabeth Spelke

a. Used looking chambers to see infants' visual preferences
b. Grasping is guided by proprioception rather than vision
c. Used the visual cliff to study infant depth perception
d. Measures babies' brain activity to determine its role in memory development
e. Infants have a biological core knowledge of the perceptual world
f. Pediatrician who observed development of infant sucking
g. Believed that newborns experience a "blooming, buzzing" world of confusion
h. Proponent of developmental biodynamics view of infant motor development
i. Early nutritional supplements have positive long-term effects on cognitive development

Essay Questions

1. A good friend of yours just had a baby and, knowing you are taking this course in life-span development, confides in you about her concerns. She says her baby sleeps "almost all the time" and doesn't seem to look at her when she feeds, rocks, or talks to the child. Because of this your friend is worried about her baby's hearing and vision, and is also concerned about whether the baby's nutritional needs are being adequately met and, her greatest concern comes from horror stories she has heard about sudden infant death syndrome. She's also told you that her baby seems to "thrash about" at things and doesn't seem coordinated. What would you tell her about sleep patterns that a normal baby experiences and the best sleeping position to reduce the risk of SIDS? What nutritional advice can you give her? How would you explain the development of motor skills as well as sensory and perceptual development, addressing issues of intermodal perception and perceptual-motor coupling and unification? What strategies might you suggest to your friend for helping her infant develop competently?

2. Your high school psychology teacher has learned that you are taking this course in life-span development and has asked you to talk to her class about the course of infant development. She has asked that you describe the patterns of cephalocaudal and proximodistal development, gross versus fine motor skills, and the development of sensation and perception. When you talked to her about this presentation, you noted she has assumed you know all about intermodal perception and perceptual-motor coupling and unification because she wants you to explain those concepts to her class as well. Remembering that this was your favorite teacher in high school, what would you tell these high school students in response to her request?

Scramblers

Unscramble the following people or terms, then describe what they are known for (people) or define them (terms):

1. BTRERO TNZAF

_____

2. IHZBAELTE PSKELE

_____

58

3. OLCAAHUPDEACL PNRATET

_____

4. LAIRZEATTAILNO

_____

5. SMRUSMAA

_____

6. PSIANRGG XREELF

_____

7. SOSRG OMTRO IKLSLS

_____

8. MPOENLETAVLED OBYDMANICSI

_____

9. ASNOESINT

_____

10. NPOEIRTCPE

_____

Key to Self-Test A

1.	b	LO 1	12.	a	LO 3	23.	c	LO 8
2.	a	LO 1	13.	c	LO 3	24.	d	LO 8
3.	d	LO 2	14.	b	LO 3	25.	b	LO 9
4.	d	LO 2	15.	b	LO 4	26.	a	LO 10
5.	b	LO 2	16.	c	LO 4	27.	a	LO 11
6.	c	LO 2	17.	b	LO 5	28.	c	LO 11
7.	a	LO 2	19.	b	LO 5	29.	a	LO 11
8.	c	LO 2	19.	d	LO 6	30.	d	LO 12
9.	b	LO 2	20.	b	LO 7	31.	c	LO 12
10.	d	LO 2	21.	d	LO 7	32.	b	LO 12
11.	d	LO 3	22.	a	LO 7	33.	b	LO 13

Key to Self-Test B

1. d	4. b	7. a
2. i	5. h	8. c
3. f	6. g	9. e

Key to Essay Questions

1. An appropriate answer should include discussion of infant states, noting that the typical neonate will sleep about 17 hours a day, but may range from 10 to 21 hours a day. Advise her that sleeping on the back is the best position for reducing the risk of SIDS. Then discuss the notions of cephalocaudal and proximodistal development, noting that development proceeds from head down and from inside out, and that infants are first learning to coordinate gross motor skills before they can develop fine motor skills. In terms of your friend's concern about eye contact, tell her about the infant's visual limitations, then explain to her what we know about development of the other sensory modalities; here you should incorporate information about intermodal perception (how the sensory modalities are linked) and perceptual-motor coupling and unification (looking at how perceptual-motor development is integrated). Finally, you would want to make some suggestions for how your friend can maximize her baby's development and ensure that the baby is well, so this would include: (a) discussing her concerns with her pediatrician; (b) being flexible about the baby's own rhythms; (c) providing good nutrition and explaining infants' nutritional needs; and (d) being supportive and encouraging while providing a safe yet stimulating environment.

2. As in the previous question, you would discuss the notions of cephalocaudal and proximodistal development, noting that development proceeds from head down and from inside out, and that infants are first learning to coordinate gross motor skills before they can develop fine motor skills (for example, a child will first grasp a crayon with her fist before she is able to control a pencil with her fingers). You would then add the discussion on intermodal perception and perceptual-motor coupling and unification outlined above, being sure to provide understandable examples.

Key to Scramblers

1. Robert Fantz: Used looking chambers to see infants' visual preferences
2. Elizabeth Spelke: Believed infants have a biological core knowledge of the perceptual world
3. Cephalocaudal pattern: The sequence in which the growth gradually proceeds from top to bottom
4. Lateralization: Specialization of functions in one hemisphere of the cerebral cortex or the other
5. Marasmus: A wasting away of body tissues in the infant's first year, caused by protein-calorie deficiency
6. Grasping reflex: A neonatal reflex; the infant tightly grasps something touching the infant's palms
7. Gross motor skills: Motor skills that involve large muscle activities, such as walking
8. Developmental biodynamics: Explains how motor behaviors are assembled for perceiving and acting
9. Sensation: Occurs when information interacts with the sensory receptors
10. Perception: The interpretation of what is sensed

Research Project 1: Observing Infants' Reflexes and Sensory Abilities

After getting parental permission (or try to get permission to visit a neonatal unit in a local hospital), observe an infant for half an hour. Record the infant's age and your observations of the infant's use of reflexes and sensory modalities. If you know the child's parents, you may want to seek permission to test some of the reflexes, so long as this does not cause any distress for the infant. Compare your observations with what you would expect of a child this age from reading Chapter 5 and from researching other reflexes. Then answer the questions that follow.

Child's Age (in days or weeks)_____   Child's Sex   Female [ ]   Male [ ]

Sense	Observed	Expected	Expected Change Over Time
Visual (Sight)			
Auditory (Sound)			
Olfactory (Smell)			
Gustatory (Taste)			
Tactile (Touch)			
Integration of Senses			

Reflex	Observed	Expected	Expected Change Over Time
Blinking			
Grasping			
Rooting			
Sucking			
Moro			
Tonic Neck			
Babinski			
Plantar			

1. How did the infant demonstrate the presence of each of the senses?
2. In what way did you observe that the infant was able to integrate the different senses?
3. Were your observations of this infant's sensory development consistent with what you would expect from reading Chapter 5?
4. Which reflexes were you able to observe? Describe the infant's reflexive behaviors.
5. What additional reflexes did you observe that were not described in the chapter?
6. Were your observations of this infant's reflexes consistent with what you would expect from reading Chapter 5 and the outside sources you found?
7. What purpose do you think each of the reflexes serves?

8. You might note from Figure 5.7 that some reflexes are permanent and others "drop out" after a certain period of time. Which reflexes remain with us, which disappear, and what might it mean if those that are expected to disappear don't?

9. What have you learned about the infant's adaptive abilities from observing this child's use of sensory modalities, coordination of senses, and reflexive behaviors?

Research Project 2: Mapping the Brain

Review the information in Chapter 5 on brain development during infancy. Then, using the diagrams below, or any others that you prefer, indicate each area of the brain and what functions it controls for the infant. Explain how the brain develops and how that affects the infant's various cognitive and motor abilities.

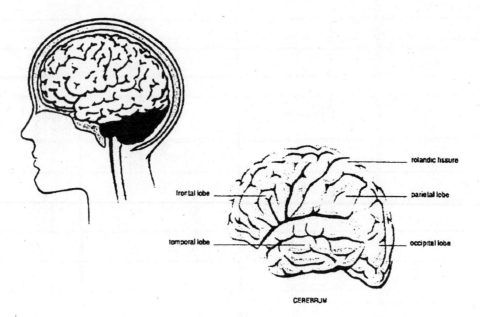

Personal Application Project 1: Reflecting on What You Learned

Consider what you read in Chapter 5, then answer the following questions:

1. What information in this chapter did you already know?
2. How can/do you use that information in your own life?
3. What information in this chapter was totally new to you?
4. How can you use that new information in your own life?
5. What information in this chapter was different from what you previously believed?
6. How was this information different?
7. How do you account for the differences between what you believed and what you learned in the chapter?
8. What is the most important thing you learned from reading this chapter?

Personal Application Project 2: Consider Your Own Development

Check with your parents or other caregivers from your early childhood to see what records, if any, they kept on your development. Consider each area of development discussed in Chapter 5, then use the chart below to complete your own developmental milestones, indicating if they were ahead of, behind, or in synchrony with the stated norms. Do you think your own rate of development (ahead/behind/in synch) affected your later life? If so, state how. If you cannot reconstruct your own early growth, look at your own child(ren) or other children with whom you have close contact (being sure to get parental consent if the children are not your own).

Aspect of Your Self	Your Development	Norms in Chapter 5	Comments
Demonstrations of Cephalocaudal Pattern			
Demonstrations of Proximodistal Pattern			
Height Age Age: Age:			
Weight Age: Age: Age:			
Evidence of Brain Growth			
Gross Motor Skills Age: Age: Age:			
Fine Motor Skills Age: Age: Age:			
Sleeping Patterns			
Other (describe)			

Internet Projects

Check out the McGraw-Hill web site for this text (http://www.mhhe.com/santrockld8). You'll find numerous activities there, in particular various quizzes, flash cards of key terms, and a challenging and fun crossword puzzle. Please note that all website addresses in this Study Guide have been checked and are correct at the time of publication, however, websites may be discontinued or addresses may change so when you search a given site it may no longer be viable. If that occurs, I apologize for the inconvenience, and would appreciate you notifying me so I could make appropriate revisions in future editions of this Study Guide.

Internet Project 1: Sudden Infant Death Syndrome (SIDS)

SIDS is a mysterious problem that is the highest cause of infant death in the United States. Go to the SIDS website at http://sids-network.org to learn more about what SIDS is, risk factors for SIDS, how many children and families are affected, and what steps parents can take to minimize the risk of their child dying from SIDS.

Internet Project 2: Healthy Starts

The Sociocultural Worlds of Development box in Chapter 5 discusses the Hawaii Family Support/ Healthy Start Program. Explore the Internet to find more information about that program and also to find other programs that offer similar support for high-risk families. Check out professional sites (e.g., medical [such as, http://www.webmd.com], psychological [such as, http://www.apa.org]) as well as general information sites (e.g., http://www.searchcactus.com, http://www.askjeeves.com, etc.

1. How many programs were you able to find?
2. Where are the programs located?
3. Who funds these programs?
4. What outcomes have these programs achieved?
5. What steps are taken to keep families in these programs?
6. Compare the professional and general information sites and state what differences you notice in terms of how the programs and the program outcomes are described?
7. Based on what you have learned about the healthy start programs and the results that have been reported, how would you design an effective program to maximize the potential of children in at-risk families?

Other Relevant Sites on the Internet

APA site
http://www.apa.org

APS site
http://www.psychologicalscience.org/

Children's Defense Fund (CDF)
http://www.childrensdefense.org is the web site for CDF, the organization headed by Marian Wright Edelman to promote child welfare (discussed in Chapter 1 of the text).

Florida State University Center for Music Research School of Music
http://otto.cmr.fsu/memt/baby/allbaby looks into research on the effects of music on intelligence (and offers parents of new babies the opportunity to participate).

New York University Infant Cognition Center
http://www.psych.nyu.edu/infant is NYU's Infant Cognition Center's site presenting the latest information on how babies think.

Pediatric Health and Safety Information
http://www.babysdoc.com is edited and reviewed by board certified pediatricians. It offers an array of information on development revolving around health and safety issues, but also promotes products for sale.

Society for Research in Child Development (SRCD)
http://srcd.org is the web site for SRCD, an organization whose purposes are to promote multidisciplinary research in the field of human development, to foster the exchange of information among scientists and other professionals of various disciplines, and to encourage applications of research findings.

Zero to Three
http://www.zerotothree.com is a site for parents and professional. Zero to Three is a non-profit organization that focuses on promoting the healthy development of babies and toddlers.

Chapter 6:   Cognitive Development in Infancy

Learning Objectives

1. Grasp the four stages in Piaget's theory of cognitive development, and the role the concepts of assimilation, accommodation, and schemes play in the individual's adaptation.
2. Describe Piaget's sensorimotor stage of development, including the six substages and object permanence.
3. Discuss the contributions of Piaget's theory to the perceptual and conceptual development of infants, and then discuss how more modern researchers might modify his views.
4. Explain how research with infants has demonstrated the role of conditioning in early cognitive abilities.
5. Describe the concepts of habituation and dishabituation.
6. Understand the infant's memory capabilities and how that relates to imitation.
7. Discuss the history of intelligence testing, the tests that are used to test infant intelligence, and the relationship between infant cognitive abilities and cognitive functioning in childhood and adolescence.
8. Describe what language is and how it relates to the concept of infinite generativity.
9. Explain the developmental milestones in language development including receptive vocabulary, the holophrase hypothesis, and telegraphic speech.
10. Describe how biological development influences the development of language and cite evidence to support Chomsky's view of language development.
11. Describe the behavioral view of language development and be able to indicate how environmental factors influence the development of language.

Chapter Outline

PIAGET'S THEORY OF INFANT DEVELOPMENT
>   The Stage of Sensorimotor Development
>   Substages
>>   Simple Reflexes
>>   First Habits and Primary Circular Reactions
>>   Secondary Circular Reactions
>>   Coordination of Secondary Circular Reactions
>>   Tertiary Circular Reactions, Novelty, and Curiosity
>>   Internalization of Schemes
>   Object Permanence
>   Evaluating Piaget's Sensorimotor Stage
>>   Perceptual Development
>>   Conceptual Development

LEARNING AND REMEMBERING
>   Conditioning
>   Habituation and Dishabituation
>   Imitation
>   Memory

INDIVIDUAL DIFFERENCES IN INTELLIGENCE

LANGUAGE DEVELOPMENT
>   Defining Language
>   How Language Develops
>   Biological Influences
>>   Biological Evolution

Self-Test A: Multiple Choice

1. Jean Piaget gathered the information for his theories about cognitive development by:
   a. reviewing the literature on cognitive development.
   b. surveying thousands of parents.
   c. observing his own children.
   d. testing hundreds of children in his laboratory.

2. In a Piagetian model, _____ is a cognitive structure that helps individuals organize and understand their experiences.
   a. a memory
   b. an image
   c. cognition
   d. a scheme

3. Piaget's theory is a qualitative theory of cognitive development, which means that it:
   a. uses standardized tests to measure and describe thought.
   b. explains what kinds of knowledge are typical of children at different ages.
   c. identifies different kinds of thinking children perform at different ages.
   d. provides ways to determine how well children think at different stages.

4. According to Piaget, during the first sensorimotor substage, infants' behaviors are:
   a. reflexive.
   b. maladaptive.
   c. unchanging.
   d. reinforced.

5. Which is the best example of Piaget's concept of a habit?
   a. learning to suck on a nipple and later being able to do it while sleeping
   b. accidentally shaking a rattle, which produces a sound, and then purposefully shaking the rattle to produce the sound
   c. initially blinking reflexively in response to a bright light and then blinking when no stimulus is present
   d. learning to laugh at people who slip on ice and fall down

6. By chance, Abigail shook her rattle. She then began to repeat this action of shaking her rattle. As a normal infant, Abigail is in which substage?
   a. reflexive
   b. first habits and primary circular reactions
   c. secondary circular reactions
   d. coordination of secondary circular reactions

7. Laurent has problems retrieving a ball that rolled out of reach, so he uses a Tinkertoy stick to hit it. He is in which substage?
   a. primary circular reactions
   b. secondary circular reactions
   c. coordination of secondary circular reactions
   d. tertiary circular reactions

8. When D'Andre was 5 months old, he looked at a toy train, but when his view of the train was blocked, he did not search for it. Now that he is 9 months old he does look for it, reflecting the presence of:
   a. object permanence.
   b. self-differentiation.
   c. assimilation.
   d. schemata.

9. Much of the new research on cognitive development in children suggests that:
   a. Piaget's view was accurate.
   b. Piaget's view was wrong.
   c. Piaget's view needs to be modified.
   d. it is impossible to replicate Piaget's research because it was done primarily on his three children.

10. Research by Renée Baillargeon has found that:
    a. infants as young as 4 months of age have intermodal perception.
    b. infants as young as 4 months of age expect objects to be substantial and permanent.
    c. equipment for testing children under 4 months of age is not yet sophisticated enough to provide useful information about perception.
    d. infants are not able to see objects as bounded, unitary, solid, and separate from their background until they are at least 4 months old.

11. Infants whose parents use sign language have been observed to start using conventional signs at about _____ months of age.
    a. 2 to 3
    b. 6 to 7
    c. 9 to 10
    d. 12 to 13

12. Carolyn Rovee-Collier (1987) has demonstrated:
    a. young infants' inability to learn from classical conditioning.
    b. young infants' inability to learn from operant conditioning.
    c. how infants can retain information through classical conditioning.
    d. how infants can retain information through operant conditioning.

13. _____ occurs when repeated exposure to the same stimulus results in a reduced reaction to that stimulus.
    a. Habituation
    b. Object permanence
    c. Transference
    d. Dishabituation

14. Which is an example of dishabituation?
    a. the excitement students exhibit when a boring professor shows a film instead of lecturing
    b. first being bothered by wearing a new wristwatch, but then getting so used to it that you forget you're wearing it
    c. realizing that when a jet flies off into the distance it still exists
    d. a drinker who believes she is not responsible for her actions

15. Having an understanding of habituation and dishabituation can benefit parent-infant interaction in that the "wise" parent does all of the following EXCEPT:
    a. presents many repetitions of a stimulus so the infant can process the information.
    b. stops repetitively presenting a stimulus when the infant redirects her attention.
    c. continues to present a stimulus to regain the infant's attention when the infant looks away.
    d. changes behaviors when the infant redirects her attention.

16. Research by Andrew Meltzoff (1992, 1999) showing the infant's ability to imitate adult facial expressions shortly after birth demonstrates that:
    a. imitative abilities are learned quickly.
    b. imitation has a biological base.
    c. infants have a full range of emotional expression at birth.
    d. imitation is a form of emotional expression.

17. Meltzoff has found that infants demonstrate the ability to engage in deferred imitation by age _____ months.
    a. 3
    b. 6
    c. 9
    d. 18

18. Lorenzo is a normal 4-month-old infant. Thus we would expect him to have _____ memory.
    a. both implicit and explicit
    b. neither implicit nor explicit
    c. implicit but not explicit
    d. explicit but not implicit

19. Sarula is 18 years old. She finds it frustrating that she cannot remember anything prior to the time she was 3 years old. According to the research on memory:
    a. she is "normal," since most adults cannot remember anything from the first 3 years of their life.
    b. her memory is deficient, since it is common for adults to remember back to the time when they were at least 2 years old.
    c. she should be concerned, because it appears she is suffering from a loss of memory called infantile amnesia.
    d. her inability to remember before age 3 may be an indicator that she was sexually molested as an infant.

20. The developmental quotient (DQ) is a global developmental score that combines subscores in all of the following domains EXCEPT:
    a. motor.
    b. language.
    c. physical.
    d. personal-social.

21. The Fagan Test of Infant Intelligence:
    a. estimates intelligence by comparing the amount of time a baby looks at a new object and the amount of time spent looking at a familiar object.
    b. assesses infants' overall development in terms of motor, language, adaptive, and personal-social domains.
    c. has been successful at measuring infant intelligence in industrialized nations, but not in third-world countries.
    d. was the first measure of infant intelligence.

22. The _____ has been predictive of academic achievement at 6 or 8 years of age.
    a. Piagetian Sensorimotor Scales
    b. Bayley Scales of Infant Development
    c. Gesell Developmental Schedules
    d. Brazelton Neonatal Behavior Assessment Scales

23. Infant intelligence scales are useful for all of the following EXCEPT:
    a. assessing the effects of malnutrition.
    b. predicting childhood intelligence.
    c. determining developmental effects of environmental stimulation.
    d. measuring detrimental effects of a mother's prenatal drug-taking habits.

24. Language is most accurately defined as a system of _____ that allow for communication with others.
    a. images
    b. vocalizations
    c. symbols
    d. words

25. The child's first word is typically uttered at around _____ months.
    a. 3 to 6
    b. 6 to 9
    c. 9 to 10
    d. 10 to 15

26. The child's first words:
    a. are the same today as they were 50 years ago.
    b. were more likely related to people than to objects 50 years ago as compared with today.
    c. are more likely related to people than to objects today than they were 50 years ago.
    d. are more complex today than they were 50 years ago.

27. Andrew sees a cat on the lawn then says to his mother, "Kitty." The notion that Andrew is using that one word to imply a whole sentence, such as "That's a kitty," would be suggestive of the _____ hypothesis.
    a. generalization
    b. generativity
    c. cognitive
    d. holophrase

28. Which statement about the two-word utterances of 18- to 24-month old children is NOT correct?
    a. The child relies heavily on gesture, tone, and context to help convey meaning.
    b. They are used by children in such diversecountries as the United States, Germany, Russia, and Samoa.
    c. They are difficult for adults to understand.
    d. They can communicate a wealth of meaning.

29. The strongest evidence for the biological basis of language is that:
    a. a language acquisition device (LAD) has been located in the brain's temporal lobe.
    b. children all over the world reach language milestones at about the same time and in the same order.
    c. language represents chains of responses and imitation.
    d. children from middle-income professional and welfare backgrounds develop normally in terms of language.

30. The best estimate is that human language evolved about _____ years ago.
    a. 20,000
    b. 50,000
    c. 100,000
    d. 500,000

31. If a child were reared in isolation from people for the first 10 or 11 years of life, that child would likely:
    a. never learn to communicate effectively with humans.
    b. learn to communicate if given speech and language therapy.
    c. learn to communicate if placed in a warm, comfortable environment.
    d. learn to communicate in that child's own personal language system understood by a few people.

32. In their study of language development in children, Hart and Risley (1995) found that:
   a. middle-income professional parents spent almost twice as much time communicating with their children as the welfare parents did.
   b. welfare parents spent almost twice as much time communicating with their children as the middle-income professional parents did.
   c. in the United States, there were few differences between the amount of time middle-income professional parents and welfare parents spent communicating with their children.
   d. the amount of time that parents spent communicating with their children made little difference in terms of the children's later language abilities.

33. Dr. Jones claims Marie can make a negative statement because that use was reinforced. Dr. Jones most likely takes which view?
   a. biological
   b. behavioral
   c. cognitive
   d. interactionist

34. Which of the following statements is NOT correct about infant-directed speech?
   a. It is sometimes called "parentese."
   b. It involves the use of simple words and sentences.
   c. Much of it is automatic when an adult is talking to a baby.
   d. It has a lower than normal pitch.

35. When Jennifer said, "The deer was running," Mother asked, "Where was the deer running?" Mother's strategy is:
   a. echoing.
   b. expanding.
   c. recasting.
   d. labeling.

Self-Test B: Matching

Match the following persons with the statement or theory that most closely reflects their perspective:

1. Arnold Gesell
2. Carol Rovee-Collier
3. Nancy Bayley
4. Andrew Meltzoff
5. Roger Brown
6. Jean Piaget
7. Jean Mandler
8. Noam Chomsky
9. Renée Baillargeon

a. Devised the most commonly used infant intelligence test
b. Contributed to cognitive theory by observing his three children
c. Studied imitation and deferred imitation by infants
d. Argued that explicit memory does not occur until the second half of first year
e. Believes humans are biologically prewired to learn language
f. No evidence supports reinforcement as responsible for language rule systems
g. Infants as young as 4 months expect objects to be substantial and permanent
h. Demonstrated detailed memory in 2- to 3-month-old infants
i. Developed a clinical measure to assess potential abnormality in infants

Essay Questions

1. Your next-door neighbor is planning to open a day-care center that caters to infants and toddlers. She has had a lot of experience with toddlers, but less experience with infants, and so she has asked you to share what you have been learning in your life-span development class. She is familiar with Piaget, but has heard some criticisms of his ideas and asks you what you know about this. She also wants your suggestions on how to provide the best possible environment for the children. What would you tell her?

2. Your 15-month-old nephew has started using two-word sentences. His father is overjoyed with what a genius his son is, and he shares his delight with you every time the two of you speak. While he constantly lets you know that this is clearly a matter of genetics, he also wants to know what he can do to encourage his child's language development. Explain the process of language development to him, including the stages of language development and explanations of the biological and behavioral theories involved, and discuss with him the research on the influence of both genetics and environment with regard to language development. On the basis of what you know, do you agree with the boy's father that his language skills are advanced? Or do you believe they are either normal or delayed? Give your reasons.

Scramblers

Unscramble the following people or terms, then describe what they are known for (people) or define them (terms):

1. AENJ DLNERAM

_____

2. MOAN MSOKYHC

_____

3. MEHCES

_____

4. YARESCDON LCUARIRC ITOCNASER

_____

5. SINDOITHBAUATI

_____

6. RERFEDED NIOMIITTA

_____

7. UGANGAEL

_____

8. PETCIEVRE UBLACAROYV

_____

9. HGIOLAROCPH HSIYPSOEHT

_____

Key to Self-Test A

1.	c	LO 1	13.	a	LO 5	25.	d	LO 9
2.	d	LO 1	14.	a	LO 5	26.	a	LO 9
3.	c	LO 1	15.	c	LO 5	27.	d	LO 9
4.	a	LO 2	16.	b	LO 6	28.	c	LO 9
5.	c	LO 2	17.	c	LO 6	29.	b	LO 10
6.	c	LO 2	18.	c	LO 6	30.	c	LO 10
7.	c	LO 2	19.	a	LO 6	31.	a	LO 10
8.	a	LO 2	20.	c	LO 7	32.	a	LO 11
9.	c	LO 3	21.	a	LO 7	33.	b	LO 11
10.	b	LO 3	22.	b	LO 7	34.	d	LO 11
11.	b	LO 3	23.	b	LO 7	35.	c	LO 11
12.	d	LO 4	24.	c	LO 8			

Key to Self-Test B

1.	i	4.	c	7.	d
2.	h	5.	f	8.	e
3.	a	6.	b	9.	g

Key to Essay Questions

1. First you would talk about Piaget's notions of schemes, then describe each of the six substages in the sensorimotor stage, so your neighbor would be familiar with what to expect. Be sure to include object permanence, as well as imitation and deferred imitation, being clear when each develops. Then you would go through the various criticisms of Piaget's theory (such as the research finding that infants go through the stages earlier than Piaget suggested). You should also present some information about the perceptual and conceptual findings, as well as sensitizing her to children's individual differences. Finally, you would want to offer some advice such as providing a stimulating, but not overstimulating, environment, in which caregivers actively communicate with the infants in their charge.

2. This question requires you to explain each stage of language development discussed in this chapter, beginning with receptive language (understanding words about 6 to 9 months of age), the one-word stage (which begins at approximately 12 months), etc. Present the biological influences, such as biological prewiring as suggested by Noam Chomsky (i.e., the language acquisition device) and the evidence for a critical period for learning language. Also discuss the evidence for environmental influences (e.g., the use of infant directed speech and the strategies such as recasting that adults use with children). The research of Hart and Risley that compares children from middle-class professional families with children from welfare families should help this father understand the importance of communicating with his son. Finally, it would appear that your nephew is, indeed, advanced in his language skills, since the two-word stage doesn't typically begin until 18 to 24 months.

Key to Scramblers

1. Jean Mandler: Argued that explicit memory does not occur until the second half of first year
2. Noam Chomsky: Believes humans are biologically prewired to learn language
3. Scheme: In Piaget's theory, a cognitive structure that helps individuals organize/understand experience
4. Secondary circular reactions: Piaget's 3rd stage; infant becomes more object-oriented
5. Dishabituation: An infant's renewed interest in a stimulus
6. Deferred imitation: Imitation that occurs after a time delay of hours or days
7. Language: A system of symbols used to communicate with others
8. Receptive vocabulary: The words an individual understands
9. Holographic hypothesis: A single word can be used to imply a complete sentence
10. Telegraphic speech: The use of short and precise words to communicate young children's utterances

Research Project 1: Observing Imitation

Something I particularly enjoy doing (as a developmental psychologist) is to observe babies when I'm standing in a line somewhere, like at the grocery store. The next time you find yourself standing behind an infant, observe the child to see what you notice that would (or would not) be consistent with what you've learned in this chapter. Then smile at the baby and see what kind of response you get—does the baby smile back, turn away, ignore you, cry (oh, I hope the baby doesn't cry—I've been lucky that in all the years I've been doing this, they've never cried)? Sometimes, though, you'll notice a baby is crying, and what I've found often stops the crying is to make a big "O" with your mouth as if you are sympathizing with the child and acknowledging the child's distress. Whenever I do this, I find the child will stop crying and look at me in wide-eyed interest. Try opening and shutting your mouth to see if the child will imitate you. You might also try wiggling your nose or your ears. Although people would clearly think you're weird if you do this in some other context, they generally understand when they see the baby, so they'll either ignore you or be amused. Typically the parent(s) will acknowledge your presence, and if they do, you might say you are taking this class and ask the baby's age. (Obviously, if the parent(s) seem annoyed or ask you to stop, do stop immediately; I've never had this happen, though.) Based on your observations, answer the questions that follow:

1. What have you noticed about the child's perceptual abilities?
2. Are they what you would expect for a child of this age (if the parent doesn't tell you how old the child is, you might be able to make an "educated" guess).
3. Did anything the child do surprise you?
4. What did you learn from observing this interaction?

Research Project 2: Charting Cognitive Development in Infancy

Describe the components of cognitive development through the first 2 years of life, stating what you would expect to observe based on what you read in the text. Then observe children during this life stage, and record your observations (unless you are watching unobtrusively, be sure to get permission from parents and, if possible, the children). (You could create a similar chart to observe language development.) Finally, answer the questions that follow.

Developmental Issue	Age Range	Expected Behavior(s)	Observed Behavior(s)
Simple reflexes			
Primary circular reactions			
Secondary circular reactions			
Coordination of secondary circular reactions			
Tertiary circular reactions			
Internalization of schemes			
Perceptual development			
Conceptual development			
Habituation/Dishabituation			
Imitation			
Deferred imitation			
Memory			

1. What did you notice when you compared what you would expect to see from reading the chapter with what you actually did see?
2. Did you observe anything that particularly surprised you with respect to what you expected after reading the chapter? Explain.
3. What observations were consistent with Piaget's theory?
4. What observations were inconsistent with Piaget's theory?
5. Based on your observations, which theories and research studies appeared to be supported?
6. What other comments do you have concerning these observations?

Personal Application Project 1: Reflecting on What You Learned

Consider what you read in Chapter 6, then answer the following questions:

1. What information in this chapter did you already know?
2. How can/do you use that information in your own life?
3. What information in this chapter was totally new to you?
4. How can you use that new information in your own life?
5. What information in this chapter was different from what you previously believed?
6. How was this information different?
7. How do you account for the differences between what you believed and what you learned in the chapter?
8. What is the most important thing you learned from reading this chapter?

Personal Application Project 2: Consider Your Own Development

This may be difficult, but if you can, give it a try. Now that you have learned about infantile amnesia (look back at the chapter if you don't remember what that is) you might understand why you can't remember back to your early life, so you will have to rely on input from older adults who were around at the time you were a baby. Ask your relatives about your developmental milestones during the first 2 years of your life. Be sure to include cognitive milestones (such as Piaget's six substages, if possible), imitation, and language development. Based on these recollections, indicate how consistent your early development was with what the theorists would predict.

Developmental Milestone	Your Development	Comments
Piaget's sensorimotor substages (describe)		
Other cognitive milestones (describe)		
Language development (describe)		
Other (describe)		

Internet Projects

Check out the McGraw-Hill web site for this text (http://www.mhhe.com/santrockld8). You'll find numerous activities there, in particular various quizzes, flash cards of key terms, and a challenging and fun crossword puzzle. Please note that all website addresses in this Study Guide have been checked and are correct at the time of publication, however, websites may be discontinued or addresses may change so when you search a given site it may no longer be viable. If that occurs, I apologize for the inconvenience, and would appreciate you notifying me so I could make appropriate revisions in future editions of this Study Guide.

Internet Project 1: Language Development in Infancy

Two of the particularly interesting web sites are http://www.parentingme.com/language.htm and http://childdevelopmentinfo.com/development/language_development.shtml. The former provides in-depth information concerning language development, the latter presents a chart of language development. Compare the information from both sites with each other and with the text. As you observe young children, can you apply what you are learning from all of these sources (text and Internet sites)? Is there a good fit between what you observe and the information you gather from these sources? Describe any discrepancies you notice.

Internet Project 2: Stimulating Cognitive and Linguistic Development

The text offers several studies that demonstrate the importance of interactions between the baby and others (parents, siblings, other adults, other children) for maximal development. (One thing to watch out for, though, is to avoid overstimulation—take your cue from the baby). One site with many excellent ideas plus suggestions for appropriate books, is http://www.babyparenting.about.com/parenting/babyparenting. Check out the information about early learning and activities that can help the child's cognitive development. Also check out the Zero to Three site, http://zerotothree.org and look particularly at the Magic of Everyday Moments section.

1. How does the information on these sites augment what you learned from the text?
2. Was there anything that particularly surprised you?
3. What information did you already know? What was new to you?
4. How will this information help you interact effectively with young children?
5. How will this information help you interact effectively with parents of young children?
6. What concerns might there be about overstimulating children? How would you address those concerns?
7. If you were to design a program that provided the optimal experience for children to encourage their cognitive (and linguistic) development, while at the same time helping them learn to **enjoy** learning, what would that program look like?

Other Relevant Sites on the Internet

Academic Press
http://www.apnet.com/inscight/09261997/grapha.htm is an interesting article titled "Babies Don't Forget What They Hear." Check this out and see how it relates to what you learned about memory in infancy from the text.

APA site
http://www.apa.org

APS site
http://www.psychologicalscience.org/

Children's Defense Fund (CDF)
http://www.childrensdefense.org is the web site for CDF, the organization headed by Marian Wright Edelman to promote child welfare (discussed in Chapter 1 of the text).

Kidsource
http://www.kidsource.com/NICHCY/speech.html discusses the various types of speech and language problems that children may develop.

Society for Research in Child Development (SRCD)
http://srcd.org is the web site for SRCD, an organization whose purposes are to promote multidisciplinary research in the field of human development, to foster the exchange of information among scientists and other professionals of various disciplines, and to encourage applications of research findings.

Web MD
http://www.webmd.com offers a wide variety of information for the medical profession and for consumers.

Chapter 7: Socioemotional Development in Infancy

Learning Objectives

1. Understand the difficulty of defining emotion and the complexity of its components.
2. Describe the use of MAX in determining a developmental timetable of emotions.
3. Discuss how crying, smiling, and stranger anxiety are important communication mechanisms for infants.
4. Explain the concept of temperament, including the types of temperament, goodness of fit, and the implications of temperamental variations for parenting.
5. Discuss early personality development, including trust and the developing sense of self and independence.
6. Define attachment, then describe the importance of the research of Harlow and Zimmerman and the theories of Erik Erikson and John Bowlby.
7. Describe the types of attachment and the Strange Situation, being sure to mention what behaviors manifest themselves for each type and what caregiving styles will predict each type.
8. Discuss criticisms of attachment theory and the Strange Situation laboratory procedure, understanding the role played by cultural differences.
9. Understand reciprocal socialization and scaffolding, and the notion of the family as a system.
10. Describe the roles of the mother and the father in the development of an infant.
11. Indicate the effects of day care on developmental processes in infancy and what constitutes high-quality day care for infants.

Chapter Outline

EMOTIONAL AND PERSONALITY DEVELOPMENT
    Emotional Development
        Defining Emotion
        Affect in Parent-Infant Relationships
        Developmental Timetable of Emotions
        Crying
        Smiling
        Stranger Anxiety
    Temperament
        Defining and Classifying Temperament
        Goodness of Fit
        Parenting and the Child's Temperament
    Personality Development
        Trust
        The Developing Sense of Self and Independence
ATTACHMENT
    What Is Attachment?
    Individual Differences
    Caregiving Styles and Attachment Classification
    Attachment, Temperament, and the Wider Social World
        Biological Factors
        Social Factors
SOCIAL CONTEXTS
    The Family
        Transition to Parenthood

Reciprocal Socialization
Family as a System
Maternal and Paternal Infant Caregiving
Day Care

Self-Test A: Multiple Choice

1. Emotion is a mixture of:
   a. unconscious and universal processes.
   b. conscious experience and unconscious processes.
   c. physiological arousal, conscious experience, and behavioral expression.
   d. physiological arousal, unconscious processes, and behavioral expression.

2. _____ represent the first language used by infants and parents.
   a. Emotions
   b. Facial expressions
   c. Words
   d. Gazes

3. Carroll Izard (1982) developed the Maximally Discriminative Facial Movement Coding System (MAX), which is a system designed to measure:
   a. attention.
   b. emotion.
   c. memory.
   d. fear.

4. Which of the following emotions develops before the others?
   a. guilt
   b. contempt
   c. surprise
   d. shame

5. Which cry is a rhythmic pattern consisting of a cry, followed by a briefer silence, then a shorter inspiratory whistle somewhat higher in pitch than the main cry, then another brief rest before the next cry?
   a. basic
   b. anger
   c. pain
   d. colicky

6. The _____ smile appears in response to an external stimulus.
   a. social
   b. internal
   c. reflexive
   d. universal

7. Which of the following situations is most likely to produce stranger anxiety in an infant?
   a. sitting on the mother's lap
   b. meeting a stranger in a research laboratory
   c. meeting a stranger in the infant's home
   d. encountering a stranger who smiles

8. Temperament is best defined as:
   a. the way an individual reacts to a special person in the environment.
   b. an individual's general behavioral style.
   c. the emotions experienced by infants and children.
   d. the reaction displayed by a parent when a child engages in an unwanted activity.

9. Chess and Thomas believe the _____ child is the most typical temperament for a child.
   a. easy
   b. feisty
   c. difficult
   d. slow-to-warm-up

10. The revised classifications of temperament proposed by Rothbart and Bates (1998) include all of the following EXCEPT:
    a. positive affect and approach.
    b. negative affectivity.
    c. emotionality.
    d. effortful control.

11. _____ influences temperament, but the degree of influence depends on _____ .
    a. Heredity/environmental experiences
    b. Environmental experiences/heredity
    c. Affectivity/situational experiences
    d. Environment/long-term experiences

12. Temperament experts Ann Sanson and Mary Rothbart (1995) concluded that:
    a. we are now able to define what is involved in "good parenting."
    b. parents should refrain from structuring their child's environment.
    c. researchers have not yet developed any effective programs for dealing with the "difficult child."
    d. parents need to be sensitive to their infant's signals and needs.

13. The human infant learns to recognize his or her image in a mirror at approximately _____ ___ months.
    a. 2
    b. 6
    c. 9
    d. 18

14. According to Erik Erikson, children will develop an excessive sense of shame and a sense of doubt about their abilities under all of the following circumstances EXCEPT when:
    a. impatient parents do things children can do for themselves.
    b. children are consistently overprotected.
    c. accidents the children have had or caused are criticized.
    d. when children are allowed to express their emotions.

15. _____ is a close emotional connection between the infant and the caregiver.
    a. Bonding
    b. Attachment
    c. Closeness
    d. Security

16. The research of Harry Harlow and Robert Zimmerman (1959) found that the critical element in the attachment process is:
    a. oral satisfaction.
    b. contact comfort.
    c. feeding the infant.
    d. consistent interaction.

17. The stage that Erik Erikson believed is most relevant to the formation of attachment is the _____ stage.
    a. anal
    b. phallic
    c. trust versus mistrust
    d. autonomy versus shame and doubt

18. Randy, a normal infant, now has increased locomotor skills, so he actively seeks contact with his mother and father. Randy is in phase _____ of attachment.
    a. 1
    b. 2
    c. 3
    d. 4

19. Mary Ainsworth believes that attachment security depends on:
    a. how sensitive and responsive the caregiver is to infant signals.
    b. the mother's love and concern for the welfare of her child.
    c. the consistency of parental responses during the child-care routine.
    d. reinforcement of attachment behaviors by the caregiver.

20. You are asked to babysit your niece for the evening. When the parents put the child down so they can finish getting dressed, she heads toward her toys while she watches her parents find their coats. Your niece is demonstrating which kind of attachment?
    a. secure
    b. avoidant
    c. resistant
    d. disorganized

21. Life-span developmentalists agree that secure attachment:
    a. is essential to adult social competence.
    b. is not essential, but is a factor in adult social competence.
    c. is not an important factor in adult social competence.
    d. cannot easily be connected to adult social competence.

22. Jerome Kagan has emphasized the importance of _____ as a determinant of social competence.
    a. bonding
    b. temperament
    c. peer responsiveness
    d. learning

23. All of the following are criticisms of attachment theories EXCEPT:
    a. genetics and temperament have not been accounted for and may play more of a role in development than the nature of the attachment.
    b. the role of multiple social agents and changing social contexts have been largely ignored in the study of attachment.
    c. cultural variations show different patterns of attachment.
    d. the relationship between the parent and the infant is not emphasized enough.

24. Reciprocal socialization is best defined in which of the following ways?
    a. Children are products of their parents' socialization techniques.
    b. Parents are products of their children's socialization techniques.
    c. Socialization is bi-directional.
    d. The interactions that children have with people other than their parents determine how they will be socialized.

25. Studies of reciprocal socialization during infancy reveal that _____ plays an important role in socialization.
    a. breast-feeding
    b. mutual gaze
    c. trust
    d. attachment

26. One of the functions of scaffolding is to:
    a. introduce infants to interactive games.
    b. provide a parent support network.
    c. teach infants social rules.
    d. ensure that parents know how to care for their infants.

27. In maternal and paternal infant interactions:
   a. fathers' interactions are more likely to include play.
   b. fathers' interactions are more likely to center around child care activities.
   c. fathers are less able than mothers to act sensitively and responsively with their infants.
   d. no big differences are seen in mothers' and fathers' interactions with infants in today's "typical" American family.

28. In a Swedish study where mothers work and fathers stay home with the baby, the fathers:
   a. reverse roles and behave like the typical mother in many respects.
   b. interact with their babies in the usual fatherly manner.
   c. are more likely to discipline and comfort the infant than the mothers.
   d. play with their infants in a less physical manner than do the mothers.

29. Which country has no national policy permitting paternity leave?
   a. Norway
   b. the United States
   c. Israel
   d. Sweden

30. Day care for American children:
   a. is primarily provided by large day-care centers.
   b. is least often provided in private homes.
   c. is run by non-profit organizations.
   d. varies extensively.

31. In his research concerning the effects of child care on children, Kagan has found in the experimental program at Harvard that:
   a. day care had long-term, detrimental effects on children.
   b. day care had no observed adverse effects.
   c. day care facilitated development.
   d. the effects of day care are dependent on the length and type of care given.

32. A longitudinal study by the National Institute of Child Health and Human Development (NICHHD) assessed the child care experiences of children and their development and found all of the following EXCEPT:
   a. infants from low-income families were more likely to receive low-quality child care than their higher-income counterparts.
   b. child care did not adversely affect the security of infants' attachments to their mothers.
   c. the quality of child care was linked with fewer child problems.
   d. children reared in the exclusive care of their mothers had higher cognitive abilities.

33. Andrea wanted to put 2-1/2-year-old Jessica in a high-quality day-care setting. In terms of the number of adults she should look for to care for children, the ratio should be:
   a. 1:4.
   b. 1:6.
   c. 1:8.
   d. 1:10.

34. If you wanted to place your child in a day care program, based on what you learned in this chapter you would look for all of the following EXCEPT:
   a. caregivers who observe and record each child's progress and development.
   b. programs designed to increase the children's language skills.
   c. a minimum of 25 square feet of usable playroom floor space indoors per child.
   d. encouragement for parents to observe, discuss policies, and work in the center's activities.

Self-Test B: Matching

Match the following persons with the statement or theory that most closely reflects their perspective:

1. Carroll Izard
2. Edward Zigler
3. Mary Ainsworth
4. John Bowlby
5. Margaret Mahler
6. Jerome Kagan
7. Harry Harlow
8. Mary Rothbart
9. Alexander Chess & Stella Thomas

a. Suggested temperament classifications focus on affect, approach, and control
b. Proposed a solution to day-care needs for many U.S. families
c. Infants are evolutionarily equipped to stay on a positive developmental course
d. Described easy, difficult, and slow-to-warm-up temperaments in infants
e. Tested Freud's theory of attachment via oral gratification using monkeys
f. Created the Maximally Discriminative Facial Movement Coding System (MAX)
g. Devised the Strange Situation to measure attachment in children
h. Developmentalist who said children go through separation and individuation
i. British psychiatrist who stated that attachment has a biological basis

Essay Questions

1. Your sister and brother-in-law both work for the same internationally based company that has branches in fifty countries and every continent around the world. Your sister has confided in you that she would like to have children but, while she feels guilty about it, she would really rather work than stay at home with them while they are growing up. She said her husband also wants children, and he has said he's willing to stay home with them for a while so your sister could continue working, but he's concerned about the loss of income if he doesn't work for several months. They both would like to spend some time at home with their children, but would want to put them into day care even though they feel guilty about doing that. Assuming that you think they would actually be good parents, what information would you give them about where in the world they might live to maximize their ability for both to have time with their newborn children; and what would you advise them about placing their children in day care?

2. The local PTA has asked you to talk to their parents and teachers about working with young children. They have specifically asked you to address the idea of attachment—what it is, the research supporting a notion of attachment, the different forms of attachment, and how to help a child develop secure attachment—and the different types of temperament, including how to deal effectively with children according to their temperamental styles. What will you tell these parents and teachers?

Scramblers

Unscramble the following people or terms, then describe what they are known for (people) or define them (terms):

1. MROEJE NKAGA

_____

2. IELHAS REMMAANK

_____

3. TMNEOIO

_____

4. ERVEIFXLE ESLMI

_____

5. GANRETRS EXINTAY

_____

6. NETMTEPMARE

_____

7. HCMAETNTAT

_____

8. CEUSRNEI DIAONVTA SBEAIB

_____

9. CCRIELAOPR ZIALTAICIOONS

_____

10. GSNCIADFLFO

_____

Key to Self-Test A

1.	c	LO 1	13. d	LO 5	25. b	LO 9
2.	a	LO 1	14. d	LO 5	26. c	LO 9
3.	b	LO 1	15. b	LO 6	27. a	LO 10
4.	c	LO 2	16. b	LO 6	28. b	LO 10
5.	a	LO 3	17. c	LO 6	29. b	LO 10
6.	a	LO 3	18. c	LO 6	30. d	LO 11
7.	b	LO 3	19. a	LO 7	31. b	LO 11
8.	b	LO 4	20. a	LO 7	32. d	LO 11
9.	a	LO 4	21. d	LO 7	33. b	LO 11
10.	c	LO 4	22. b	LO 7	34. c	LO 11
11.	a	LO 4	23. d	LO 8			
12.	d	LO 4	24. c	LO 9			

Key to Self-Test B

1. f
2. b
3. g
4. i
5. h
6. a
7. e
8. c
9. d

Key to Essay Questions

1. You would need to explore the maternity and paternity leave policies of different countries around the world, including the United States, which presently does not have a paternity leave policy, and also discuss the various child care policies around the world (Sweden, of course, comes to mind as an excellent example of a country that provides paid leave to both parents during the fist year of a child's life). You would also need to discuss the benefits and problems that would arise from having only one or both parents involved in early child rearing, and placement of infants and young children into day care facilities. The issue of day care for both infants and young children needs to be discussed, including the different types of day care that exist in the United States and abroad, the effects of day care on children based on the research to date, and how widely the quality of day care varies. Give tips from the chapter for determining what defines quality day care. As for the issue of feeling guilty, sometimes it is not an option (either financially or emotionally) for the mother to stay home with the children, so you would want to address this issue as well.

2. Here you would define attachment, then look at the various research studies that have explored attachment, including, among others, the research of Harry and Margaret Harlow and Robert Zimmerman with the rhesus monkeys, and Ainsworth's Strange Situation research. Talk about the different types of attachment that Ainsworth described, and discuss ways to promote secure attachment so children will feel safe to explore new environments and take on new challenges (be sure to include Erikson's stage of trust versus mistrust in your discussion). Then look at the work by Chess and Thomas on temperament, discussing the three types they describe (note that only 65 percent of children are clearly able to be designated into one of the three types), as well as the factors that Rothbart and Bates suggest (e.g., positive affect and approach). Finally, using the guidelines in the chapter, provide some strategies for the parents and teachers to use to work most effectively with children's different temperaments.

Key to Scramblers

1. Jerome Kagan: Believes that infants are evolutionarily equipped to stay on a positive developmental course
2. Sheila Kamerman: Looked at child care policies around the world
3. Emotion: Feeling or affect that can involve physiological arousal, conscious experience, and behavior
4. Reflexive smile: A smile that does not occur in response to external stimuli
5. Stranger anxiety: An infant's fear and wariness of strangers
6. Temperament: An individual's behavioral style and characteristic way of emotional response
7. Attachment: A close emotional bond between an infant and a caregiver
8. Insecure avoidant babies: Show insecurity by avoiding the mother
9. Reciprocal socialization: Children socialize parents just as parents socialize children
10. Scaffolding: Parental behavior that supports children's efforts and promotes skills

Research Project 1: Observing Developmental Periods

Bearing in mind the three temperaments described by Thomas and Chess (i.e., easy, difficult, slow-to-warm-up) and the three temperament classifications of affect, approach, and control suggested by Rothbart and Bates, observe six different infants and, using the chart below, describe which category(ies) each child fits. Indicate each child's sex and age in months and state the specific behaviors that justify this categorization.

	Child 1 Sex:___ Age:___	Child 2 Sex:___ Age:___	Child 3 Sex:___ Age:___	Child 4 Sex:___ Age:___	Child 5 Sex:___ Age:___	Child 6 Sex:___ Age:___
Temperament Style						
Affect						
Approach						
Control						
Behaviors observed to justify classification						

1. How easy was it to classify each child?
2. What effect do you believe the child's age or sex had on that child's behavior?
3. If you were able to observe the child interacting with parents or other adults, describe the nature of the interactions and what effect you believe that had on the child's behavior.
4. In terms of classification, which system (Chess & Thomas or Rothbart & Bates) works best for you? Explain.
5. Describe what you would include in your own system for classifying temperament.
6. Based on your observations, what advice would you give to parents to maximize the positive and minimize the negative aspects of their children's temperaments?

Research Project 2: Parental Leave and Child Care

In a group with other students in your class, prepare a chart that compares parental leave policies around the world, different types of child-care facilities, and what the research indicates are the effects that parental leave and various forms of child care have on the developing child. After comparing and contrasting each of these variables, write a paper that presents a policy statement concerning what you believe would be the best possible situation in the United States to ensure optimal development of our next generation. You may wish to go a step further and write a letter based on your findings to your elected officials in Washington and in your own home state. You would then want to report back to the class whether you received any response to your letter, what the response was, and how it relates to the information in this chapter.

Personal Application Project 1: Reflecting on What You Learned

Consider what you read in Chapter 7, then answer the following questions:

1. What information in this chapter did you already know?
2. How can/do you use that information in your own life?
3. What information in this chapter was totally new to you?
4. How can you use that new information in your own life?
5. What information in this chapter was different from what you previously believed?
6. How was this information different?
7. How do you account for the differences between what you believed and what you learned in the chapter?
8. What is the most important thing you learned from reading this chapter?

Personal Application Project 2: Comparing Temperaments

A common question among siblings is, "Did we really grow up in the same family?" This puzzling dilemma stems from each child's unique temperament, which in turn affects the child's experiences and perceptions. Observe your own family (or, if you have no siblings, look at your parents and their siblings, or your friends who are not only children) and consider the temperament of each child in the family (if it's your parents, for purposes of this exercise, consider them as children of their family). Using the chart below, indicate the temperament type and the different characteristics of each individual included. Feel free to add siblings as needed.

	Temperament Type	Positive Affect/ Approach	Negative Affectivity	Effortful Control
Self				
Sibling 1				
Sibling 2				
Sibling 3				
Sibling 4				

1. How similar are you (or are your parents or your friends) to the siblings listed?
2. Do you have similar or dissimilar temperaments? In what ways are you similar or dissimilar?
3. Do your dissimilarities complement each other or create conflict?

4. How can you use this information to improve your relationships with your siblings?
5. Were you or any of your siblings difficult to categorize? (Note that not everyone is easily described using the Chess and Thomas labels.)
6. What do you think would be the best way to categorize a child's temperament? Describe your "labels" and the characteristics each would have.
7. What have you learned about yourself and your family by looking at temperament?

Internet Projects

Check out the McGraw-Hill web site for this text (http://www.mhhe.com/santrockld8). You'll find numerous activities there, in particular various quizzes, flash cards of key terms, and a challenging and fun crossword puzzle. Please note that all website addresses in this Study Guide have been checked and are correct at the time of publication, however, websites may be discontinued or addresses may change so when you search a given site it may no longer be viable. If that occurs, I apologize for the inconvenience, and would appreciate you notifying me so I could make appropriate revisions in future editions of this Study Guide.

Internet Project 1: Child Care Guidelines

Go to http://nccic.org, which is the website for the National Child Care Information Center. This center, which is supported by a contract from the U.S. Department of Health and Human Services, provides information and resources to promote the delivery of high-quality child-care services to children and families. Scroll down to the link Tribal Child Care Technical Assistance Center, then link to Minimum Standards for Tribal Child Care Centers and pull up the document at that site. (You'll need Adobe to get the document, but if you don't have it you can go to the necessary links and get it for free—it's extremely useful for downloading and/or printing documents on line.) After reviewing the guidelines set out in this document, compare them with the characteristics of high-quality day care that are outlined in the text. How do they compare? What differences do you find? If you were to design your own child-care facility, what would you take from each of these sets of guidelines?

Internet Project 2: How Important Is Temperament?

Go to http://www.temperament.com and scroll down to the link for Things to Do at This Website, then link onto "Practical Importance of Temperament." After reading the article, indicate:

1. What did you learn from the article that wasn't in the text?
2. In what ways is understanding temperament important in your own personal life?
3. How is understanding temperament a valuable tool for parents and teachers?
4. In what ways can a child's temperament traits be used to enhance that child's life?
5. We often think of certain traits that a child has as harmful (particularly for the "difficult" child). How can these traits be used to help the child develop in a healthy direction?
6. How can you use this information in your personal and professional life?

Other Relevant Sites on the Internet

The Administration for Children and Families (Department of Health and Human Services) http://www.acf.dhss.gov offers links and information concerning child care, child welfare, and agencies to assist children, parents, and families.

Attachment Deficit

http://www.attachmentdeficit.com was created by psychoanalyst Aaron Lederer, who has included his e-mail address if you have questions. The site discusses attachment, problems that arise when children do not learn attachment, and ways to treat attachment deficit.

Attachment Homepage

http://www.attach-bond.com offers assistance to parents and children to develop healthy attachment, and addresses issues of both healthy attachment and attachment disorders.

Attachment Theory

http://www.caen.it/psicologia/spa_emjc.htm offers an in-depth look at Bowlby's research on attachment.

Children's Defense Fund (CDF)

http://www.childrensdefense.org is the web site for CDF, the organization headed by Marian Wright Edelman to promote child welfare (discussed in Chapter 1 of the text).

Drake University

http://www.educ.drake.edu/doc/dissertatin/TMPR/home.htm presents a dissertation on "Temperament Theory," including its history, theorists, types, characteristics, influences, assessment, suggested readings, and other useful information to expand on what was presented in Chapter 7.

Kidsource

http://www.kidsource.com/NICHCY/speech.html discusses the various types of speech and language problems that children may develop.

Society for Research in Child Development (SRCD)

http://srcd.org is the web site for SRCD, an organization whose purposes are to promote multidisciplinary research in the field of human development, to foster the exchange of information among scientists and other professionals of various disciplines, and to encourage applications of research findings.

The Temperament Project

http://www.temperamentproject.bc.ca is sponsored by the Difficult Child Support Association of B.C., a Canadian non-profit organization that "seeks early intervention by providing support, education and information to those who live or work with children who have been temperamentally challenging to raise from an early age."

Web MD

http://www.webmd.com offers a wide variety of information for the medical profession and for consumers.

Zero to Three

http://www.zerotothree.com is a site for parents and professionals. Zero to Three is a non-profit organization that focuses on promoting the healthy development of babies and toddlers.

Chapter 8: Physical and Cognitive Development in Early Childhood

Learning Objectives

1. Understand the changes in height and weight during the preschool years and note factors associated with individual differences in height and weight.
2. Define myelination and discuss its contribution to brain development.
3. Explain how gross motor skills and fine motor skills change during the preschool years and the role that handedness plays in motor skills and intellect.
4. Define basal metabolism rate (BMR), and explain why early exposure to fast food worries developmentalists.
5. Discuss the state of illness and health in the world's children, including the leading cause of childhood death in the world, relevant treatment, and prevention.
6. Define Piaget's preoperational stage and be able to give examples of behaviors that differentiate children in the symbolic function and intuitive thought substages.
7. Explain Vygotsky's theory of development, including the zone of proximal development (ZPD), scaffolding, language and thought, and the educational applications of Vygotsky's theory, and compare Vygotsky's theory with that of Piaget.
8. Indicate what changes occur in attention, memory, and use of strategies in early childhood.
9. Explain the development of the young child's theory of the mind.
10. Identify observations that indicate children understand rules of morphology, semantics, and pragmatics.
11. Compare and contrast the child-centered kindergarten with the Montessori approach, and discuss developmentally appropriate and inappropriate practices in educating young children.
12. Be able to answer the question, "Does preschool matter?" by addressing developmental consequences for all children, including those who are economically disadvantaged.

Chapter Outline

PHYSICAL DEVELOPMENT IN EARLY CHILDHOOD
  Body Growth and Change
    Height and Weight
    The Brain
  Motor Development
    Gross Motor Skills
    Fine Motor Skills
    Handedness
  Nutrition
    Energy Needs
    Eating Behavior
  Illness and Death
    The United States
    The State of Illness and Health of the World's Children
COGNITIVE DEVELOPMENT IN EARLY CHILDHOOD
  Piaget's Preoperational Stage of Development
    Symbolic Function Substage
    Intuitive Thought Substage
  Vygotsky's Theory of Development
    Zone of Proximal Development

Self-Test A: Multiple Choice

1. Two important factors that can produce individual differences in height are:
   a. ethnic origin and nutrition.
   b. genetic predisposition and early behavior.
   c. central nervous system functioning and reduction of fat intake.
   d. standard of living and cost of living.

2. Which of the following is NOT a condition that can produce unusually short children?
   a. physical problems
   b. congenital factors
   c. emotional difficulties
   d. ethnic origin

3. The Nortons love their son, but are concerned about his lack of height and his slow rate of growth. A medical examination would likely reveal a malfunction of the:
   a. pineal gland.
   b. adrenal gland.
   c. pituitary gland.
   d. medulla.

4. Myelination improves the efficiency of the central nervous system in the same way that:
   a. talking to an infant speeds his ability to produce a first word.
   b. reducing the distance between two children playing catch reduces the time it takes for a baseball to travel form one child to the other.
   c. the ingestion of certain chemicals (e.g., steroids) can improve overall muscle development.
   d. the insulation around an electrical extension cord improves its efficiency.

5. Recent research using brain scans has found that from ages 3 to 15:
   a. the overall size of the brain shows dramatic growth.
   b. there are dramatic changes in local patterns within the brain.
   c. there are dramatic changes in brain size from age 3 to age 6, then a slowing of growth thereafter.
   d. many diseases that are manifested later in life can be seen early on.

6. The most rapid growth in the brain for children aged 3 to 6 takes place in the:
   a. frontal lobe areas.
   b. temporal lobe areas.
   c. parietal lobes.
   d. occipital lobe.

7. Which of the following would be considered a fine motor skill?
   a. bouncing a ball
   b. walking a straight line
   c. sorting blocks
   d. writing your name

8. Left-handedness is associated with:
   a. early maturation of motor skills.
   b. imagination and creativity.
   c. cognitive and perceptual deficits.
   d. delinquent tendencies.

9. What a child eats during the early childhood period affects all of the following EXCEPT:
   a. skeletal growth.
   b. body shape.
   c. susceptibility to disease.
   d. basal metabolism rate.

10. Your child is overweight. What is the best recommendation to help him slim down?
    a. Give him snacks only when he has been good.
    b. Put him on a diet that will help him lose weight.
    c. Encourage him to get more exercise.
    d. Punish him when you find him eating snacks.

11. Exposure to _____ increases children's risk for developing such medical problems as pneumonia, bronchitis, middle ear infections, burns, and asthma.
    a. tobacco smoke
    b. cocaine
    c. lead
    d. pesticides

12. The most likely cause of death in the world among children younger than 5 years is:
    a. birth defects.
    b. polio.
    c. diarrhea.
    d. German measles.

13. An easy solution to the high child mortality rate from diarrhea around the world would be low cost:
    a. vaccinations.
    b. oral rehydration therapy.
    c. birth control.
    d. immunizations.

14. In the _____ substage the young child gains the ability mentally to represent an object that is not present.
    a. symbolic function
    b. intuitive thought
    c. tertiary circular reactions
    d. preoperational

15. Wendy was listening as her mother told a friend how to get to their house. Mrs. Jones said, "Come south on Main, then turn left on Ash, then right on Cedar, and we are the second house on the right." Wendy said, "No, you turn right on Ash." She said this because from where she sat, Ash was to her right. Assuming Mrs. Jones is correct, Wendy would be demonstrating:
    a. animism.
    b. egocentrism.
    c. centration.
    d. conservation.

16. Three-year-old Henry tripped on an uneven sidewalk and ran crying to his mother saying, "The sidewalk made me fall on purpose!" Henry is demonstrating:
    a. animism.
    b. egocentrism.
    c. centration.
    d. conservation.

17. The typical "human tadpole" that preschoolers draw to represent a person probably best reflects:
    a. limited knowledge of the human body.
    b. a confusion between fantasy and reality.
    c. a symbolic representation of a human.
    d. limited perceptual motor skills.

18. When her father asked Kim how she concluded that two apples and two apples make five apples, she believed her answer was correct and confidently replied, "I know it because I know it!" Kim is in which substage of development?
    a. primary circular reactions
    b. tertiary circular reactions
    c. symbolic function
    d. intuitive thought

19. _____ is clearly evidenced in young children's lack of conservation when they focus their attention on one characteristic (such as height or length) to the exclusion of others.
    a. Egocentrism
    b. Centration
    c. Concentration
    d. Overregulation

20. Professor Rosen showed 4-year-old Clarence two balls of clay that were the same size. As he watched, she rolled one of the balls into a snake shape, neither adding nor taking away any clay. When asked if both the ball and the "snake" had the same amount of clay, Clarence responded that the snake had more. This demonstrates Clarence's:
    a. imagination.
    b. inability to reverse actions mentally.
    c. shape preferences.
    d. developing conservation abilities.

21. Rochel Gelman suggests that children fail conservation tasks because they:
    a. cannot think about more than one aspect of a task.
    b. do not notice important features of the tasks.
    c. cannot mentally reverse the sequence of actions in the tasks.
    d. do not understand why researchers are testing them.

22. Which of the following questions is typical of the preoperational child?
    a. "How many different piles of toys can I make from my toys?"
    b. "How much is two plus two?"
    c. "Where does the moon go when it's light out?"
    d. "Do you see the same thing I do, Daddy?"

23. Lev Vygotsky BELIEVED some tasks are too difficult for children to handle alone, but can be done with the help of someone more skilled. Such tasks:
    a. fall into the zone of proximal development.
    b. are difficult because they are not salient to the child.
    c. are best taught by having the child observe a skilled teacher.
    d. will be frustrating for the child and should be left to a time when the child can more easily accomplish them.

24. The zone of proximal development (ZPD) is a measure of:
    a. intelligence.
    b. potential.
    c. skill.
    d. achievement.

25. Which of the following reflects Lev Vygotsky's beliefs about language and thought?
   a. Children who engage in high levels of private speech are usually socially incompetent.
   b. Children use internal speech earlier than they use external speech.
   c. All mental functions have external or social origins.
   d. Language and thought initially develop together and then become independent.

26. Vygotsky believed that cognitive development was most influenced by which of the following factors?
   a. biological
   b. social
   c. personality
   d. emotional

27. According to Vygotsky, an institutional component that influences cognitive development is:
   a. a child's interactions with a teacher.
   b. watching educational programs on television.
   c. the traditions of a child's ethnic group.
   d. the use of computers to teach math concepts.

28. Compared to that of a toddler, a preschooler's ability to pay attention enables her to:
   a. ignore unimportant but distracting details of a task.
   b. habituate more quickly to repeated stimulation.
   c. concentrate on an activity for longer periods of time.
   d. pay attention to several things simultaneously.

29. All of the following have been found to account for differences in memory between older and younger children EXCEPT:
   a. use of rehearsal.
   b. speed and efficiency of processing.
   c. use of strategies.
   d. increased intelligence.

30. According to information-processing theorists, which of the following IS NOT one of the developmental steps in children's thoughts about the human mind?
   a. realizing the mind exists
   b. realizing the mind has connections to the physical world
   c. realizing that there is a true reality that will come to be understood
   d. understanding that the mind can represent objects and events accurately or inaccurately

31. Evidence that children understand the rules of their language includes all of the following EXCEPT:
   a. observations of overgeneralizations.
   b. application of rules to nonsense words.
   c. correct word order placement.
   d. identifying the names of objects they have never previously seen.

32. Overgeneralization of language rules indicates:
   a. a failure to apply language rules.
   b. children's guesses about language rules.
   c. the use of language rules.
   d. the imitation of language rules.

33. Jesus is attending a child-centered kindergarten, so we would expect to see all of the following EXCEPT:
    a. instruction organized around Jesus' needs, interests, and learning style.
    b. an emphasis on the process of what Jesus is learning.
    c. an emphasis on what Jesus learns.
    d. play as an important aspect of Jesus' development.

34. An instructor who uses developmentally inappropriate methods for teaching the alphabet would:
    a. have the children recite the alphabet three times a day every day.
    b. use music to teach the alphabet.
    c. use animal names and shapes to teach the alphabet.
    d. use the sandbox to let children draw the letters of the alphabet.

35. According to David Elkind, preschool:
    a. is a critical element of the young child's socialization.
    b. is not necessary if home schooling approximates the experiences available at a competent preschool.
    c. education should not begin until the child is socially mature.
    d. can produce excessive stress and anxiety.

36. Project Head Start was designed to:
    a. provide low-income children a chance to acquire skills that would help them succeed at school.
    b. assess the advantages and disadvantages of preschool educational programs.
    c. give parents an educational day-care center.
    d. determine the feasibility of starting formal education at an earlier age.

37. Which type of approach was related to good school attendance in Project Follow Through?
    a. an academic, direct-instruction approach
    b. a Montessori-type approach
    c. a Head Start approach
    d. an effective education approach

38. Schooling for young children in Japan is most like:
    a. a developmentally appropriate kindergarten.
    b. a program of concentrated academic instruction.
    c. the kind of program most Americans want.
    d. the typical American kindergarten.

Self-Test B: Matching

Match the following persons with the statement or theory that most closely reflects their perspective:

1. Jean Berko   a. Early childhood education should be part of public education on its own terms
2. Lev Vygotsky   b. Used fictional words to test children's understanding of language rules
3. Teresa Amabile   c. Uses information-processing approach to analyze children's inability to conserve
4. Jean Piaget   d. Language and thought, initially independent, eventually merge
5. Rochel Gelman   e. Revolutionized teaching by allowing children freedom and spontaneity
6. Maria Montessori   f. Underscores the importance of motivation in children's creativity
7. David Elkind   g. Documented that children as young as 2 can learn problem-solving strategies
8. Robert Siegler   h. Preoperational thought moves from primitive to sophisticated use of symbols

Essay Questions

1. Your neighbor has just become aware that his son is left-handed. He's particularly concerned because he remembers that as a child he was left-handed and was forced by his teachers and parents to use his right hand, something he believes caused him emotional problems, but he has observed that people who are left-handed have problems with even simple things, like using scissors. What would you advise him about his son?

2. You are stuck in the middle of an argument among your three best friends concerning cognitive development during early childhood. One of them thinks that Piaget had the best explanations of how children develop, the second believes Vygotsky has the most plausible theory, while the third says that Gelman and information processing offer the best explanations, not to mention criticisms of (especially) Piaget's theory. Discuss all three of these theories and sate which you think makes the most sense and why.

3. Your cousin has told you that it is not an option for her to stay home to be a full-time mother, so she needs to put her child into a day-care setting. She considers you to be a wise person, especially now that you are taking this class in life-span development. What would you suggest to her in terms of finding the best type of day-care option for her child?

Scramblers

Unscramble the following people or terms, then describe what they are known for (people) or define them (terms):

1. NAJE RKBEO

_____

2. HEZ NHEC

_____

3. NETCROIGSEM

_____

4. MISNIAM

_____

5. REVSANTOICNO

_____

6. GSNCIAFLFOD

_____

7. ICAOLS TCSOINVSITTRCU ORAPCPHA

_____

8. YOHTER FO NDIM

_____

9. OMIRTNOSES PAHCRPAO

_____

10. EJORPCT AEDH RATTS

_____

Key to Self-Test A

1.	a	LO 1	14.	a	LO 6	27.	a	LO 7
2.	d	LO 1	15.	b	LO 6	28.	c	LO 8
3.	c	LO 1	16.	a	LO 6	29.	d	LO 8
4.	d	LO 2	17.	c	LO 6	30.	c	LO 9
5.	b	LO 2	18.	d	LO 6	31.	d	LO 10
6.	a	LO 2	19.	b	LO 6	32.	c	LO 10
7.	d	LO 3	20.	b	LO 6	33.	c	LO 11
8.	b	LO 3	21.	b	LO 6	34.	a	LO 11
9.	d	LO 4	22.	c	LO 6	35.	c	LO 12
10.	c	LO 4	23.	a	LO 7	36.	a	LO 12
11.	a	LO 5	24.	b	LO 7	37.	d	LO 12
12.	c	LO 5	25.	c	LO 7	38.	a	LO 12
13.	b	LO 5	26.	b	LO 7			

Key to Self-Test B

1.	b	4.	h	7.	a
2.	d	5.	c	8.	g
3.	f	6.	e		

Key to Essay Questions

1. A proper answer would acknowledge that we do, indeed, live in a "right-handed world," but would address the positive aspects of being left-handed, particularly in terms of athletics, intelligence, and creativity.

2. To answer this question you will need to explain the three cognitive approaches that describe development at this point in time, i.e., Piaget, Vygotsky, and information processing. This will involve a discussion of the various facets of the two substages (symbolic function and intuitive thought) of the preoperational stage (e.g., animism, egocentrism), how Piaget arrived at his ideas, and how they have been supported; then address the criticisms of Piaget's findings (e.g., problems with his research designs, the fact that children

demonstrate certain abilities earlier than he suggested); then contrast Piaget's theory with that of Vygotsky, which states that development is embedded within the sociocultural context (be sure to discuss the zone of proximal development and scaffolding); then compare those theories with the information-processing approach concerning attention, memory, and children's theory of mind. After presenting these three perspectives, state which makes most sense to you (or whether all three are needed together), and explain the rationale for your choice.

3. There are many issues to address here, including: the educational applications of Vygotsky's theory (e.g., use of scaffolding); the various types of early childhood education programs (e.g., child-centered kindergarten, the Montessori approach, Project Head Start for educationally disadvantaged children); developmentally appropriate and inappropriate practices (e.g., providing experiences in all developmental areas rather than narrowly focusing on cognitive development); non-sexist education; and a discussion of what factors predict a successful early education program. Note, too, Elkind's position that young children do need early education, whether by parents who are willing and able to provide it, or by competent preschools.

Key to Scramblers

1. Jean Berko: Uses fictional words to test children's understanding of language rules
2. Zhe Chen: With Siegler documented that children as young as 2 can learn problem-solving strategies
3. Egocentrism: Inability to distinguish one's own perspective from that of someone else
4. Animism: Belief that inanimate objects have "lifelike" qualities and are capable of action
5. Conservation: Awareness that altering an object's/substance's appearance does not change its properties
6. Scaffolding: In teaching session, skilled person adjusts guidance to fit child's current performance level
7. Social constructivist approach: Emphasizes the social contexts of learning
8. Theory of mind: Individuals' thoughts about how mental processes work
9. Montessori approach: Educational philosophy in which children have freedom and spontaneity
10. Project Head Start: Compensatory education; helps low-income children acquire school success skills

Research Project 1:Designing a Developmentally Appropriate Preschool Curriculum

Considering everything you have learned in this chapter concerning developmentally appropriate and inappropriate practices, avoiding sexist education, and creating an atmosphere that will optimize children's learning abilities while minimizing stress, design a developmentally appropriate preschool curriculum. What will you specifically include? What will you specifically omit? Describe your "dream" preschool, explaining the kinds of personnel, activities, curriculum, and physical environment you would want, and why you think these would be important. Which theories would you consider to be most relevant when designing this curriculum? How are they important and how would they be incorporated into your design?

Research Project 2: Early Childhood Memory

This project will assist you in understanding memory changes for young children. First, get permission from the parents of three children of the same sex, ages 2-4, 6-8, and 11-13, being sure to ask the children themselves if they are willing to help you with this project (if a child is reluctant to participate, find another child). Using the number sets below, ask the children (separately) to listen as you read the number set. Tell them you will begin each set by saying "Start," and will end by saying "Go," at which time they should write down the numbers of each set in the order they were read. Read the numbers clearly, with 4 seconds between each number in the set. Record their answers in the chart below, then answer the questions that follow. After you have finished, ask the children how they were able to remember the numbers that they did remember, and what they felt were the reasons they did not remember all of the numbers.

Number Set	Child 1 Age___/Sex___	Child 2 Age___/Sex___	Child 3 Age___/Sex___
2-6			
7-4-9			
8-1-7-2			
5-3-0-9-4			
6-1-8-3-9-2			
9-2-4-3-5-7-1			
4-3-7-9-5-1-2-8			
3-9-4-6-5-1-8-0-2			

1. According to the text, what would you expect to find in terms of each child's ability to remember these numbers? Were your findings consistent with these expectations?
2. What strategies (e.g., rehearsal), if any, did each child use to try to remember these numbers? Were these behaviors consistent with what you read in the text? If so, explain how; if not, explain how they were not consistent.
3. What reasons did the children give for their ability to remember or not remember? Were these reasons consistent with the literature on cognitive development? Explain how they were or were not consistent.
4. Based on your observations of these children, which theory do you think best explains cognitive development for these age groups?
5. What similarities did you notice among the children in the way they performed? What differences did you notice.

Personal Application Project 1: Reflecting on What You Learned

Consider what you read in Chapter 8, then answer the following questions:

1. What information in this chapter did you already know?
2. How can/do you use that information in your own life?
3. What information in this chapter was totally new to you?
4. How can you use that new information in your own life?
5. What information in this chapter was different from what you previously believed?
6. How was this information different?
7. How do you account for the differences between what you believed and what you learned in the chapter?
8. What is the most important thing you learned from reading this chapter?

Personal Application Project 2: Consider Your Own Development

Consider the story in the beginning of the chapter about Teresa Amabile and her experiences in school that served to frustrate her creativity. Reflect on your own early years in school and think about what experiences you had that hindered your creative talents and what experiences nurtured them. What long-term effects can you attribute to each of these factors? How can you use this information to foster young children's creativity?

Internet Projects

Check out the McGraw-Hill web site for this text (http://www.mhhe.com/santrockld8). You'll find numerous activities there, in particular various quizzes, flash cards of key terms, and a challenging and fun crossword puzzle. Please note that all website addresses in this Study Guide have been checked and are correct at the time of publication, however, websites may be discontinued or addresses may change so when you search a given site it may no longer be viable. If that occurs, I apologize for the inconvenience, and would appreciate you notifying me so I could make appropriate revisions in future editions of this Study Guide.

Internet Project 1: Poverty in Childhood

The chapter addresses some issues of poverty in childhood, particularly in the sections on illness and health and early education. Go to http://drkoop.com (which is the website developed by Dr. C. Everett Koop, former U. S. Surgeon General) and do a search for children in poverty. How does that information augment what you learned in the chapter? What are the consequences of living in poverty to the children involved? What are the societal consequences of having **any** children living in poverty, and of having 20 percent of our children living **below the poverty level**? Combining what you have learned from the chapter with information you gather from this website (and any other sources), design a program that you believe would help these children.

Internet Project 2: Children's Health

The website http://www.intelihealth.com, a subsidiary of Aetna U.S. Healthcare, presents information from sources such as Harvard Medical School and Pennsylvania School of Dental Medicine. Go to the site and click on "Children's Health." Look at the various sections, such as news articles, features, and "Ask the Doc." In the news and features sections, check out the types of articles presented. Then, reflecting on Chapter 8, think about what questions come to mind that either weren't answered in the text or that were generated by what you read. Then go ahead and "Ask the Doc" that question. Feel free to do a search for any other topic that seems relevant.

1. What articles did you find at this website?
2. How did these articles relate to what you read in Chapter 8?
3. Was the information consistent with what you read? Explain.
4. What question came to mind that you decided to "Ask the Doc"?
5. What answer did you get back? Was it helpful?
6. What other topics did you decide to check out at this website?
7. How credible do you believe the information is from this site?

Other Relevant Sites on the Internet

APA site
http://www.apa.org

APS site
http://www.psychologicalscience.org/

The Administration for Children and Families (Department of Health and Human Services)
http://www.acf.dhss.gov offers links and information concerning child care, child welfare, and agencies to assist children, parents, and families.

Child Nutrition, Health, and Physical Activity
http://www.ificinfo.health.org/index3.htm provides current information about children's nutrition.

Children's Defense Fund (CDF)
http://www.childrensdefense.org is the web site for CDF, the organization headed by Marian Wright Edelman to promote child welfare (discussed in Chapter 1 of the text).

Drake University
http://www.educ.drake.edu/doc/dissertatin/TMPR/home.htm presents a dissertation on "Temperament Theory," including its history, theorists, types, characteristics, influences, assessment, suggested readings, and other useful information to expand on what was presented in Chapter 7.

Kidsource
http://www.kidsource.com/NICHCY/speech.html discusses the various types of speech and language problems that children may develop.

Lorin's Left-Handedness Site
http://duke.usask.ca/~elias.left/ provides information about being left-handed.

Pediatric Health and Safety Information
http://www.babysdoc.com is edited and reviewed by board certified pediatricians. It offers an array of information on development revolving around health and safety issues, but also promotes products for sale.

Society for Research in Child Development (SRCD)
http://srcd.org is the web site for SRCD, an organization whose purposes are to promote multidisciplinary research in the field of human development, to foster the exchange of information among scientists and other professionals of various disciplines, and to encourage applications of research findings.

Web MD
http://www.webmd.com offers a wide variety of information for the medical profession and for consumers.

Zero to Three
http://www.zerotothree.com is a site for parents and professionals. Zero to Three is a non-profit organization that focuses on promoting the healthy development of babies and toddlers.

Chapter 9: Socioemotional Development in Early Childhood

Learning Objectives

1. Discuss young children's self-understanding, incorporating Erikson's view of the initiative versus guilt stage.
2. Explain how children attempt to make sense of their own and other people's emotional reactions and feelings.
3. Understand the Piagetian, social cognitive, and Freudian theories of moral development.
4. Describe the biological, social, and cognitive factors that influence gender development.
5. Understand the four major parenting styles and how parenting styles are affected by developmental changes in the child, as well as by culture, social class, and ethnicity.
6. Describe the multifaceted nature of child abuse, including contextual aspects, risk factors, and consequences of abuse.
7. Describe the complexity of sibling relationships.
8. Summarize the research that has examined birth-order effects and the criticism that birth order has been overdramatized and overemphasized.
9. Consider how families are changing in a changing society, including concerns of working mothers or both parents working.
10. Discuss the many factors involved in divorce such as the effects of divorce on children, whether parents should stay together for the sake of their children, the influence of family processes, factors involved in children's risk and vulnerability, and socioeconomic factors.
11. Outline the cultural, ethnic, and socioeconomic variations in families.
12. Indicate the role that peers play in early development and be able to differentiate peer interaction and parent-child interaction.
13. Describe the functions of play and the types of play.
14. Describe the effects of television viewing on development, including both positive and negative behavior.

Chapter Outline

EMOTIONAL AND PERSONALITY DEVELOPMENT
    The Self
        Initiative Versus Guilt
        Self-Understanding
    Emotional Development
        Developmental Timetable of Young Children's Emotion Language and Understanding
    Moral Development
        What Is Moral Development?
        Piaget's View of How Children's Moral Reasoning Develops
        Moral Behavior
        Moral Feelings
    Gender
        What Is Gender?
        Biological Influences
        Social Influences
        Cognitive Influences
FAMILIES
    Parenting

Self-Test A: Multiple Choice

1. In the opening story for this chapter, 4-year-old Sara raised money for endangered species and helped feed the homeless. According to our text:
   a. Sara was born innately good.
   b. Sara's sense of morality and values were encouraged by sensitive parenting.
   c. Sara was taught to do these things because her parents were extremely religious.
   d. there is no clear way to know how Sara developed her sense of morality and values.

2. Olivia's parents openly value Olivia's participation in family conversations. Although she frequently misunderstands the topic, they answer her questions, help her to join in, or simply enjoy her sometimes fantastic ideas. According to Erik Erikson, these parents are encouraging:
   a. initiative.
   b. conscience.
   c. identification.
   d. self-concept.

3. Preschoolers most often describe themselves in terms of their:
   a. thoughts.
   b. physical characteristics.
   c. emotions.
   d. relationships to other people.

4. Children show an increased ability to reflect on emotions by age:
   a. 18 to 24 months.
   b. 2 to 3 years.
   c. 4 to 5 years.
   d. 6 to 7 years.

5. A major distinction between autonomous morality and heteronomous morality is that autonomous moral thinkers focus on the:
   a. consequences of behavior.
   b. intentions of someone who breaks a rule.
   c. way a specific behavior makes them feel.
   d. rewards moral behavior will bring.

6. Piaget believed that the social understanding of autonomous children comes about through:
   a. parental modeling.
   b. what they learn in their educational settings.
   c. biological maturation.
   d. the mutual give-and-take of peer relations.

7. Dr. Emory believes that when children are rewarded for behavior that is consistent with laws and social conventions, they are likely to repeat that behavior. Dr. Emory most likely takes a _____ view of development.
   a. Piagetian
   b. social cognitive
   c. Freudian
   d. Pavlovian

8. According to social cognitive theorists, the ability to resist temptation is closely tied to the development of:
   a. empathic behavior.
   b. spontaneity.
   c. abstract reasoning.
   d. self-control.

9. Which cognitive ability is essential to the capacity for empathy?
   a. conservation
   b. logical reasoning
   c. decentration
   d. perspective taking

10. Gender identity refers to the:
   a. biological dimension of being male or female.
   b. social and psychological dimensions of being male or female.
   c. sense of being male or female.
   d. set of expectations that prescribe how males or females should think, act, or feel.

11. Female sex hormones are called _____; male sex hormones are called _____.
   a. estrogens/androgens
   b. testosterones/estrogens
   c. androgens/testosterones
   d. androgens/estrogens

12. The Freudian belief that "biology is destiny":
   a. is well-accepted by most developmentalists.
   b. overlooks the importance of socialization experiences.
   c. has been disproved.
   d. overlooks the role of heredity.

13. Which of the following statements is most accurate about identification theory and social cognitive theory with respect to gender-role development?
   a. Both assume that children adopt the characteristics of their parents.
   b. Both assume that rewards directly shape gender-role development.
   c. Both assume that children actively acquire gender roles.
   d. Identification theory rejects the idea that anatomy is destiny, while social cognitive theory accepts it.

14. In terms of parental influences on their children's gender development:
    a. fathers are more consistently given responsibility for physical care.
    b. mothers are more likely to engage in playful interaction.
    c. mothers are more likely to be given responsibility for ensuring their children conform to cultural norms.
    d. fathers are more involved than mothers in socializing their children.

15. The tendency for children to show a clear preference for being with and liking same-sex peers usually becomes stronger during:
    a. the toddler years.
    b. the preschool years.
    c. the middle and late childhood years.
    d. early adolescence.

16. According to Sadker and Sadker (1994), girls and boys might receive an education that is not fair in all of the following ways EXCEPT:
    a. boys' learning problems are not identified as often as girls' are.
    b. boys are given the lion's share of attention in schools.
    c. boys are most often at the top of their classes, but also are most often at the bottom as well.
    d. pressure to achieve is more likely to be heaped on boys than on girls.

17. _____ theory states that an individual's attention and behavior are guided by an internal motivation to conform to gender-based sociocultural standards and stereotypes.
    a. Social cognitive
    b. Identification
    c. Gender schema
    d. Cognitive developmental

18. When Del showed up at kindergarten with a barrette in his hair, Andrew got very upset because he thought if Del wore a barrette he was a girl, not a boy. Andrew has not yet developed:
    a. gender constancy.
    b. gender schema.
    c. sexual identification.
    d. gender typing.

19. In the 1930s, John Watson argued that parents:
    a. should provide their children with a nurturing environment.
    b. should put their children on a regular schedule for feeding, toileting, and sleeping.
    c. are too affectionate with their children.
    d. are not sufficiently affectionate with their children.

20. All of the following characterize children of authoritarian parents EXCEPT that they:
    a. fail to initiate activity.
    b. have weak communication skills.
    c. are anxious about social comparison.
    d. lack self-control.

21. Mr. Williams was talking to Ms. Jones on the phone and they got disconnected. When he called Ms. Jones back, he explained that his daughter had cut the phone cord. Ms. Jones asked, "Didn't you see her with the scissors?" to which Mr. Williams replied, "Oh, we don't like to put limits on our children–they need to experience life to the fullest." It sounds like Mr. Williams is _____ parent.
    a. an authoritarian
    b. an authoritative
    c. a neglectful
    d. an indulgent

22. All of the following are dimensions of Baumrind's parenting styles EXCEPT:
   a. acceptance.
   b. responsiveness.
   c. rejection.
   d. control.

23. According to the text, the most common form of abuse is by:
   a. a raging, uncontrolled father who physically abuses his child.
   b. an overwhelmed single mother in poverty who neglects her child.
   c. an alcoholic socialite who emotionally rejects her child.
   d. authoritarian parents who demand strict obedience to their rules.

24. Developmentalists are now using the term "child maltreatment" rather than "child abuse" because:
   a. child abuse is a legal term, not a psychological term.
   b. they believe that changing the term is likely to reduce the incidence of abuse.
   c. the term "maltreatment" includes several different conditions, not just abuse.
   d. they want to be able to differentiate the two in terms of severity.

25. Reductions in incidents of child abuse have been shown to be related to all of the following EXCEPT:
   a. the presence of community support systems.
   b. the availability of support from relatives and friends.
   c. harsher laws punishing abusers.
   d. crisis centers.

26. Maltreated children are likely to develop which attachment pattern?
   a. disorganized
   b. avoidant
   c. anxious
   d. rebellious

27. Research on the relationship between the role of parenting and children's development has demonstrated that:
   a. parenting is primarily responsible for children's development.
   b. heredity is primarily responsible for children's development.
   c. parenting and peer relations are jointly responsible for children's development.
   d. parenting, heredity, and peer relations are jointly responsible for children's development.

28. Parents are likely to treat their firstborns differently than their later-born children in that they:
   a. have higher expectations for later-born children.
   b. put more pressure on the firstborn for achievement and responsibility.
   c. interfere less with the firstborn's activities.
   d. give the firstborn more attention than later-born children.

29. Compared to historical times, children today are growing up in _____ family structures.
   a. about the same kinds of
   b. entirely different
   c. a smaller variety of
   d. a greater variety of

30. To reduce the guilt parents feel when both work outside the home, a good suggestion is to:
   a. rationalize.
   b. pay closer attention to how their children are doing.
   c. explain to their children why both parents need to work.
   d. try to get split shifts so one or the other can be home with their children.

31. The research on the effects of divorce on children suggests that:
    a. most children competently cope with their parents' divorce.
    b. older children are better able to cope with their parents' divorce.
    c. children from divorced families have slightly more adjustment problems than children from nondivorced families.
    d. generally speaking, it is better for the children if parents remain in a marriage even if there is a great deal of conflict.

32. Sarah and Tina's parents have recently divorced. Sarah now lives with their father, and Tina now lives with their mother. Based on the research in this area, which of the following might we expect?
    a. Sarah will adjust better than Tina.
    b. Tina will adjust better than Sarah.
    c. Both girls will adjust well in time.
    d. Neither girl will adjust well since they've been separated from each other.

33. You are going through a divorce and must talk to your children about it. Which of the following is a good recommendation?
    a. Do not explain the separation because no matter what you say, the children are likely to believe it's somehow their fault.
    b. Explain that it may take time to feel better.
    c. Help them understand the divorce by being honest about your ex-spouse's shortcomings as well as your own.
    d. Make a "clean break" by starting fresh and getting rid of as many reminders of the marriage as possible.

34. It is more common for low-income families than middle- or upper-income families to:
    a. use verbal praise.
    b. use criticism.
    c. use reasoning.
    d. encourage questions.

35. One of the most important functions of the peer group is to:
    a. foster love and understanding.
    b. act as a surrogate for the parents.
    c. teach the importance of friendship.
    d. teach about the world outside the family.

36. Experimental studies of monkeys and case studies of humans support all of the following conclusions EXCEPT:
    a. peer relationships are not necessary for normal social development in children.
    b. peer relationships contribute to the normal social development of children.
    c. attachment to peers produces different effects than does attachment to adults.
    d. isolation from peers can produce social maladjustment.

37. Play therapy is based on the notion that:
    a. play relaxes children and acts as a calming influence.
    b. if the child feels less threatened, true feelings will be displayed.
    c. the child will model adaptive behavior during play.
    d. increased cognitive functioning during play allows the child to understand whatever problem is being experienced.

38. Parten's play categories are examples of increasingly complex and interactive:
    a. pretense/symbolic play.
    b. social play.
    c. instructional play.
    d. academic play.

39. Practice play differs from sensorimotor play in that practice play:
   a. is common in the infancy stage of development.
   b. involves coordination of skills.
   c. revolves around the use of symbols.
   d. is done for its own sake.

40. One conclusion that is evident about watching television is that:
   a. children should not be allowed to watch television unless supervised by an adult.
   b. there is no relationship between watching violence on television and aggressive behavior.
   c. children who watch violence on television get it out of their systems and are actually less likely to fight.
   d. children who view violence on television are more likely to engage in aggressive behavior.

41. Aimee Leifer (1973) found television viewing to be associated with young children's:
   a. hostile behavior.
   b. prosocial behavior.
   c. capacity to use their imaginations.
   d. cognitive functioning.

Self-Test B: Matching

Match the following persons with the statement or theory that most closely reflects their perspective:

1. Lawrence Kohlberg
2. Anna Freud
3. Daniel Berlyne
4. Mildred Parten
5. Lois Hoffman
6. Diana Baumrind
7. William Damon
8. Erik Erikson

a. Play satisfies an exploratory drive in each of us
b. Analyzed and characterized children's play
c. Stated that maternal employment is part of modern life
d. Described the crisis of early childhood as one of initiative versus guilt
e. Emphasized the role of empathy in moral development
f. Gender constancy develops at around 6-7 in concert with conservation
g. Psychiatrist who showed peers are important for social development
h. Parenting style is related to children's socioemotional development

Essay Questions

1. You are considering opening a child-care center after you complete your education and get the appropriate degrees and certifications. Your center will accept children who have been potty-trained, including toddlers, preschoolers, and children in the primary grades (for after-school care). You anticipate opening in an ethnically, culturally, and/or racially diverse area, and expect that the parents of these children will come from diverse educational and socioeconomic backgrounds. You want to incorporate the parents as partners to provide an optimal developmental context for the children. Based on the information in this chapter: (a) what kinds of facilities/activities would you need to provide for the children, and (b) what kinds of training might you provide to the parents?

2. Your next-door neighbor comes to you for advice. She confides in you that her husband has been repeatedly unfaithful and she has recently learned that he is having unprotected sex with multiple partners.

His behavior has been "erratic" in that she never knows if or when he'll be home, he does not participate in the children's school and extracurricular activities, and the two of them spend most of their time together either arguing or in icy silence. She has suggested they see a marriage counselor, but he says he is perfectly happy with the way things are. She tells you she is considering leaving him and asks you what the effect might be on her children if she divorces him. She has heard that even in the worst of relationships, it is better for the couple to stay together "for the sake of the children." Short of giving her legal advice (other than "see an attorney to learn what you can do and what your rights are"), what can you tell her about the effects of divorce on children and how she can minimize the trauma to her children in the event of a divorce?

Scramblers

Unscramble the following people or terms, then describe what they are known for (people) or define them (terms):

1. NREWCAEL GKROEHBL

   _____

2. ENIALD LYNREBE

   _____

3. LMARO OLPEMVEENDT

   _____

4. NIEMNMTI TSIUCJE

   _____

5. DNEERG

   _____

6. DNEERG ASMCEH RYHTEO

   _____

7. IRTOAHTTIUVAE NETRIANPG

   _____

8. SYORLAIT LAPY

   _____

9. AICLOS YPLA

_____

10. MAESG

_____

Key to Self-Test A

1.	b	LO 1	15.	c	LO 4	29.	d	LO 9
2.	a	LO 1	16.	a	LO 4	30.	b	LO 9
3.	b	LO 1	17.	c	LO 4	31.	a	LO 10
4.	d	LO 2	18.	a	LO 4	32.	b	LO 10
5.	b	LO 3	19.	c	LO 5	33.	b	LO 10
6.	d	LO 3	20.	d	LO 5	34.	b	LO 11
7.	b	LO 3	21.	d	LO 5	35.	d	LO 12
8.	d	LO 3	22.	c	LO 5	36.	a	LO 12
9.	d	LO 3	23.	b	LO 6	37.	b	LO 13
10.	c	LO 4	24.	c	LO 6	38.	b	LO 13
11.	a	LO 4	25.	c	LO 6	39.	b	LO 13
12.	b	LO 4	26.	a	LO 6	40.	d	LO 14
13.	a	LO 4	27.	d	LO 7	41.	b	LO 14
14.	c	LO 4	28.	b	LO 8			

Key to Self-Test B

1.	f	4.	b	7.	e
2.	g	6.	c	8.	d
3.	a	7.	h		

Key to Essay Questions

1. In answering this question you would want to look at the types of facilities that would encourage age-appropriate play, so you would need to discuss the purpose of play and the different categories of play that children engage in as they develop, being sensitive to what are and what are not age-appropriate social interactions with peers and adults. You would also want to consider the issue of television, and how its use can be both beneficial and harmful; and look at the types of caregiver-to-child activities that would be appropriate for these children, listing the strategies for enriching quality of children's play outlined in the text (e.g., allowing uninterrupted time for sociodramatic and constructive play; providing adequate space to play effectively); be sensitive to gender differences (e.g., boys get more attention than girls while girls' learning deficits are not identified as often as boys'); and incorporate activities that will assist the children in developing empathy. With respect to parents, it would be helpful to teach them about Baumrind's parenting styles and the effect each style has on children, and provide them with guidelines for improving their children's socioemotional development (authoritative parents, adapting to the child's developmental changes); provide information concerning the effects of divorce on children and how to minimize the negative effects; and discuss with them the research concerning the most effective ways to use television (as well as its problems).

2. Here you will need to discuss what the text has presented about how children adjust to divorce (although more children from divorced families have adjustment problems than children from nondivorced families, most children competently cope with their parents' divorce); the factors involved in children's risk and vulnerability (e.g., adjustment prior to divorce, temperament, gender, age); and change in socioeconomic status. Since she specifically asked whether they should "stay together for the sake of the children," you will need to address the research in that regard. It would be particularly important also to discuss with her the guidelines for communicating with young children about divorce (e.g., explaining the separation, explaining that it is not the children's fault, etc.).

Key to Scramblers

1. Lawrence Kohlberg: Gender constancy develops around age 6-7 in concert with conservation
2. Daniel Berlyne: Play satisfies an exploratory drive in each of us
3. Moral development: Development regarding rules/conventions of how people interact with others
4. Imminent justice: The concept that immediate punishment follows the breaking of rules
5. Gender: The social and psychological dimension of being male or female
6. Gender schema theory: Internal motivation to conform to gender-based standards guides behavior
7. Authoritative parenting: Parenting style encouraging independence while placing limits and controls
8. Solitary play: Play in which the child plays alone and independently of others
9. Social play: Play that involves social interactions with peers
10. Games: Activities engaged in for pleasure; include rules & often competition with one or more individuals

Research Project 1: Sibling Birth Order

The text provides interesting findings concerning the effects of birth order on later development, but notes that these effects may be "overdramatized and overemphasized." Using the chart below as a starting point, track as many of your friends and relatives as you practically can, indicating each person's birth order (e.g., only child, firstborn of six, second of four, etc.), sex, their personal characteristics (per those indicated in the text or otherwise), their job title/position, and other information that you believe is relevant. Then answer the questions that follow.

Person	Birth Order	Sex	Characteristics	Job Title/ Position	Other

1. Looking at your data overall, understanding that there will be individual differences, were your observations consistent with what you might expect from the research described? Explain your response.
2. What patterns did you notice when comparing persons of similar birth order in terms of the material discussed in this chapter?
3. What differences did you notice when comparing persons of similar birth order in terms of the material discussed in this chapter?
4. What might you conclude about the effects of birth order based on your observations (e.g., did you find that there really are consistent effects of birth order, or did you find that the effects have been "overdramatized and overemphasized")?

Research Project 2: Parental Guidelines for Children's Television Viewing

Apply the life-span developmental concepts in this chapter to devise guidelines that would assist parents in using television as a positive influence on their children's lives. Consider the different roles that television plays, the types of influence that it has on children, the characteristics of children that are attracted to specific types of programs, how the amount of television watching may affect children, and how parents can most effectively use television as a positive factor for their children's socioemotional development. Suggest possible guidelines and how parents might interact with their children to discuss what they view on television.

Personal Application Project 1: Reflecting on What You Learned

Consider what you read in Chapter 9, then answer the following questions:

1. What information in this chapter did you already know?
2. How can/do you use that information in your own life?
3. What information in this chapter was totally new to you?
4. How can you use that new information in your own life?
5. What information in this chapter was different from what you previously believed?
6. How was this information different?
7. How do you account for the differences between what you believed and what you learned in the chapter?
8. What is the most important thing you learned from reading this chapter?

Personal Application Project 2: Consider Your Own Development (Your Parents' Parenting Style)

As discussed in the text, Diana Baumrind describes four primary styles of parenting: authoritative, authoritarian, neglectful, and indulgent. Of course, none of us is perfectly consistent, and oftentimes two parents may have different parenting styles. Further, as discussed in the text, parents may shift their style and become less controlling as their children grow up. Consider your own parents and the style(s) they used with you and your siblings (they may have used different styles of parenting for each child—this is not a really clean-cut system). Indicate which style was used primarily by each of your parents, together with the types of behaviors that would indicate to you that this was, indeed, the style that parent used; then indicate what other styles might have been used and the situations that elicited that style. Also indicate the style(s) used for your siblings, and any changes in parenting style as you got older. After filling in the chart, answer the questions that follow.

	Primary Style with You	Other Style(s) with You	Primary Style with Siblings
Mother (you were a toddler)			
Mother (you were in early childhood)			
Mother (you were in middle & late childhood)			
Mother (you were an adolescent)			
Father (you were a toddler)			
Father (you were in early childhood)			
Father (you were in middle & late childhood)			
Father (you were an adolescent)			

1. What was the primary parenting style each of your parents used with you? What other style(s) did they use? When?
2. How consistent were your parents in terms of their parenting style? If they were not consistent, what do you think accounted for the lack of consistency?
3. Did both of your parents use the same parenting style?
4. If your parents used different styles, how do you think that affected you?
5. Did they change parenting styles as you got older? In what way?
6. If you can, describe these styles to your parents and ask them which style they think best fits the one they used as you were growing up. Is this consistent with your assessment?
7. How can you relate the research on parenting styles to who you are today?

Internet Projects

Check out the McGraw-Hill web site for this text (http://www.mhhe.com/santrockld8). You'll find numerous activities there, in particular various quizzes, flash cards of key terms, and a challenging and fun crossword puzzle. Please note that all website addresses in this Study Guide have been checked and are correct at the time of publication, however, websites may be discontinued or addresses may change so when you search a given site it may no longer be viable. If that occurs, I apologize for the inconvenience, and would appreciate you notifying me so I could make appropriate revisions in future editions of this Study Guide.

Internet Project 1: The Effects of Television on Children

It should be clear from Chapter 9 that watching television is associated with both beneficial and detrimental outcomes. Check out two sites to find more information on this topic. First, go to the APA website (http://www.apa.org) and type "children and television" in the search box ("What Are You Looking For?") and review some of the articles; then go to http://library.thinkquest.org/17067/you/pgender.html to look more specifically at issues of gender inequity on television. After reviewing several articles about the effects on children of watching television, consider the following questions:

1. What are the problems associated with watching television?
2. What are the benefits associated with watching television?
3. With respect to aggression and television violence, does watching violence make children more aggressive, or is it that the more aggressive children watch violent programs?
4. The "Thinkquest" article describes how providing strong female role models has had a backlash of providing aggressive female role models. What do you think?
5. How can parents use television to increase their children's sensitivity, empathy, and intellectual growth?
6. Consider the various guidelines presented in the text and the articles you've read on-line, then develop a set that you believe would be useful for people you know who have children (this may be you).

Internet Project 2: Child Sexual Abuse

Go to the APA website (http://www.apa.org) and type "child abuse" in the search box ("What Are You Looking For?"). Review several of the articles that come up, but pay particular attention to the article titled "Statement on Child Sexual Abuse: Childhood Sexual Abuse Causes Serious Harm to Its Victims." What are the issues here? This article is in response to concerns that a previous article published in *American Psychologist* seemed to downplay the effects of child sexual abuse and raised questions about whether a child actually is harmed when sexually molested by an adult. Discuss the various interpretations of the first article, the response of the APA (and its members), and what you would conclude about the harm that occurs to a child (both as a child and later as an adult) resulting from child sexual abuse. (Another good non-web source is a book by Catherine Cameron, *Resolving Childhood Trauma: A Long-Term Study of Abuse Survivors* (2000, Sage Publications), which presents in a most readable fashion the results of her longitudinal research with women who had been sexually molested as children.) How can you use this information to reduce the occurrence of child sexual abuse?

Other Relevant Sites on the Internet

APS site
http://www.psychologicalscience.org/

Brown University
http://search.brown.edu/search/texis/webinator/search is an excellent site to search for issues concerning gender equity; a particularly good article is the one by Lorie N. Sutter titled "Achieving Gender Equity in Science Classrooms."

Children's Defense Fund (CDF)
http://www.childrensdefense.org is the web site for CDF, the organization headed by Marian Wright Edelman to promote child welfare (discussed in Chapter 1 of the text).

Positive Discipline
http://www.positivediscipline.com is a good site for parents and teachers to find useful solutions for discipline problems.

Society for Research in Child Development (SRCD)
http://srcd.org is the web site for SRCD, an organization whose purposes are to promote multidisciplinary research in the field of human development, to foster the exchange of information among scientists and other professionals of various disciplines, and to encourage applications of research findings.

Web MD
http://www.webmd.com offers a wide variety of information for the medical profession and for consumers.

Zero to Three
http://www.zerotothree.com is a site for parents and professionals. Zero to Three is a non-profit organization that focuses on promoting the healthy development of babies and toddlers.

Chapter 10: Physical and Cognitive Development in Middle and Late Childhood

Learning Objectives

1. Explain the physical changes that take place during middle and late childhood, including motor development.
2. Discuss the importance of exercise and the effects of sports.
3. Discuss the most prevalent health issues of this time period—accidents and injuries, obesity, and childhood cancer.
4. Discuss what a learning disability is and the types of learning disabilities children have.
5. Consider how the educational system helps children with disabilities.
6. Understand Piaget's theory of concrete operations, and examine how his theories are applied to teaching as well as criticisms of his theory.
7. Describe how information processing examines cognitive development, including changes in memory, critical thinking, and metacognition.
8. Discuss what intelligence is, how it is measured, and the difficulty in measuring it.
9. Explain Sternberg's and Gardner's alternative theories of intelligence.
10. Examine the controversies surrounding intelligence, including culturally-biased tests and the misuse of intelligence tests.
11. Discuss mental retardation and its two causes.
12. Explain what giftedness is and the characteristics of a gifted child.
13. Understand what creativity is and ways to foster it in children.
14. Describe the two approaches to reading and the effectiveness of each.
15. Discuss bilingual education and the positions of both its critics and its supporters.

Chapter Outline

PHYSICAL DEVELOPMENT
    Body Growth and Proportion
    Motor Development
    Exercise and Sports
    Health, Illness, and Disease
        Accidents and Injuries
        Obesity
        Cancer
    Children with Disabilities
        Who Are Children with Disabilities?
        Learning Disabilities
        Attention Deficit Hyperactivity Disorder
        Educational Issues
COGNITIVE DEVELOPMENT
    Piaget's Theory
        Piaget and Education
        Evaluating Piaget's Theory
    Information Processing
        Memory
        Critical Thinking

Self-Test A: Multiple Choice

1. The story related in the text about Jessica Dubroff suggests that:
   a. parents need to be sensitive to and encourage the special talents and desires of their children.
   b. parents can subtly guide their children in a way that the parents are able to fulfill their own desires.
   c. children should be allowed to have a well-rounded life.
   d. parents need to restrict their children's activities to prevent them from injuring themselves.

2. The period of middle and late childhood involves:
   a. slow, consistent growth.
   b. rapid, consistent growth.
   c. rapid spurts of growth.
   d. moderate growth with occasional spurts.

3. During the elementary school years, body changes occur:
   a. at close to the same rate as they occurred during early childhood.
   b. much more rapidly than they did during early childhood.
   c. in the skeletal and muscular systems.
   d. most significantly in the dermal and subdermal systems.

4. Duran is a normal, healthy second-grader. He is most likely to become fatigued by long periods of:
   a. sitting.
   b. running.
   c. jumping.
   d. bicycling.

5. Which pattern best portrays changes in gross and fine motor skills in the elementary school years?
   a. Boys outperform girls in fine motor skills.
   b. Girls outperform boys in fine motor skills.
   c. Girls outperform boys in gross motor skills.
   d. There are no sex differences in the development of gross and fine motor skills.

6. A 1997 national poll found that _____ percent of elementary school children were physically active for 30 minutes every day of the week.
   a. 12
   b. 22
   c. 32
   d. 42

7. Which of the following sports settings present special concern for child developmentalists?
   a. special olympics
   b. highly competitive, win-oriented sports
   c. gymnastics
   d. highly physical interactive sports

8. The most common cause of severe injury and death in middle and late childhood is:
   a. cancer.
   b. skate-boarding.
   c. ingestion of poisons.
   d. motor vehicle accidents.

9. Nine-year-old Fernando has had a weight problem since he was an infant. One of the best strategies he could use to lose weight would be:
   a. stomach surgery.
   b. wiring his mouth to reduce food intake.
   c. a high-protein, low-carbohydrate diet.
   d. exercise and a moderate reduction in calories.

10. The most common cancer in children is:
    a. leukemia.
    b. lymphoma.
    c. brain cancer.
    d. neuroblastoma.

11. The most frequent disability among school children in the United States is:
    a. visual impairment.
    b. learning disabilities.
    c. mental retardation.
    d. speech handicaps.

12. Jason, a second-grader, has no trouble with math, science, or art, but he cannot spell, read, or write. Jason is likely to be found to have:
    a. a vision impairment.
    b. a speech handicap.
    c. a learning disability.
    d. an attention deficit.

13. Tyisha suffers from attention deficit hyperactivity disorder (ADHD). She is most likely to be experiencing all of the following symptoms EXCEPT:
    a. she has a short attention span.
    b. she engages in high levels of physical activity.
    c. her intelligence is below normal for her age.
    d. she is extremely impulsive.

14. Which of the following class of drugs is most likely to be given to a child to control attention deficit hyperactivity disorder?
    a. stimulants
    b. depressants
    c. tranquilizers
    d. relaxants

15. In 1983, Public Law 94-142 was renamed the Individuals with Disabilities Education Act (IDEA). This act requires that students with disabilities have:
    a. special classrooms to enhance their education.
    b. funding for special education.
    c. an individualized education plan.
    d. tutors or aides to assist them.

16. Today, the term "mainstreaming" means educating a child with:
    a. disabilities in the regular classroom.
    b. special education needs full-time in the general school program.
    c. special education needs partially in a special education classroom, partially in a regular classroom.
    d. disabilities in the least restrictive environment possible.

17. Reversible mental actions are called:
    a. focal points.
    b. symbolic thought.
    c. abstractions.
    d. operations.

18. Tyrell understands that his father can also be a son and a brother all at the same time. This suggests that Tyrell is in the _____ stage.
    a. sensorimotor
    b. preoperational
    c. concrete operational
    d. formal operational

19. Which of the following is an application of Piaget's ideas to education?
    a. We need to know how children understand the world to teach them effectively.
    b. Children's illogical or distorted ideas about the world make it hard for them to learn.
    c. The pattern of mental development is universal, so one curriculum could be developed and used for all children.
    d. By the third or fourth grade, children are ready for abstract learning.

20. All of the following are criticisms of Piaget's work EXCEPT:
    a. not all concepts of a cognitive stage develop at the same time.
    b. changing the tasks that measure cognitive development changes skills children can exhibit.
    c. children can be trained to do tasks that they should not be able to do given the cognitive stage they are in.
    d. some of the skills Piaget identified appear much later than he suggested.

21. The cognitive processes that do not occur automatically but require work and effort are called:
    a. control processes.
    b. strategic methods.
    c. critical thinking skills.
    d. motivation.

22. _____ involves grasping the deeper meaning of ideas, keeping an open mind about different approaches and perspectives, and deciding for oneself what to believe or do.
    a. Reflection
    b. Critical thinking
    c. Use of strategies
    d. Abstract learning

23. Aaron is aware of his thinking and understands that he uses certain strategies to help him remember. These skills demonstrate:
    a. memory.
    b. cognition.
    c. metacognition.
    d. abstract reasoning.

24. Summarizing and getting the "gist" of what an author is saying are important strategies for:
    a. planning.
    b. writing.
    c. reading.
    d. rereading.

25. _____ is defined as verbal ability, problem-solving skills, and the ability to adapt to and learn from life's everyday experiences.
    a. Creativity
    b. Intelligence
    c. Metacognition
    d. Wisdom

26. The purpose of the first intelligence test designed by Alfred Binet and Theophile Simon was to:
   a. identify students who should be placed in special classes.
   b. identify gifted students who should be placed in accelerated training programs.
   c. measure intelligence so that future success could be predicted.
   d. form a basic definition of intelligence and find definitive answers to what intelligence is.

27. Ashley has a mental age of 13 and a chronological age of 10. Thus her intelligence quotient (IQ) is:
   a. 130.
   b. 100.
   c. 77.
   d. 10.

28. Robert Sternberg's triarchic theory of intelligence includes all of the following abilities EXCEPT:
   a. analytical.
   b. creative.
   c. motivational.
   d. practical.

29. Indira grew up in poverty and first learned to care for herself and her younger brother by selling newspapers and developing "street smarts." Although she never went to school, she has become successful in business. In terms of Robert Sternberg's triarchic theory, which type(s) of intelligence does Indira have?
   a. analytical
   b. creative
   c. practical
   d. all three factors

30. Ariadne is an architect. According to Howard Gardner's theory of intelligence, which type of intelligence would Ariadne have?
   a. spatial
   b. mathematical
   c. kinesthetic
   d. naturalist

31. Many of the early intelligence tests favored urban, middle-income, White individuals. These tests are considered to be:
   a. culture-fair.
   b. culture-biased.
   c. culturally differentiating.
   d. normative.

32. Why does it seem to be impossible to devise a universal, culture-fair intelligence test?
   a. We cannot establish norms for the different populations of people who take the test.
   b. Languages are so different that some languages cannot express what other languages can.
   c. Different cultures appear to encourage the development of different intellectual skills or knowledge.
   d. We are beginning to doubt that IQ tests actually measure intelligence.

33. All of the following are potential problems with IQ tests EXCEPT:
   a. scores on an IQ test can easily lead to stereotypes.
   b. IQ tests can be used as the sole indicator of a person's competence.
   c. there may be problems in interpreting the meaningfulness of the overall IQ score.
   d. IQ tests can be used to predict how well a student might be expected to perform in school.

34. Information about the causes of mental retardation suggests that:
    a. the causes are primarily organic.
    b. environment is more important than biology.
    c. most retardation is due to genetic factors.
    d. both biological and environmental factors are involved.

35. Ellen Winner (1996) has described three criteria that characterize gifted children. Which of the following is NOT a criterion?
    a. ingenuity
    b. precocity
    c. marching to their own drummer
    d. a passion to master

36. Hyun-Joo is asked to come up with as many possible uses of a paper clip as possible. This task requires her:
    a. verbal comprehension.
    b. convergent thinking.
    c. divergent thinking.
    d. critical thinking.

37. Isaac's parents want to encourage him to become more creative. Which of the following should they AVOID doing?
    a. Encourage Isaac to brainstorm.
    b. Provide Isaac with an environment that stimulates creativity.
    c. Introduce Isaac to creative people.
    d. Encourage Isaac's external motivation.

38. Xanath is a normally developing 8-year-old. If you were to ask her to say the first thing that comes to mind when you say the word "dog," she would most likely say:
    a. "black."
    b. "big."
    c. "sit."
    d. "animal."

39. Mrs. Kumin believes that in early reading instruction, children should be presented with materials in their complete form, such as stories and poems. Which approach does Mrs. Kumin support?
    a. whole-language
    b. basic-skills-and-phonetics
    c. balanced
    d. classical

40. Researchers have found that bilingualism:
    a. has a negative effect on children's cognitive development.
    b. has a positive effect on children's cognitive development.
    c. confuses children in regard to language development.
    d. results in children scoring lower than monolingual children on intelligence tests.

Self-Test B: Matching

Match the following persons with the statement or theory that most closely reflects their perspective:

1.	Alfred Binet	a.	Created the major alternative to the Stanford-Binet intelligence test
2.	Howard Gardner	b.	Created the first test to determine which children would do well in school
3.	David Wechsler	c.	Proposed a theory of seven kinds of intelligence
4.	Ellen Winner	d.	Developed the triarchic theory of intelligence
5.	Robert Sternberg	e.	Talked about the importance of getting students to think reflectively
6.	John Dewey	f.	Metacognition should be a strong focus to help children think critically
7.	Deanna Kuhn	g.	The key to education is helping students learn a rich repertoire of strategies
8.	Michael Pressley	h.	Described gifted children in terms of precocity, own drummer, and passion

Essay Questions

1. You have been approached by your favorite elementary school teacher, who has asked you for your ideas on creating a healthy, holistic atmosphere for his students. He wants to address their physical, emotional, and cognitive needs, but also wants a special emphasis on teaching children to read. Bearing in mind all of the developmental issues you have studied in this chapter, what would you suggest?

2. Your roommates are arguing about whose ideas were more appropriate for application to education, Piaget's or Sternberg's. On another note, though, they have agreed with each other that intelligence tests are biased and should not be used. Because you are taking this class in life-span development, they turn to you to determine whether Piaget's or Sternberg's theories and applications are more useful, and they also want you to confirm their stand on intelligence tests. What can you tell them?

Scramblers

Unscramble the following people or terms, then describe what they are known for (people) or define them (terms):

1. VIDAD HCSELWRE

   _____

2. EBROTR RNEBTESRG

   _____

3. ELXSYIAD

   _____

4. ULSCINOIN

   _____

5. YTTRIAVNISTI

   _____

6. GONCIATTIEOMN

   _____

7. LILGEENTCNEI

   _____

8. HCIRCARIT OERHYT

   _____

9. VIITTAYECR

_____

10. ALIBLUIGN NEODIUTCA

_____

Key to Self-Test A

1.	b	LO 13	15.	c	LO 5	29.	c	LO 9
2.	a	LO 1	16.	c	LO 5	30.	a	LO 9
3.	c	LO 1	17.	d	LO 6	31.	b	LO 10
4.	a	LO 1	18.	c	LO 6	32.	c	LO 10
5.	b	LO 1	19.	a	LO 6	33.	d	LO 10
6.	b	LO 2	20.	d	LO 6	34.	d	LO 11
7.	b	LO 2	21.	a	LO 7	35.	a	LO 12
8.	d	LO 3	22.	b	LO 7	36.	c	LO 13
9.	d	LO 3	23.	c	LO 7	37.	d	LO 13
10.	a	LO 3	24.	c	LO 7	38.	d	LO 13
11.	b	LO 4	25.	b	LO 8	39.	a	LO 14
12.	c	LO 4	26.	a	LO 8	40.	b	LO 15
13.	c	LO 4	27.	a	LO 8			
14.	a	LO 4	28.	c	LO 9			

Key to Self-Test B

1.	b	4.	h	7.	f
2.	c	5.	d	8.	g
3.	a	6.	e		

Key to Essay Questions

1. Your answer here should encompass the entire chapter, including physical changes in the skeletal and muscular systems and increased motor skills (gross and fine) and how that relates to proper diet and their need to exercise, as well as the positive and negative consequences of participating in sports; sensitivity to various issues of children's disabilities (e.g., learning disabilities, ADHD) and socioeconomic issues; then move on to the developmental changes in children's cognitive abilities (they are now in the concrete operational stage), addressing application of Piaget's theory to education, what information-processing theory says about development during this period (e.g., memory, metacognition, critical thinking). Then address the issues of intelligence, creativity, language development, and the debate on teaching reading using the whole language approach or the basic-skills-and-phonetics approach. After addressing all of these developmental issues, suggest how you would use this information to assist your teacher in creating a model classroom with a developmentally appropriate curriculum to achieve optimal outcomes for all of the students. (To **really** be a star, you might also want to include the benefits of bilingualism and a discussion of how it would be appropriate for children at this age to start to learn a second language if they do not come from a bilingual home.)

2. Here, of course, you will need to lay out the theories of both Piaget and Sternberg, discussing what Piaget said about children's abilities in the concrete operational stage and how that information can be applied to education (e.g., assuming the constructivist approach, children need to be actively involved in seeking solutions for themselves) and the criticisms of his theory (e.g., some cognitive abilities emerge earlier than he thought). Then you will need to address Sternberg's triarchic theory of intelligence with its three separate components and explain how each of those can be incorporated into the teaching/learning process, discussing what he believes is important in teaching (i.e., balanced instruction related to the three types of intelligence in addition to traditional memorization). Bringing in any of the other theories you wish to consider, state which approach you think works best and explain your rationale. Then move on to the concerns about use of intelligence tests (understanding why Binet and Simon developed them in the first place, you can understand their use as a general predictor for how well a student may be expected to perform, **but** discuss the many issues of bias, inability to create a truly culture-free test, and other misuses) and develop a clear argument presenting the safeguards, limitations, and cautions you believe are necessary for these tests to be used effectively.

Key to Scramblers

1. David Wechsler: Created the major alternative to the Stanford-Binet intelligence test
2. Robert Sternberg: Developed the triarchic theory of intelligence
3. Dyslexia: Category of learning disabilities involving severe impairment in reading & spelling abilities
4. Inclusion: Educating a child with special education needs full-time in the regular classroom
5. Transitivity: Mental concept underlying the ability to combine relations logically, understand conclusions
6. Metacognition: Thinking about thinking or knowing about knowing
7. Intelligence: Verbal ability, problem-solving skills, ability to learn from/adapt to everyday experience
8. Triarchic theory: Intelligence consists of componential, experiential, and practical components
9. Creativity: Ability to think in novel, unusual ways and come up with unique solutions
10. Bilingual education: Teaching academic subjects in child's native language, gradually adding English

Research Project 1: Fine and Gross Motor Activity

This is a way to see developmental changes in fine and gross motor activity over time. After obtaining parental permission and the permission of the children with whom you will be working, have five children from five different age groups (ranging from 2 through 10) write (or print, as appropriate) their first name and their age and draw a picture of themselves (note that only one chart is provided—be sure to make four more copies before using this one). Compare the handwriting and the drawings in terms of what you have learned so far. Then answer the questions below.

Name:	Age:

Self-Portrait:

1. What similarities and what differences did you notice in how the children held their writing/drawing utensil (pencil, crayon, etc.)?
2. What patterns of development did you notice when comparing the writing and drawing of the children in terms of the material discussed in this chapter?
3. Were your observations consistent with what you might expect from the research described? Explain your response.
4. What might you conclude about development of these skills based on your observations?

Research Project 2: Conservation Tasks

Work with two children, one between the ages of 4 and 5, the other between 6 and 7. Be sure to obtain written consent from the parents; it is also appropriate to have the children sign (or print, as the case may be) the consent form indicating their willingness to participate—even if they don't sign the consent form, you should be sure to ask them for permission to work with them. Usually if you tell them you are working on a project for school and ask if they would be willing to help you out, they are more than happy to do so. In the event parent and/or child wishes to have the parent present while you are doing these tasks, instruct the parent to say nothing, merely to observe. Also, be sure that you do not have both of these children present and observing each other as that might influence the outcome.

Referring back to Chapter 8 of the text, look at Figures 8.6 and 8.7, which contain conservation tasks. You may administer any or all of these to the children to demonstrate differences in conservation ability. For example, to do the conservation of liquid (volume) task, you will need a pitcher of colored water (use a couple of drops of food coloring), two glasses (glasses A and B) that are the same size, and one glass (glass C) that is taller and thinner than the other two. In the presence of the child, pour water into glass A; then, as you pour water into glass B, ask the child to tell you when there is exactly the same amount of water in glass B as in glass A. When the child is sure they're the same, ask: "Do both of these glasses have the same amount of water?" If the child says yes, then pour water from glass B into glass C, saying: "I'm pouring the water from this glass into this glass. I'm not adding any, I'm not taking any away." After you have poured all the water into glass C, ask the child: "Do both glasses have the same amount of water, or does one have more?" Typically, the younger child will say one has more. If so, ask: "Which has more?" In either case, whether the child says one has more or they're the same, ask: "How do you know?" Then pour the water back into glass B and ask: "Are they both the same, or does one have more?" Unless you've spilled some in the process, the child will almost always say they're the same. Repeat the entire process again.

You can do a similar task for conservation of number using twelve objects of the same size, shape, and color (pennies, the plastic tops of water bottles, whatever). Lay them out in two rows of six, being sure that they are completely aligned with each other. Ask the child whether there are the same amount (don't say "number") of pennies (or whatever) in the top row as in the bottom row. Then spread out the bottom row and ask the child again if there are the same amount in the top row as in the bottom row. Whatever the answer, ask: "How do you know?" Then put the items back into aligned rows and repeat the process.

You can do similar tasks with all of the forms of conservation discussed in Figure 8.7. You may also wish to look at the children's degree of animism—whether they consider inanimate objects to be alive. A well-used question is: "Have you ever watched the moon at night when you're riding in a car? What does it do?" The typical animistic (preoperational) response is: "It follows me."

Using the charts on the next page, record the two children's responses. Then answer the questions that follow.

Task	Child 1 (age:___/sex___) Response 1	Reason for Response	Child 1 (age:___/sex___) Response 2	Reason for Response
Conservation of Liquid				
Conservation of Number				

Task	Child 2 (age:___/sex___) Response 1	Reason for Response	Child 2 (age:___/sex___) Response 2	Reason for Response
Conservation of Liquid				
Conservation of Number				

1. What similarities and what differences did you notice in how the children responded?
2. What patterns of development did you notice when comparing the responses of the children in terms of the material discussed in Chapters 8 and 10?
3. Were your observations consistent with what you might expect from the research described? Explain your response.
4. Recalling the criticisms of and support for Piaget's theory, how were the responses of the children you observed consistent/inconsistent with what Piaget and his critics would predict?
5. What might you conclude about development of these skills based on your observations?

Personal Application Project 1: Reflecting on What You Learned

Consider what you read in Chapter 10, then answer the following questions:

1. What information in this chapter did you already know?
2. How can/do you use that information in your own life?

3. What information in this chapter was totally new to you?
4. How can you use that new information in your own life?
5. What information in this chapter was different from what you previously believed?
6. How was this information different?
7. How do you account for the differences between what you believed and what you learned in the chapter?
8. What is the most important thing you learned from reading this chapter?

Personal Application Project 2: Sternberg's Triarchic Theory

Think about your own intellectual growth over the years, including where you are today. Consider the three components of Sternberg's Triarchic Theory of Intelligence and use the chart below to indicate what evidence you have concerning your own strengths and challenges in each of these categories as you have developed.

	Analytical	Creative	Practical
Early Childhood			
Middle to Late Childhood			
Adolescence			
Present time			
Comments:			

Internet Projects

Check out the McGraw-Hill web site for this text (http://www.mhhe.com/santrockld8). You'll find numerous activities there, in particular various quizzes, flash cards of key terms, and a challenging and fun crossword puzzle. Please note that all website addresses in this Study Guide have been checked and are correct at the time of publication, however, websites may be discontinued or addresses may change so when you search a given site it may no longer be viable. If that occurs, I apologize for the inconvenience, and would appreciate you notifying me so I could make appropriate revisions in future editions of this Study Guide.

Internet Project 1: How Intelligent Are the Intelligence Tests?

This is a really fun project (well, I had fun working on it). Go to http://www.queendom.com/tests/iq/index.html and select the Classical Intelligence Test-R. Take the test (it takes about 30-45 minutes, depending on how quickly you read, how many interruptions you have, how fast your modem is—obviously faster if you have DSL) and see what it tells you your IQ is. PLEASE DO NOT TAKE THIS TOO SERIOUSLY–WE SPEND A LOT OF TIME TAKING CLASSES ON HOW TO ADMINISTER AND ASSESS TESTS, SO JUST DO THIS AS A FUN PROJECT (my first series of assessment classes were an entire academic year, and I've taken several others since then, but this can give you some idea about the verbal, spatial, and mathematical nature of a classic intelligence test). After completing the test, consider the following questions:

1. How accurate do you think this test is?
2. What parts were most challenging for you?
3. There are several questions on the test that ask you to determine which of five words does not fit. What are the different classifications that you can think of for those questions? Can you think of other ways that the words could be classified so that an answer other than the one they consider "correct" might be correct (although they don't tell you what the "correct" answers are)?
5. Note in the "Adventures for the Mind" section the question of whether parents should test their children's IQ. Consider what you learned in the chapter and what you gained from this website and answer the questions in that box.
4. To what degree do you think this test is culturally biased?
5. What problems might someone from another culture have taking a test like this?
6. How might you put the results of a test like this to good use?

Feel free to take any of the other tests at that website–a relatively new area of interest is in emotional intelligence, so you might want to look at that as well. You might also want to try the Culture-Fair IQ Test to see if you think it really is culture-fair. Have fun with this☺

Internet Project 2: Nutrition and Exercise

As indicated in Chapter 10, nutrition and exercise are major concerns for children today—it often seems either they are "couch potatoes" who stuff themselves in front of the television set and get too little exercise, or they are overly concerned with diet and push themselves beyond health limits in competitive sports. Check out what the "experts" are saying by going to two by-now-familiar websites: American Psychological Association (http://www.apa.org) and Dr. Koop (http://www.drkoop.com). At each site do a search for "children and sports" and review the articles that you see.

1. How does the information of each site compare with what you learn at the other?
2. How does the information compare with what you have read in the chapter?
3. What additional information did you learn?
4. Based on what you learned, what advice would you give to parents about their children's (and their own) participation in children's sports?
5. Based on the information in the text and from the websites, what type of intervention would you design to ensure that school children today are protecting their health in terms of diet, nutrition, and exercise?

Other Relevant Sites on the Internet

APS site
http://www.psychologicalscience.org/

Children's Defense Fund (CDF)
http://www.childrensdefense.org is the web site for CDF, the organization headed by Marian Wright Edelman to promote child welfare (discussed in Chapter 1 of the text).

Middle Childhood Physical Development
http://www.fractaldomains.com/devpsych/midchildphys.htm is a nice site that adds additional perspectives about physical development in middle childhood to the information contained in our text.

The National Institute of Child Health
http://www.nichd.nih.gov is one of the many information sites of the National Institutes of Health. This one is devoted to all aspects of children's health.

Society for Research in Child Development (SRCD)
http://srcd.org is the web site for SRCD, an organization whose purposes are to promote multidisciplinary research in the field of human development, to foster the exchange of information among scientists and other professionals of various disciplines, and to encourage applications of research findings.

Web MD
http://www.webmd.com offers a wide variety of information for the medical profession and for consumers.

Chapter 11: Socioemotional Development in Middle and Late Childhood

Learning Objectives

1. Understand the shift in development of self-understanding during middle and late childhood.
2. Define self-esteem and self-concept, and discuss ways to increase children's self-esteem.
3. Explain Erik Erikson's fourth stage of psychosocial development.
4. Examine the changes in emotional development that take place in this period and discuss emotional intelligence.
5. Describe Kohlberg's theory of moral development, as well as criticisms of it.
6. Discuss Carol Gilligan's alternate theory of moral development.
7. Define prosocial behavior and altruism, and understand ways to increase altruism in children.
8. Examine gender stereotypes and gender similarities and differences.
9. Discuss gender-role classification, including androgyny and gender-role transcendence, and the importance of considering gender in context.
10. Explain how parent-child interactions in the family change during middle and late childhood.
11. Describe both the short-term and long-term effects of living in stepfamilies.
12. Define the term latchkey children and elaborate on ways to reduce the risk to these children.
13. Expound on the four peer statuses.
14. Identify the parent-child relationships that characterize bullies and victims, as well as the effects of bullying and strategies to reduce bullying.
15. Explain what social cognition is and why it is important.
16. Examine the importance of children's friendships.
17. Discuss the transition to elementary schools, how socioeconomic status and ethnicity impact education, and ways to improve relations among ethnically diverse groups.
18. Examine the cross-cultural differences in levels of achievement.

Chapter Outline

EMOTIONAL AND PERSONALITY DEVELOPMENT
    The Self
        The Development of Self-Understanding
        Self-Esteem and Self-Concept
        Industry Versus Inferiority
    Emotional Development
        Developmental Changes
        Emotional Intelligence
    Moral Development
        Kohlberg's Theory
        Prosocial Behavior and Altruism
    Gender
        Stereotypes
        Similarities and Differences
        Gender-Role Classification
        Gender in Context
FAMILIES
    Parent-Child Issues

Self-Test A: Multiple Choice

1. As a normal third-grader, Nora is most likely to define herself in terms of all of the following EXCEPT:
   a. her feelings.
   b. her eye color.
   c. her religious affiliation.
   d. how she compares with other third graders.

2. _____ refers to global evaluations of the self.
   a. Self-esteem
   b. Self-perception
   c. Self-concept
   d. Self-efficacy

3. Which of the following is NOT one of the ways the text suggests for increasing a child's self-esteem?
   a. setting high goals with a need to succeed
   b. identifying the causes of low self-esteem and the domains of competence important to the self
   c. providing emotional support and social approval
   d. achievement and effective coping

4. Amara is a single mother with one child, 8-year-old Aslam. Amara decides to enroll Aslam in a local Boys' Club program. In doing so, Amara is attempting to raise her son's self-esteem through:
   a. achievement.
   b. coping.
   c. emotional support.
   d. identifying areas of competence.

5. Children in the middle and late childhood period of development are also in which of Erikson's psychosocial stages?
   a. trust versus mistrust
   b. autonomy versus shame and doubt
   c. initiative versus guilt
   d. industry versus inferiority

6. Hermione is experiencing emotional changes that are characteristic of children in elementary school. Thus we would expect her to exhibit all of the following EXCEPT:
   a. emotions becoming more externalized.
   b. increased understanding that more than one emotion can be experienced in a particular situation.
   c. improved ability to conceal negative emotions.
   d. use of self-initiated strategies to redirect her feelings.

7. _____ intelligence initially was proposed as a form of social intelligence that involves the ability to monitor one's own and others' feelings and emotions, to discriminate among them, and to use this information to guide one's thinking and action.
   a. Practical
   b. Emotional
   c. Intellectual
   d. Experiential

8. Daniel Goleman believes that when it comes to predicting an individual's competence:
   a. IQ matters more than emotional intelligence.
   b. emotional intelligence matters more than IQ.
   c. practical intelligence matters more than IQ.
   d. practical intelligence matters more than emotional intelligence.

9. The Nueva School near San Francisco has developed a class called "self science," which includes all of the following topics EXCEPT:
   a. understanding that apathy is a key dimension of getting along in the social world.
   b. seeing the consequences of alternative choices.
   c. taking responsibility for decisions and actions.
   d. learning to be assertive rather than passive or aggressive.

10. In building on Piaget's theory of moral development, Kohlberg emphasized the importance of:
   a. understanding intentions.
   b. opportunities to take the perspective of others.
   c. reducing conflict.
   d. punishment.

11. Lawrence Kohlberg's theory of moral development stresses that a child's moral level is determined by:
   a. how well the child defends a correct answer to a moral dilemma.
   b. the nature of the child's ideas about morality.
   c. how a child processes information about moral problems.
   d. the child's reasoning about moral decisions.

12. "Heinz should steal the drug. It isn't like it really cost $2,000, and he'll be really unhappy if his wife dies." This statement is characteristic of a stage of morality called:
   a. heteronomous morality.
   b. individualism, purpose, and exchange.
   c. mutual interpersonal expectations.
   d. social contract and individual rights.

13. A pacifist who is thrown in jail for refusing to obey the draft laws because he believes that killing is morally wrong is at what stage of moral development?
   a. individualism, purpose, and exchange
   b. mutual interpersonal expectations
   c. social contract and individual rights
   d. universal ethical principles

14. Research on Kohlberg's theory of moral development in 27 diverse cultures around the world:
   a. has provided no universal support for this theory.
   b. has provided support for the universality of the first four stages.
   c. has provided support for the universality of all six stages.
   d. has found conflicting results in terms of the theory's universality.

15. Criticisms of Kohlberg's theory of moral development include all of the following EXCEPT:
    a. it places too much emphasis on moral thought, not enough on moral behavior.
    b. it is culturally biased.
    c. it considers family processes essentially unimportant in children's moral development.
    d. it places females at a higher level of morality than males.

16. Carol Gilligan (1996) has found that as girls reach adolescence they:
    a. become increasingly moral.
    b. adopt a justice perspective of morality.
    c. increasingly silence their "distinctive voice."
    d. become more outspoken about their inner feelings.

17. William Damon (1988) has found that by the time children enter elementary school, they share with others:
    a. for the fun of the social play ritual.
    b. out of imitation of older people.
    c. out of obligation, but don't think they need to be as generous to others as they are to themselves.
    d. from a sense of fairness involving principles of equality, merit, and benevolence.

18. Mr. Edwards wants to increase the prosocial behavior of children in his fifth-grade class. An effective strategy would be to:
    a. lecture the students about prosocial behavior.
    b. punish students for antisocial behavior.
    c. model prosocial behaviors.
    d. use a lot of external rewards for prosocial behavior.

19. When reviewing research comparing males and females, it is important to keep in mind that:
    a. even when differences are found, most of the individuals in the groups are virtually identical.
    b. it is unfair to compare the groups because almost all gender differences are the result of uncontrollable biological factors.
    c. it is only when statistically significant scores are found that you can conclude there is little overlap between male and female scores.
    d. even when differences are reported, there is considerable overlap between the sexes.

20. Which of the following has been found in terms of the physical comparisons of males and females?
    a. Females are more vulnerable than males.
    b. Females are more likely than males to develop physical or mental disorders.
    c. Analyses of metabolic activity in the brain show females to demonstrate greater emotionality than males.
    d. Analyses of metabolic activity in the brain show males to demonstrate greater physical expressiveness than females.

21. For which of the following do investigators continue to find gender differences?
    a. verbal skills
    b. visuospatial skills
    c. social skills
    d. suggestibility

22. A recent study by the U.S. Department of Education (2000) found that:
    a. girls significantly surpassed boys in math skills.
    b. boys significantly surpassed girls in verbal skills.
    c. boys did slightly better than girls at math and science, but girls were better students than boys.
    d. girls did slightly better than boys at math and science, and were also better students than boys..

23. According to Alice Eagly (2000), gender differences:
    a. are small or nonexistent.
    b. are stronger than feminists acknowledge.
    c. demonstrate females are more resistant to illness than males.
    d. are irrelevant in today's society.

24. J. O. Halliwell's (1844) poem in which he describes girls as being made of "sugar and spice and all that's nice" provides a good example of:
    a. gender-role transcendence.
    b. gender-role classification.
    c. gender stereotyping.
    d. gender-based prejudice.

25. The term "androgyny" refers to a gender role that is:
    a. highly masculine.
    b. highly feminine.
    c. both highly masculine and highly feminine.
    d. neither masculine nor feminine.

26. Researchers have found that high-masculinity adolescent boys:
    a. often engage in problem behaviors.
    b. do exceptionally well in school.
    c. are highly protective and nurturing of others.
    d. are more flexible, competent, and mentally healthy than other adolescent boys.

27. A woman would most likely be expected to carry on domestic duties, marry, and rear children, but least likely to work in the public sphere in which country?
    a. the United States
    b. Egypt
    c. Israel
    d. China

28. Which parent-child issue will most likely emerge in the middle and late childhood period?
    a. getting dressed
    b. getting the chores done
    c. attention-seeking behavior
    d. bedtime

29. The most common reason for elementary school children to be referred for clinical help is:
    a. school-related difficulties.
    b. problems getting along with siblings.
    c. problems getting along with parents.
    d. depression.

30. During the elementary school years, coregulation results in:
    a. more control taken by parents.
    b. moment-to-moment self-regulation by children, but general parental supervision.
    c. transfer of control to children.
    d. no change from early childhood in the amount of control exercised by parents.

31. Which of the following is a good example of boundary ambiguity?
    a. parents in a blended family deciding on who should discipline the children
    b. children of divorce who are deciding which parent they will stay with
    c. fighting parents who are unsure if they should divorce or separate
    d. children from a blended stepfamily attending the birthday party of a step-sibling

32. Marlene, a single parent, works full time, so her 11-year-old daughter Beth is an after-school latchkey child. To minimize the negative impact of this situation, Marlene should:
    a. encourage Beth to make friends that she can hang out with after school.
    b. use authoritative parenting and monitor Beth's activities.
    c. explain the importance of independence and provide at-home responsibilities so Beth learns independent living.
    d. hire a baby-sitter.

33. All of the following children are likely to be popular with their peers EXCEPT those who:
    a. give out lots of reinforcement.
    b. listen carefully to what others have to say.
    c. try to please others even if it means compromising themselves.
    d. are self-confident.

34. Samantha has few friends at school. Other children pay little attention to her and no one invites her home. Samantha is probably a _____ child.
    a. rejected
    b. neglected
    c. latchkey
    d. controversial

35. In terms of peer relations, Pedro is a rejected child. To teach him how to gain popularity with his peers, Pedro's counselor should encourage him to:
    a. join a group of peers, but avoid asking them questions.
    b. gain status by talking about items of personal interest to him, even if they are of no interest to others.
    c. get peers to pay attention to him through some positive activity (e.g., treating the class to pizza).
    d. ask questions, listen in positive ways, and say things about himself that relate to his peers' interests.

36. In a study by Olweus (1980), victims of bullies were found to have parents who were:
    a. rejecting, authoritarian, or permissive.
    b. anxious and overprotective.
    c. authoritative or permissive.
    d. victims themselves.

37. To reduce bullying, the text suggests all of the following EXCEPT:
    a. get older peers to serve as monitors for bullying and intervene when they see it taking place.
    b. suspend bullies from school for victimizing other children.
    c. form friendship groups for children who are regularly bullied by peers.
    d. incorporate the antibullying message into community activities where the children are involved.

38. The correct order of Kenneth Dodge's (1983) stages of processing social information is:
    a. enacting, searching for a response, decoding social cues, interpreting, selecting an optimal response.
    b. decoding social cues, interpreting, searching for a response, selecting an optimal response, enacting.
    c. searching for a response, decoding social cues, selecting an optimal response, enacting, interpreting.
    d. interpreting, selecting an optimal response, decoding social cues, enacting, searching for a response.

39. Tamara's friend Shelley is someone she can confide in and get good advice from, and her friend Tanya is interesting and introduces her to many new things to do. The functions each of these friendships serves, respectively, are:
    a. companionship; social comparison.
    b. intimacy/affection; stimulation.
    c. ego support; physical support.
    d. intimacy/affection; similarity.

40. In the latter part of elementary school, children's self-esteem:
    a. is lower than it was in the earlier part.
    b. is higher than it was in the earlier part.
    c. does not change from where it was in the earlier part.
    d. is lower for girls but higher for boys than it was in the earlier part.

41. Research by Jonathan Kozol (1991) found that many inner-city schools:
    a. are receiving funds to increase the quality of education for inner-city youth.
    b. have done an excellent job of integrating students from diverse backgrounds.
    c. do not provide adequate opportunities for children to learn effectively.
    d. are where the older teachers about to retire get placed.

42. John Santrock (in press) suggests teachers use all of the following strategies to improve relations between ethnically diverse students EXCEPT:
    a. turn the class into a jigsaw classroom.
    b. teach students the harmful effects of segregation.
    c. encourage students to engage in perspective taking.
    d. be a competent cultural mediator.

43. In Stevenson's research comparing students in the United States with students in Asian countries, he found that:
    a. students in the United States scored higher on math than students in Taiwan.
    b. American teachers spent more of their time teaching math than did the Asian teachers.
    c. students in the United States spent more time in school than their Asian counterparts.
    d. Asian parents were more likely than American parents to help their children with their math homework.

Self-Test B: Matching

Match the following persons with the statement or theory that most closely reflects their perspective:

1.	Carol Gilligan	a.	Described some of the problems children of poverty face in school
2.	Sandra Bem	b.	Found gender differences to be stronger than feminists acknowledge
3.	Susan Harter	c.	Devised an inventory to measure gender orientation
4.	William Damon	d.	Believed that minority students are in a position of subordination & exploitation
5.	Lawrence Kohlberg	e.	Used self-perception profile to measure children's self-esteem in many domains
6.	Kenneth Dodge	f.	Described a developmental model of children's altruism
7.	Elliot Aronson	g.	Stressed that moral development is based on moral reasoning
8.	John Ogbu	h.	A critic of Kohlberg; distinguished between justice & care perspectives
9.	Jonathan Kozol	i.	Analyzed how children process information about peer relations
10.	Alice Eagly	j.	Created the jigsaw classroom

Essay Questions

1. One of your best friends has given you the great news that she is planning to remarry after having been divorced for 2 years. Her major concern, though, is the effect this will have on her 12-year-old daughter. Your friend's fiancé has a daughter about the same age, and she is very different from your friend's daughter. Your friend's fiancé also has a 10-year-old son. Your friend has a secondary concern about the fact that both she and her fiancé have full-time jobs that neither can afford to quit, which means the children will be left home alone for several hours after school. What advice would you give her about

providing the best possible environment for the children's safety and most risk-free development?

2. You have decided to open a day-care center for elementary school children to provide an optimum environment for them between the hours that school lets out and the time their parents finish working. You've already talked to some of the parents and, while they may not tell you **their** child has problems, each has been quite open about some of the other children's problems, including low self-esteem, difficulties establishing friendships, and even bullying. The parents have also asked if you would be willing to help their children (not to mention the others!) develop in a morally appropriate manner, but they come from different religious perspectives, so they want to keep religion out of the picture in your center. Further, it appears that all five "peer statuses" are represented among the population of children you are anticipating will be enrolled (popular, average, neglected, rejected, and controversial). How would you help all of these children have the best possible growth experience in your day-care facility? How would you assist them in developing a healthy sense of self-esteem, altruism, and a solid foundation for moral development?

Scramblers

Unscramble the following people or terms, then describe what they are known for (people) or define them (terms):

1. LIELOT NOSONAR

   _____

2. HOJN UGOB

   _____

3. PSERCETPVIE KIANGT

   _____

4. FSLE-ETEMSE

   _____

5. EVRISNAUL LEATCIH SPRELINPIC

   _____

6. REAC EPCSTRIEVPE

   _____

7. SLMAITUR

   _____

8. ORGDYNNAY

_____

9. LEGCTEEDN DLIREHNC

_____

10. MIATCIYN NI DSHNEIPIRSF

_____

Key to Self-Test A

1.	b	LO 1	16.	c	LO 6	31.	a	LO 11
2.	a	LO 2	17.	d	LO 7	32.	b	LO 12
3.	a	LO 2	18.	c	LO 7	33.	c	LO 13
4.	c	LO 2	19.	d	LO 8	34.	b	LO 13
5.	d	LO 3	20.	c	LO 8	35.	d	LO 13
6.	a	LO 4	21.	b	LO 8	36.	b	LO 14
7.	b	LO 4	22.	c	LO 8	37.	b	LO 14
8.	b	LO 4	23.	b	LO 8	38.	b	LO 15
9.	a	LO 4	24.	b	LO 9	39.	b	LO 16
10.	b	LO 5	25.	c	LO 9	40.	a	LO 2
11.	d	LO 5	26.	a	LO 9	41.	c	LO 17
12.	c	LO 5	27.	b	LO 9	42.	b	LO 17
13.	d	LO 5	28.	b	LO 10	43.	d	LO 18
14.	b	LO 5	29.	a	LO 10			
15.	d	LO 5	30.	b	LO 10			

Key to Self-Test B

1.	h	5.	g	9.	a	
2.	c	6.	i	10.	b	
3.	e	7.	j			
4.	f	8.	d			

Key to Essay Questions

1. Here you will need to look at the relationship between custodial parents and their children; the issues of boundary ambiguity and who will make which decisions; the need to use effective parenting techniques (noting that the authoritative parenting style is the most effective for stepfamilies and for latchkey children); how to get the children communicating and working together; and finally, the issues of dealing with latchkey children, such as carefully monitoring their activities and getting them involved in academically, socially, and emotionally supportive after-school activities.

2. You will need to describe the five peer statuses, explain the stages of moral development and development of altruism, and describe how these can be facilitated in children. You will also need to address self-esteem

building and the various domains where a child can learn to acquire skills; and you will need to address how to incorporate the less socially competent students (e.g., rejected) into supportive peer groups. Finally, you will need to address the issues concerning bullying both in terms of reducing (hopefully, eliminating) the behavior and helping the victimized children learn not to be bullied.

Key to Scramblers

1. Elliot Aronson: Created the jigsaw classroom to reduce negative interracial/interethnic interactions
2. John Ogbu: Believed that minority students are in a position of subordination & exploitation
3. Perspective taking: The ability to assume another person's perspective/understand his/her feelings
4. Self-esteem: The global evaluative dimension of the self
5. Universal ethical principles: Kohlberg's 6th stage; moral standards based on universal human rights
6. Care perspective: Gilligan's perspective; views people in terms of connectedness with others
7. Altruism: Unselfish interest in helping others
8. Androgyny: The presence of desirable masculine & feminine characteristics in the same individual
9. Neglected children: Children infrequently nominated as a best friend but are not disliked by their peers
10. Intimacy in friendships: Self-disclosure and the sharing of private thoughts

Research Project 1: The Jigsaw Classroom

Elliot Aronson (1986) developed the jigsaw classroom in response to a major crisis in the education system in Austin, Texas. As described in your text, students from different cultural backgrounds are placed in a cooperative group in which they have to construct different parts of a project to reach a common goal. Each student is responsible for one part of the project (e.g., learning about ways to improve relations among ethnically diverse students), each student learns his or her part, then all of the students in the group come back and teach their respective parts to the entire group. There is a great deal of research to indicate that the best way to smooth out relations among persons of diverse views is to have them cooperate with each other on a project where they have a common goal. Try this technique either with your classmates or with a group of children from different cultural orientations.

Take note of: (a) how the individuals interact with each other **before** the intervention; (b) their scores on tests/quizzes **before** the intervention; (c) how they interact with each other **after** the intervention; and (d) their scores on tests/quizzes **after** the intervention. What differences do you notice? Did the results of your intervention coincide with those found in the literature? If they are different, what do you think would explain the difference?

Research Project 2: Helping the "Challenged" Child

Consider the problems of the rejected, neglected, and controversial children discussed in this chapter, as well as the problem of bullying. Understand that these children may become the bane of society in years to come, so it would benefit us all to have some early intervention. Design a program that looks at the underlying factors that lead to these children adopting their respective behaviors, then present appropriate interventions to teach them to interact effectively with other children and with adults. This will need to include development of friendships, perspective taking, altruism, and morality. Present your ideas to your professor for critique and streamlining, then present it to your local school districts or community center to see if they would be willing to put it into action.

1. When designing this program, what do you believe are the underlying factors that will lead a child to attain a status of rejected, neglected, or controversial, or to become a bully?
2. Would the same types of interventions help all of these children? What will work for each?
3. Considering their current level of development (ignoring their peer status), based on the research, what could reasonably be expected from them in terms of perspective taking, altruism, and moral development?
4. How can you teach these children to develop friendships; perspective taking; altruism; or morality; or to become more assertive or less aggressive?

Personal Application Project 1: Reflecting on What You Learned

Consider what you read in Chapter 11, then answer the following questions:

1. What information in this chapter did you already know?
2. How can/do you use that information in your own life?
3. What information in this chapter was totally new to you?
4. How can you use that new information in your own life?
5. What information in this chapter was different from what you previously believed?
6. How was this information different?
7. How do you account for the differences between what you believed and what you learned in the chapter?
8. What is the most important thing you learned from reading this chapter?

Personal Application Project 2: Consider Your Own Development

Refer to Figure 11.5 in the text, which contains the 60 items of the Bem Sex-Role Inventory. First, assess your own score on the scale, then administer the items to other people—your friends, family, classmates—to assess how they score. Note that although not included in Figure 11.5, Bem does have a fourth category, "undifferentiated," which is low on both masculinity and femininity. You may also wish to locate a self-esteem scale (you might check out Stanley Coopersmith's, which is short and easy to administer [see, Coopersmith, S. (1981) *The Antecedents of Self-esteem*, Palo Alto, CA: Consulting Psychologists Press, Inc.] or Harter's scale for adolescents [*Self-perception Profile for Adolescents*], or adults [Messer, B., & Harter, S, 1986, *Adult Self-Perception Profile*.] You might write to Dr. Harter at the University of Denver to obtain her self-esteem profiles and manuals.) If you do both the sex-role inventory and the self-esteem assessment, you could then do a correlational analysis to see if there is any particular relationship between the sex-role statuses and self-esteem.

1. Based on the research, which status (masculine, feminine, androgynous, undifferentiated) do you think would rank highest on self-esteem? Explain your rationale.
2. Considering your own ranking on the sex-role inventory and the self-esteem scale, what do you think explains how you developed in that way (consider both nature and nurture)?
3. What would be the benefits of falling into any of the four sex-role categories?
4. If you chose to change your sex-role status or raise your level of self-esteem, how would you go about doing this?
5. Refer to the Adventures of the Mind feature titled "Rethinking the Words We Use in Gender Worlds." Are there any particular words you've noticed that seem to be biased in favor of or against males or females?
6. Listen to people speaking and notice if their language seems gender biased (you may be so used to hearing gender biased language that it may take a while to tune in). Listen for such things as use of male pronouns to represent all people or to represent high-ranking professions, or female pronouns used in more low status contexts. Listen, too, for the way people address each other—are women and children more likely than men to be called "dear," "sweety," or "honey" even by people they don't know? What effect do you think this

has on an individual's self-esteem, self-perceptions, and attitudes about gender roles? What effect does it have on **your** attitudes?

The matrix below may help you conceptualize Bem's four sex-role statuses (bear in mind that masculinity and femininity are two separate dimensions, not polar opposites):

High Masculinity

	High Masculinity		
High Femininity	Androgynous	Masculine	Low Femininity
	Feminine	Undifferentiated	

Low Masculinity

Internet Projects

Check out the McGraw-Hill web site for this text (http://www.mhhe.com/santrockld8). You'll find numerous activities there, in particular various quizzes, flash cards of key terms, and a challenging and fun crossword puzzle. Please note that all website addresses in this Study Guide have been checked and are correct at the time of publication, however, websites may be discontinued or addresses may change so when you search a given site it may no longer be viable. If that occurs, I apologize for the inconvenience, and would appreciate you notifying me so I could make appropriate revisions in future editions of this Study Guide.

Internet Project 1: Talking to Kids about Tough Issues

Kaiser Permanente Health Care has an excellent website titled "Talk With Your Kids," located at http://www.talkingwithkids.org. The suggestion is to start talking with children about tough issues when they are between 8 and 12; if children haven't received guidance by the time they are teenagers, it becomes much harder to establish good communication with them. When you go to the site, consider the following questions:

1. What topics on the site are related to Chapter 11?
2. Are there other topics at this site that you might consider including in a chapter on socioemotional development for elementary school children that weren't already included? (Remember, of course, that no textbook can include everything—students would have to be in the class for a year or two!)
3. What have you learned from this site about ways to talk to children about difficult issues?
4. Is there someone you know who could benefit from this information? How would you go about approaching such a discussion (or would you just send them to the website and say, "after you've looked at it, come back and let's talk")?

If you'd like, you can order the booklet free from Kaiser at the website.

Internet Project 2: Testing Your Emotional Intelligence ("EI")

In the last chapter I sent you to http://www.queendom.com/tests/iq/index.html to try out an intelligence test. This time I'm suggesting you take the Emotional Intelligence Test, which is based on Daniel Goleman's research (remember the four main areas of emotional intelligence he talks about: developing emotional self-awareness, managing emotions, reading emotions, and handling relationships). After taking the test, answer the following questions:

1. How well did you score on this test? How accurate do you think the test is? How are the results of the test useful for you?
2. What parts of the test were most challenging for you?
3. Do you think someone could "fake good" on this test and come out with a high score while, at the same time, really having low emotional intelligence? What would be their rationale for doing so?
4. What would be the benefits of having high emotional intelligence?
5. You may have noticed a link toward the end of the introduction (before the actual test) to "Cyberia's Bookshelf." If you go there, you'll notice a couple of books are featured and several other books are listed. What kind of information do you think you could find in these books that might be useful to you? Based on the information in Chapter 11 and on the questions in this test, how do you think you might increase your own emotional intelligence?
6. Throughout Chapter 11 there are topics in addition to the section early on about emotional intelligence (EI), that relate directly to emotional intelligence (e.g., peer status, bullying, blended families, moral development, altruism, schools, etc.). In what way does EI fit into each of these other topics?
7. How can you apply what you've learned about EI to helping children overcome some of the problems presented in this chapter?

(By the way, while we're talking about emotional intelligence, or EI, the results of the test are often referred to as EQ, or emotional quotient, to parallel the IQ tests.) Have fun with this☺

Other Relevant Sites on the Internet

APA site
http://www.apa.org

APS site
http://www.psychologicalscience.org/

Children's Defense Fund (CDF)
http://www.childrensdefense.org is the web site for CDF, the organization headed by Marian Wright Edelman to promote child welfare (discussed in Chapter 1 of the text).

Divorce Page
http://www.divorcesupport.com offers information about divorce, including child custody and support, the effects of divorce on children, and how to minimize the negative effects.

Kohlberg's Theory of Moral Development
http://snycorva.cortland.edu/~andersmd/kohl/content.html is a tutorial that summarizes Kohlberg's theory with several useful links, particularly those that suggest application of Kohlberg's theory to the classroom.

NLDLine
http://www.nldline.com/dr.htm is a nice little site by Dr. Stephen Rothenberg presenting some case studies of children who have problems with social skills and different therapeutic strategies that could be useful.

Society for Research in Child Development (SRCD)
http://srcd.org is the web site for SRCD, an organization whose purposes are to promote multidisciplinary research in the field of human development, to foster the exchange of information among scientists and other professionals of various disciplines, and to encourage applications of research findings.

WebMD
http://www.webmd.com offers a wide variety of information for the medical profession and for consumers.

Chapter 12: Physical and Cognitive Development in Adolescence

Learning Objectives

1. Understand the nature of adolescence including how adolescents view themselves and how others view them.
2. Describe the physical, hormonal, and psychological changes that take place during puberty.
3. Discuss how the timing of pubertal changes impacts females and males.
4. Elaborate on adolescent sexuality, including development of a sexual identity, progression of sexual behaviors, contraceptive use, and STDs.
5. Examine adolescent pregnancy, including statistics, consequences, and ways to reduce rates.
6. Discuss substance abuse among adolescents, being certain to identify which drugs are on the rise and which are declining in use.
7. Address the rates and effects of alcohol and nicotine use among teens.
8. Identify the role development, parents, and peers play in the decision to partake in alcohol, drug, and nicotine use.
9. Differentiate between anorexia nervosa and bulimia nervosa.
10. Describe adolescent health and the leading causes of death in adolescence.
11. Discuss Piaget's stage of formal operational thought.
12. Define adolescent egocentrism and distinguish between Elkind's two types of social thinking.
13. Elaborate on how decision making and critical thinking change during adolescence.
14. Examine the transition from elementary school to junior high school, including the criteria of an effective school.
15. Address the rate, causes, and effects of high school dropouts.
16. Discuss how schools in the United States differ from schools in other countries.
17. Discuss programs and services designed to teach moral education.

Chapter Outline

THE NATURE OF ADOLESCENCE
PUBERTY
    Puberty's Boundaries and Determinants
    Hormonal Changes
    Height, Weight, and Sexual Maturation
    Body Image
    Early and Late Maturation
ADOLESCENT SEXUALITY
    Developing a Sexual Identity
    The Progression of Adolescent Sexual Behaviors
    Risk Factors for Sexual Problems
    Contraceptive Use
    Sexually Transmitted Diseases (STDs)
    Adolescent Pregnancy
        Consequences
        Reducing Adolescent Pregnancy
ADOLESCENT PROBLEMS AND HEALTH
    Substance Use and Abuse
        Alcohol

Self-Test A: Multiple Choice

1. Today's adolescents face _____ demands, expectations, and risks compared with those faced by adolescents a generation ago.
   a. more
   b. fewer
   c. just as many
   d. less strenuous

2. Public attitudes about adolescence that emerge from personal experience and media portrayals are:
   a. relatively accurate.
   b. generally inaccurate.
   c. consistent with today's adolescents' acting out behaviors.
   d. accurate from personal experiences, inaccurate from media portrayals.

3. _____ is a period of rapid physical development involving hormonal and bodily changes that occur primarily during early adolescence.
   a. Puberty
   b. Menarche
   c. Spermarche
   d. Maturation

4. The age at which puberty arrives is _____ with each passing decade.
   a. increasing
   b. decreasing
   c. staying the same
   d. slowing down

5. For menarche to begin and continue:
   a. a girl must be at least 12 years old.
   b. pubic hair must have begun to emerge, demonstrating uterine development.
   c. calorie intake must exceed the amount of calories a girl burns up.
   d. fat must make up 17 percent of the girl's body weight.

6. The _____ important endocrine gland(s) for controlling growth and regulating other glands.
   a. hypothalamus is an
   b. pituitary gland is an
   c. thalamus is an
   d. gonads are

7. Whereas _____ is responsible for development of genitals, increase in height, and changes in boys' voices, _____ is a hormone associated with breast, uterine, and skeletal development in girls.
   a. testosterone/estradiol
   b. estradiol/testosterone
   c. estrogen/progesterone
   d. serotonin/dopamine

8. The most noticeable changes in body growth for females include all of the following EXCEPT:
   a. height spurt.
   b. tendencies toward obesity.
   c. breast growth.
   d. menarche.

9. Recent research about puberty suggests all of the following EXCEPT:
   a. it is advantageous to be an early-maturing rather than a late-maturing boy.
   b. early-maturing girls experience more problems in school than late-maturing girls.
   c. pubertal variations are less dramatic than is commonly thought.
   d. in early adolescence, early-maturing girls show less satisfaction with their figures than do late-maturing girls.

10. As a child matures into adolescence, interest in sexuality:
    a. is considered normal.
    b. is a risk factor.
    c. becomes abnormal.
    d. inhibits cognitive development.

11. Adolescents who engage in homosexual behavior in adolescence:
    a. will increase their homosexual practices into adulthood.
    b. do not necessarily continue the practice into adulthood.
    c. may benefit from counseling aimed at helping them become heterosexual.
    d. are usually only exploring their newly budding sexuality.

12. David, a homosexual male, engaged in "passing" during adolescence. This would mean David:
    a. frequented gay bath houses.
    b. encouraged his heterosexual friends to engage in homosexual activities.
    c. hid his homosexual identity.
    d. let people close to him know that he was homosexual.

13. According to a 1998 study by the Alan Guttmacher Institute, initial sexual intercourse occurs _____ for a majority of teenagers.
    a. around age 12
    b. by age 15
    c. in the early- to mid-adolescent years
    d. in the mid- to late-adolescent years

14. With respect to use of contraceptives:
    a. adolescent girls are increasing their use, but adolescent boys are decreasing their use.
    b. adolescent boys are increasing their use, but adolescent girls are decreasing their use.
    c. both adolescent boys and girls are increasing their use.
    d. both adolescent boys and girls are decreasing their use.

15. The teenage birth rate:
    a. is lower now than it was in the 1950s and 1960s.
    b. is about the same as it was in the 1950s and 1960s.
    c. is higher than it was in the 1950s and 1960s.
    d. has been growing steadily since the 1950s.

16. All of the following are health risks for infants of adolescent mothers EXCEPT:
    a. low birthweight.
    b. neurological problems.
    c. childhood illness.
    d. chlamydia.

17. The Teen Outreach Program, which involves adolescents in volunteer community service, has been successful in lowering all of the following EXCEPT:
    a. teen smoking.
    b. adolescent pregnancy.
    c. school failure rate.
    d. academic suspension.

18. The drug most widely used by adolescents in our society is:
    a. marijuana.
    b. alcohol.
    c. ecstacy.
    d. inhalents.

19. _____ is more important than _____ in predicting genetic damage to lungs.
    a. Age of onset of smoking/how much the individual smokes
    b. How much the individual smokes/age of onset of smoking
    c. An inherited genetic trait/how much the individual smokes
    d. Whether an individual's parents smoked/how much the individual smokes

20. Annette has an eating disorder that involves the relentless pursuit of thinness through starvation, which ultimately may lead to her death. Annette suffers from:
    a. bulimia nervosa.
    b. anorexia nervosa.
    c. body dysphoric disorder.
    d. failure to thrive syndrome.

21. Which of the following adolescents is most likely to suffer from anorexia?
    a. Bill, an African-American male honor student from a low-income family
    b. Kim, an Asian-American female honor student from an upper-income family
    c. Jarod, a White male from a middle-income family who has dropped out of school
    d. Emily, a White female honor student from an upper-income family

22. Adolescents in which country do the LEAST amount of exercise?
    a. the United States
    b. Ireland
    c. Germany
    d. the Slovak Republic

23. Which of the following is the LEAST likely cause of motor vehicle accidents among adolescents?
    a. speeding
    b. tailgating
    c. lack of driving experience
    d. driving under the influence of drugs

24. A child in the formal operational thought stage of cognitive development is MOST likely to engage in which of the following activities?
    a. using building blocks to determine how houses are constructed
    b. writing a story about a clown who wants to leave the circus
    c. drawing pictures of a family using stick figures
    d. writing an essay about patriotism

25. When playing the modified "Twenty Questions" game in which she is supposed to determine which picture of 42 the experimenter has in mind, Elnora asks questions in a systematic way, such as "Is it in the top half of the display?" Elnora is exhibiting:
    a. hypothetical-deductive reasoning.
    b. hypothetical-inductive reasoning.
    c. concrete operational thought.
    d. preoperational thought.

26. Jean Piaget's ideas on formal operational thought are being challenged in all of the following ways EXCEPT:
    a. Not all adolescents are formal operational thinkers.
    b. Not all adults in every culture are formal operational thinkers.
    c. There is more individual variation in the development of formal operations than Piaget thought.
    d. Only those with scientific training use hypothetical-deductive reasoning.

27. Jennifer, who is having unprotected sex with her boyfriend, comments to her best friend, "Did you hear about Barbara? You know how she fools around so much. I heard she's pregnant. That would never happen to me!" This is an example of the:
    a. imaginary audience.
    b. false-belief syndrome.
    c. personal fable.
    d. adolescent denial syndrome.

28. Sydney calls her best friend Aisha in a panic. She has a date with Jason, someone she has wanted to date for months, but now she has a blemish on her forehead, which she knows Jason (and everyone else) will notice. This is an example of the:
    a. imaginary audience.
    b. false-belief syndrome.
    c. personal fable.
    d. personal absorption syndrome.

29. Research on driver-training courses in high school has found that the courses:
    a. are not generally effective for improving adolescents' cognitive skills related to driving.
    b. are not generally effective for improving adolescents' motor skills related to driving.
    c. have not been effective in reducing adolescents' high rate of traffic accidents.
    d. have been effective in reducing adolescents' high rate of traffic accidents.

30. All of the following are cognitive changes that allow improved critical thinking in adolescents EXCEPT:
    a. more breadth of content knowledge in a variety of domains.
    b. increased ability to construct new combinations of knowledge.
    c. slower speed of information processing demonstrating focus and concentration.
    d. a greater range and more spontaneous use of strategies for applying knowledge.

31. A trend in adolescent development that has formulated the creation of middle schools is:
    a. an increase in formal operational thinking among early adolescents.
    b. the appearance of greater autonomy from adults.
    c. the earlier onset of puberty in recent decades.
    d. the fact that today's teens spend more time with peers than with parents or adults.

32. Students experiencing the top-dog phenomenon are most likely to exhibit:
    a. high achievement motivation.
    b. lowered satisfaction with school.
    c. good relations with peers.
    d. power over other students.

33. Joan Lipsitz (1984) said that the common thread among schools that have been successful in diminishing the trauma often associated with the middle-school experience is that they all emphasized:
   a. gender equity.
   b. curricular flexibility.
   c. discipline.
   d. the importance of high academic standards.

34. The Carnegie Corporation (1989) recommendations for improving middle schools in the United States included all of the following EXCEPT:
   a. lower the student counselor ratios to 10:1.
   b. get parents involved.
   c. integrate physical health into the curriculum.
   d. promote continuity by keeping all class sessions the same length.

35. Rumberger (1983) found all of the following are reasons that students drop out of schools EXCEPT:
   a. family pressures.
   b. not liking school.
   c. economic reasons.
   d. marriage.

36. Which is the only country in the world in which sports are an integral part of the public school system?
   a. the United States
   b. Russia
   c. Japan
   d. Brazil

37. _____ is conveyed by the moral atmosphere that is a part of every school.
   a. The hidden curriculum
   b. Character education
   c. Values Clarification
   d. Cognitive moral education

38. Research on service learning has shown:
   a. grades decline because students have less time for their studies.
   b. students' self-esteem improves.
   c. students become alienated from their families.
   d. students are resentful of the extra pressures placed on them.

Self-Test B: Matching

Match the following persons with the statement or theory that most closely reflects their perspective:

1. Lloyd Johnston
2. Jean Piaget
3. David Elkind
4. Joan Lipsitz
5. Lawrence Kohlberg
6. Daniel Offer
7. John Dewey

a. Imaginary audience & personal fable are part of adolescent egocentrism
b. Identified the best middle schools in the United States
c. One of three researchers who surveyed adolescents about their drug use
d. Contradicted the stereotype that most adolescents are disturbed
e. Said schools provide moral education through a "hidden curriculum"
f. Recognized the importance of the moral atmosphere in schools
g. Said adolescents can think about abstract ideas & hypothetical possibilities

Essay Questions

1. Your former high school counselor has invited you to speak to the students at your old high school. She has asked you to talk to them about high-risk behaviors—what they are, how kids get involved with them, the consequences, and how to avoid getting involved. Which issues would be important for you to address, what would you tell them about each of these, and what suggestions would you have for avoiding them?

2. Your favorite aunt and uncle have come to you because they say they cannot understand their teenage daughter. One minute she's loving and adoring, the next she's a total monster. They try to comfort her when she's upset, but she screams, "You can't possibly understand how I feel"; if she is having a "bad hair day," she refuses to go out in public, even to accompany them to religious services. How would you explain these behaviors to your aunt and uncle, and what would you suggest for helping them work with their daughter?

Scramblers

Unscramble the following people or terms, then describe what they are known for (people) or define them (terms):

1. LADEIN FOFRE

   _____

2. NOHJ EDYWE

   _____

3. RETBUYP

   _____

4. AHLTAOMPUYSH

   _____

5. ROENXAIA VOSREAN

   _____

6. SONREALP BLAFE

   _____

7. DDEINH IRUCRULUMC

   _____

8. AVEULS CNOLAITRAIFCI

   _____

9. INTGIOCVE LMARO ACTUIDOEN

   _____

Key to Self-Test A

1.	a	LO 1	14.	c	LO 4	27.	c	LO 12
2.	b	LO 1	15.	a	LO 5	28.	a	LO 12
3.	a	LO 2	16.	d	LO 5	29.	c	LO 13
4.	b	LO 2	17.	a	LO 5	30.	c	LO 13
5.	d	LO 2	18.	b	LO 6	31.	c	LO 14
6.	b	LO 2	19.	a	LO 7	32.	b	LO 14
7.	a	LO 2	20.	b	LO 9	33.	b	LO 14
8.	b	LO 2	21.	d	LO 9	34.	d	LO 14
9.	d	LO 3	22.	a	LO 10	35.	a	LO 15
10.	a	LO 4	23.	c	LO 10	36.	a	LO 16
11.	b	LO 4	24.	d	LO 11	37.	a	LO 17
12.	c	LO 4	25.	a	LO 11	38.	b	LO 17
13.	d	LO 4	26.	d	LO 11			

Key to Self-Test B

1.	c		5.	f
2.	g		6.	d
3.	a		7.	e
4.	b			

Key to Essay Questions

1. You would need to address the issues of dropping out of school, drugs, adolescent pregnancy, suicide and homicide, accidents, sexually transmitted diseases (STDs), and eating disorders. As a backdrop to understanding the issues, briefly present the physiological changes in adolescence, Piaget's notion of formal operations (abstract thought and metacognition—i.e., thinking about thinking), and Elkind's adolescent egocentrism. Then present ways to avoid these problems, such as developing effective ways to cope rather than turning to drugs, learning about contraception, working on ways to increase self-esteem, etc.

2. To answer this question, you will first need to discuss Elkind's notion of adolescent egocentrism with its two components of the imaginary audience and the personal fable. Then go into the suggestions about teaching decision making and critical thinking. Also useful here would be some of the more general discussions of how character education, values clarification, cognitive moral education, and service learning have proven beneficial to adolescents as well as the community.

Key to Scramblers

1. Daniel Offer: Contradicted the stereotype that most adolescents are disturbed
2. John Dewey: Said schools provide moral education through a "hidden curriculum"
3. Puberty: A period of rapid skeletal and sexual maturation that occurs mainly in early adolescence
4. Hypothalamus: A structure in the higher portion of the brain that monitors eating, drinking, and sex
5. Anorexia nervosa: Eating disorder involving relentless pursuit of thinness through starvation
6. Personal fable: Part of adolescent egocentrism; adolescent's sense of uniqueness & invulnerability
7. Hidden curriculum: Concept that every school has a pervasive moral atmosphere
8. Values clarification: Approach to moral education aimed at helping people clarify purpose in life
9. Cognitive moral education: Approach to moral education based on need to develop values like democracy
10. Service learning: A form of education that promotes social responsibility & service to the community

Research Project 1: Cross-Cultural Comparison of Secondary Schools

The text presents a cross-cultural comparison of secondary schools. Using that information, as well as information you can gather from the Internet, library research, and/or interviews of students or educators from other countries, compare and contrast the following aspects of secondary schools around the world with the United States:

Country	Mandatory Age	No. of Levels	Entrance/ Exit Exams	Sports	Content & Philosophy	Foreign Languages
United States						

1. What similarities do you see between these countries and the United States? What differences?
2. What effect do you think the differences have on children's intellectual development? What effect do these differences have on social and/or behavioral outcomes?
3. Some educators believe that students in the United States should spend more time in school (i.e., the school year and/or school day should be longer so students in the United States can catch up with those in other countries academically). What do you think about this suggestion? Explain your rationale.

Research Project 2: Helping Youth Avoid Problem Behaviors

Consider all of the problem behaviors presented in this chapter. What do you believe are the antecedents of such behaviors? What are the consequences? What can be done to avoid each of these problem behaviors? What type of interventions would be useful?

Behavior	Antecedents	Consequences	Prevention/Intervention
Dropping Out of School			
Alcohol & Other Drug Use/Abuse			
STDs			
Adolescent Pregnancy			
Accidents & Suicides			
Eating Disorders			

On the basis of what you have learned about these problems, design a program that could be implemented in middle schools, junior high schools, and/or high schools to help confront and eliminate these problems. Meet with a local high school counselor and/or principal to discuss your ideas, then report your findings and your revised (or not revised) program to your class.

Prepare a resource guide that can be distributed to teens and pre-teens offering them help with problems they face. There are many toll-free numbers for organizations, such as Covenant House (crisis intervention, referral, and information services for troubled teens and their families: 1-800-999-9999); Youth Crisis Hotline (counseling and referrals for tens in crisis: 1-800-448-4663 [1-800-HIT HOME]); The Centers for Disease Control and Prevention's National STD Hotline (1-800-227-8922); National Clearinghouse for Alcohol and Drug Information (alcohol and drug information and referrals: 1-800-729-6686); and National Runaway Switchboard (24-hour hot line for runaway and homeless youth and their families: 1-800-621-4000). Alcoholics Anonymous (AA), AlAnon, AlaTeen, and Narcotics Anonymous (NA) are all listed in local phone books too. Check out the Internet section for this chapter for some on-line resources that can be included as well.

Personal Application Project 1: Reflecting on What You Learned

Consider what you read in Chapter 12, then answer the following questions:

1. What information in this chapter did you already know?
2. How can/do you use that information in your own life?
3. What information in this chapter was totally new to you?
4. How can you use that new information in your own life?
5. What information in this chapter was different from what you previously believed?
6. How was this information different?
7. How do you account for the differences between what you believed and what you learned in the chapter?
8. What is the most important thing you learned from reading this chapter?

Personal Application Project 2: Consider Your Own Development

Consider your own physical development during adolescence.

Aspects of Physical Development	Early/Late/ On-Time	Effect on Life Satisfaction	Effect on Self-Image
Menarche (Females) Penile Growth (Males)			
Height Spurt			
Weight Gain			
Breast Growth (Females) Testicular Development (Males)			
Growth of Pubic Hair			

1. Was your development consistent with that described in the text?
2. Were you early, late, or on-time?
3. What effect did that have on your adjustment and satisfaction with yourself and your life?
4. Did you find adolescence to be a time of "storm and stress," or, as Daniel Offer suggests, did you have a positive self-image?
5. Did you exhibit (or, if you are now a teen, are you exhibiting) any aspects of David Elkind's notion of adolescent egocentrism (consisting of the imaginary audience and the personal fable)? If so, explain.
6. What other observations can you make when you compare your own development with the information in Chapter 12?

Internet Projects

Check out the McGraw-Hill web site for this text (http://www.mhhe.com/santrockld8). You'll find numerous activities there, in particular various quizzes, flash cards of key terms, and a challenging and fun crossword puzzle. Please note that all website addresses in this Study Guide have been checked and are correct at the time of publication, however, websites may be discontinued or addresses may change so when you search a given site it may no longer be viable. If that occurs, I apologize for the inconvenience, and would appreciate you notifying me so I could make appropriate revisions in future editions of this Study Guide.

Internet Project 1: Teen Pregnancy

Although rates of adolescent pregnancy have decreased somewhat in the past few years, this still remains a major problem, particularly for adolescent girls and their babies. It can also create problems for adolescent fathers, even if they choose not to accept responsibility. Go to the site for Planned Parenthood, http://www.plannedparenthood.org and explore the many options available. One link is designed specifically for adolescents, teenwire.com. (at the time of this writing it was located at the lower right-hand side of the home page). When investigating the Planned Parenthood site and the link to teenwire.com, what have you learned about the problems inherent in a teenager having a child (include physical, social, economic, educational, and emotional)? Consider not only the problems encountered by the mother, but also those the child, the child's father, the grandparents, and society will face. What are the risk factors that might predict teen pregnancy?

Based on what you learned from this site and from the text, design an intervention that could:
1. Help reduce teen pregnancy; and
2. Offer assistance to adolescent parents, their children, and their families to prevent the negative consequences (e.g., dropping out of school) of starting a family so early.

Internet Project 2: Sexually Transmitted Diseases

AIDS, HIV, and other STDs are considered a pandemic problem today (i.e., they are spreading quickly among populations around the world). Go to the Dr. Koop website (http://www.drkoop.com) and conduct a search for "Sexually Transmitted Diseases and Teens."

1. What types of articles did you find?
2. As you read these articles, did you notice that there are many more types of sexually transmitted diseases than were described in Chapter 12?
3. What suggestions were offered for reducing the risks of acquiring a sexually transmitted disease?
4. Based on what you read, what types of interventions do you believe would be helpful in getting adolescents to use "safe sex" practices?
5. What would you suggest to an adolescent about sexual behavior? State your reasons.
6. If you were to design a global intervention to stop the spread of HIV, AIDS, and other STDs around the world, what would that intervention look like?

Other Relevant Sites on the Internet

APA site
http://www.apa.org

APS site
http://www.psychologicalscience.org/

Intelihealth
http://www.intelihealth.com/IH/ihtIH offers health information from a variety of sources, including Harvard Medical School. Feel free to search the site for any of the topics covered in this chapter (and others), but I recommend that you do a search for "Dieting and Preteens" or "Dieting and Teens" to see how early eating problems arise.

Mothers Against Drunk Driving (MADD)
http://www.madd.org is the website for this political action group that was formed to stop drunk driving, prevent underage drinking, and to support those who have been victims of drunk drivers. The site offers information on how to join, news articles, statistics, chat rooms, etc.

National Clearinghouse for Alcohol and Drug Information
http://www.health.org provides information and links regarding any aspect of alcohol and other drug use.

Web MD
http://www.webmd.com offers a wide variety of information for the medical profession and for consumers on physical and mental health issues.

Chapter 13: Socioemotional Development in Adolescence

Learning Objectives

1. Discuss the development of identity proposed by Erikson and Marcia.
2. Examine how family, culture and ethnicity, and gender influence adolescent development.
3. Describe how families change as adolescents seek autonomy, being sure to include factors related to parent-adolescent conflict.
4. Elaborate on the changes that take place with peer groups and the importance of friendships.
5. Discuss adolescent dating, including the functions of dating and dating scripts.
6. Define "rite of passage" and examine its importance in this culture and in other cultures around the world.
7. Determine what role ethnicity and socioeconomic status play in adolescent development in this country.
8. Differentiate between assimilation and pluralism, indicating how these concepts impact the development of an ethnic identity.
9. Discuss the causes and antecedents of juvenile delinquency, and the recent research conducted on youth violence.
10. Examine the nature of depression and causes of suicide in adolescents.
11. Discuss prevention and intervention programs that have been successful with at-risk youth.

Chapter Outline

IDENTITY
    Some Contemporary Thoughts about Identity
    Identity Statuses and Development
    Family Influences on Identity
    Culture, Ethnicity, and Gender
        Gender and Identity Development
FAMILIES
    Autonomy and Attachment
    Parent-Adolescent Conflict
PEERS
    Peer Groups
        Cliques
        Adolescent Groups Versus Children Groups
    Friendships
    Dating and Romantic Relationships
        Types of Dating and Development Changes
        Dating Scripts
        Emotion and Romantic Relationships
        Sociocultural Contexts and Dating
CULTURE AND ADOLESCENT DEVELOPMENT
    Cross-Cultural Comparisons and Rites of Passage
    Ethnicity
        Ethnicity and Socioeconomic Status
        Differences in Diversity
        Values Conflicts, Assimilation, and Pluralism
ADOLESCENT PROBLEMS
    Juvenile Delinquency

Causes of Delinquency
Youth Violence
Depression and Suicide
The Interrelation of Problems and Successful Prevention/Intervention Programs

Self-Test A: Multiple Choice

1. The adolescent identity crisis refers to a period:
   a. of confusion during which youth are choosing between attachment and autonomy.
   b. when adolescents are actively making decisions about who they want to be.
   c. when adolescents actively avoid commitment to ideas or occupations.
   d. of intense turmoil and stress that lasts a short time and determines an adolescent's identity status.

2. The term that James Marcia uses to refer to the part of identity development in which adolescents show a personal investment in what they are going to do is:
   a. value.
   b. desire.
   c. commitment.
   d. involvement.

3. Asked whether they ever had doubts about their religion, four students gave the following answers. Which of these students has arrived at identity achievement?
   a. Kristin: "Oh, I don't know. It really doesn't bother me. I figure one's about as good as another."
   b. Joe: "No, not really. Our family is pretty much in agreement about these things."
   c. Alicia: "Yes, I guess I'm going through that right now. How can there be a god with so much evil in the world?"
   d. Phil: "Yeah, I even started wondering if God existed. I've pretty much resolved that by now, though."

4. A high school student who has explored all potential employment and educational options and has chosen to attend the state college near home is experiencing identity:
   a. achievement.
   b. moratorium.
   c. foreclosure.
   d. diffusion.

5. Many identity status researchers believe that a common pattern of individuals who develop positive identities is to follow what are called _____ cycles.
   a. "PAPA"
   b. "MAMA"
   c. life
   d. spiraling

6. Authoritarian parents are most likely to have adolescents experiencing identity:
   a. achievement.
   b. moratorium.
   c. foreclosure.
   d. diffusion.

7. Jessica's parents have never "forced" their opinions on her, and have always allowed her to try anything she wanted to because they did not want to put any limits on her development. Based on the research, we would expect Jessica to experience identity:
   a. achievement.
   b. moratorium.
   c. foreclosure.
   d. diffusion.

8. According to Cooper and Grotevant (1989), both _____ are important in the adolescent's identity development.
   a. separation and conflict
   b. individuality and connectedness
   c. obedience and self-regulation
   d. family and peer relations

9. Which statement best reflects Erik Erikson's (1968) belief about the relationship between culture and identity development?
   a. Culture plays a critical role in identity development.
   b. In some individuals, cultural factors may play a role in identity development.
   c. For all individuals, cultural factors play a minor role in identity development.
   d. Cultural factors have no influence on identity development.

10. Most ethnic minorities first consciously confront their ethnicity in:
   a. early childhood.
   b. middle childhood.
   c. adolescence.
   d. young adulthood.

11. Jean Phinney (1996) defined _____ as an enduring, basic aspect of the self that includes a sense of membership in an ethnic group and the attitudes and feelings related to that membership.
   a. ethnicity
   b. nationality
   c. culture
   d. ethnic identity

12. What relationship did Phinney and Alipuria (1990) find between ethnic identity and self-esteem for ethnic minority college students?
   a. Those who had thought about and resolved issues involving their ethnicity had lower self-esteem than their counterparts who had not.
   b. Those who had thought about and resolved issues involving their ethnicity had higher self-esteem than their counterparts who had not.
   c. There were no differences in self-esteem between those who had thought about and resolved issues involving their ethnicity and their counterparts who had not.
   d. They found no relationship between ethnic identity and self-esteem.

13. Gilligan (1990), investigating gender and identity development, has found:
   a. relationships and emotional bonds are more important concerns of females, while autonomy and achievement are more important concerns of males.
   b. relationships and emotional bonds are more important concerns of males, while autonomy and achievement are more important concerns of females.
   c. the differences in focus toward relationships and autonomy that were noted by Erikson are now so minimal that they barely exist today.
   d. because of the women's liberation movement, males and females are now both focusing more on relationships and emotional bonds than on autonomy and achievement.

14. Parents who want their adolescents to make a smooth transition into adulthood should:
    a. relinquish control in all areas and let the adolescent take over.
    b. maintain control in as many areas as possible for as long as possible.
    c. relinquish control in areas where the adolescent has shown competence and maintain control in those areas where the adolescent's knowledge is limited.
    d. maintain control of issues dealing with family and relinquish control for those issues having to do with peer relations.

15. Talia, age 16, has a secure attachment with her parents. One might expect she will:
    a. have trouble breaking away from her parents to form peer relationships.
    b. tend to be more dependent in her relationship with her best friend.
    c. have a lower sense of her self-worth.
    d. have better relations with her peers than her insecurely attached counterparts.

16. Parent-adolescent conflicts likely revolve around all of the following EXCEPT:
    a. keeping bedrooms clean.
    b. getting home on time.
    c. taking drugs.
    d. talking on the phone.

17. Which best characterizes the new model of parent-adolescent relationships?
    a. As adolescents mature, they detach from parents and move into a world of autonomy apart from parents.
    b. Parent-adolescent conflict is intense and stressful throughout adolescence.
    c. Everyday negotiations and minor disputes between parents and adolescents are harmful to developmental functions.
    d. Serious, highly stressful parent-adolescent conflict is associated with juvenile delinquency, school dropout, pregnancy, and drug abuse.

18. Cross-cultural research on parent-adolescent relationships conducted by Reed Larson (1999) shows that:
    a. at least some amount of severe conflict between parents and their adolescents is universal.
    b. there is more conflict between parents and their adolescents in the United States than in other industrialized nations.
    c. although parents in India generally use an authoritarian parenting style, there appears to be less conflict between parents and their adolescents than in the United States.
    d. parents in India generally use an authoritative parenting style, which results in less conflict between parents and their adolescents than in the United States.

19. Competent adolescent development is most likely to happen when adolescents have parents who:
    a. display authoritative ways of dealing with problems and conflict.
    b. display authoritarian ways of dealing with problems and conflict.
    c. insist that their adolescents learn to resolve problems and conflict on their own.
    d. develop more flexible boundaries and learn to become friends with their children.

20. Which of the following children is most likely to conform to peer pressure to engage in antisocial acts such as shoplifting or drawing graffiti?
    a. Andrew, who is in seventh grade
    b. Brandon, who is in ninth grade
    c. Charles, who is a high school sophomore
    d. Dale, who is a high school senior

21. A study of clique membership by Brown and Lohr (1987) revealed that the individuals with the lowest self-esteem were the:
    a. jocks.
    b. populars.
    c. druggies.
    d. nobodies.

22. Children's groups differ from those formed by adolescents in that children's groups:
    a. are more informal.
    b. rely more on the leaders of the groups.
    c. have more interests in common.
    d. include a greater diversity of individuals.

23. Research by Harry Stack Sullivan (1953) suggests that:
    a. adolescents who do not have close friendships experience loneliness and a reduced sense of self-worth.
    b. adolescents depend more on their parents than on their friends for a sense of self-worth.
    c. adolescents with no close friends learn to develop a sense of autonomy.
    d. as adolescents get older, they begin to spend as much time with their friends as with their parents.

24. John and Mary, juniors in high school, have been dating for the past two months and are in love with each other. According to research on dating scripts, which of the following is LEAST likely to occur?
    a. John calls Mary to ask her out, she accepts.
    b. John invites Mary out to dinner, and she drives to the restaurant.
    c. John asks Mary what she would like to eat and she says, "Why don't you order for me?"
    d. John kisses Mary goodnight and she responds accordingly.

25. Which of the following best reflects societal attitudes toward sex in adolescence?
    a. Over the past century, attitudes toward sexuality for females have become more permissive in the United States.
    b. The Mangaian culture in the South Sea islands has more restrictive attitudes toward adolescent sexuality than in the United States.
    c. The Ines Beag culture off the coast of Ireland has more permissive attitudes toward adolescent sexuality than in the United States.
    d. With only a few exceptions (i.e., cultures that are either extremely permissive or extremely conservative), attitudes toward adolescent sexuality are relatively universal.

26. A ceremony that marks an individual's transition from one status to another (such as adolescence to adulthood) is called a:
    a. rite of passage.
    b. transitory stage.
    c. period of transition.
    d. ritualistic transition.

27. Which of the following is true regarding the rite of passage from adolescence to adulthood in American culture?
    a. There are many points of transition to adulthood in American culture.
    b. There is an abrupt entry into adulthood in American culture.
    c. The end of adolescence in American culture is more clearly marked by biological change than by social milestones.
    d. No specific event marks the end of adolescence in American culture.

28. One of the major limitations of studies on the effects of ethnicity is that _____ may play a larger causal role than ethnic heritage, but it is difficult to tease the two variables apart.
    a. race
    b. innate physical variation
    c. socioeconomic status
    d. language

29. As immigration among minorities continues to contribute to the growth in the proportion of ethnic minorities in the United States population, psychologists have:
    a. been slow to study these families.
    b. begun a series of studies to assess adaptation to American culture.
    c. attempted to develop new ways to administer old tests.
    d. worked hard to understand how cultural values play a role in adaptation.

30. Stanley Sue (1990) suggests one way to resolve value conflicts about sociocultural issues is to:
    a. restrict immigration for a period of time.
    b. design a national referendum to determine what the majority of individuals within a culture believe is appropriate.
    c. eliminate all culturally specific institutions.
    d. conceptualize or redefine these value conflicts in innovative ways.

31. Which would you likely find in a country driven by ethnic pluralism?
    a. high schools being required to teach courses in the history of minority cultures
    b. tremendous internal racism
    c. great consensus on what the "average" person within that country is like
    d. virtually no foreign characters on prime-time television shows

32. The text states that all of the following have been proposed as causes of juvenile delinquency EXCEPT:
    a. heredity.
    b. identity problems.
    c. family experiences.
    d. boredom.

33. A parenting practice that is associated with an adolescent becoming delinquent is:
    a. disciplining adolescents for antisocial behavior.
    b. indulgence of an adolescent's wants.
    c. low monitoring of adolescents.
    d. restrictively controlling an adolescent's behavior.

34. Which of the following teenagers is most likely to turn violent?
    a. Katy, who feels powerless against her father's sexual molestation
    b. Ken, who feels powerless against the bullying of his classmates
    c. Karen, who is failing all of her classes
    d. Konrad, whose girlfriend just broke up with him

35. Based on his interviews with adolescent killers, Garbarino (1999) concludes that:
    a. many young people are potential killers.
    b. there is a spiritual or emotional emptiness in which the youth sought meaning in the dark side of life.
    c. the clues to predict that these young people will become killers are being overlooked by parents and teachers.
    d. the spiral of violence will continue to increase until society begins to acknowledge the emotional needs of adolescents.

36. Which of the following is NOT a reason given for the sex differences in rates of depression among adolescent males and females?
    a. females tend to ruminate in their depressed mood and amplify it.
    b. males' self-images are more negative than self-images of females.
    c. females' body images are more negative than body images of males.
    d. females face more discrimination than males.

37. Which method of suicide is more likely to be used by a male?
    a. sleeping pills
    b. guns
    c. knives
    d. carbon monoxide poisoning

38. Joy Dryfoos (1990) has described the common components of programs that have been successful in preventing or reducing adolescent problems. These include all of the following EXCEPT:
    a. intensive individualized attention.
    b. communitywide multiagency collaborative approaches.
    c. more clear structure of appropriate behavior.
    d. early identification and intervention.

Self-Test B: Matching

Match the following persons with the statement or theory that most closely reflects their perspective:

1.	James Marcia	a. Believes adolescence is a critical point in ethnic identity for minorities
2.	Jean Phinney	b. Intimacy needs intensify for teens & motivates them to have close friends
3.	Margaret Beale Spencer	c. Explored the hazards of contemporary life in families with adolescents
4.	Erik Erikson	d. Researched ways to improve the social skills of bicultural individuals
5.	Reed Larson	e. Developed the most comprehensive view of identity in adolescence
6.	Harry Stack Sullivan	f. Found a spiritual or emotional emptiness in youth killers
7.	Teresa LaFromboise	g. Described four identity statuses involving crisis and commitment
8.	James Garbarino	h. Found a relationship between ethnic identity and self-esteem

Essay Questions

1. You are giving a talk to a group of parents about adolescent development. One of the mothers asks you, "What do you do if your teenager is going to parties where alcohol is served and you know your teen is drinking? I know that if I tell him he can't go, he'll go anyway." How would you respond to her question?

2. The principal and school counselor of your former high school have asked for your advice on dealing with issues of diversity they are facing at school. The diversity is being noticed in terms of the cliques that are forming, as well as racial and ethnic conflict that seems to be a growing problem. What advice could you give them?

Scramblers

Unscramble the following people or terms, then describe what they are known for (people) or define them (terms):

1. YOJ SRYDOOF

   _____

2. NAJE NYPNIHE

   _____

3. SIRISC

   _____

4. TNIETDYI UFSFIIODN

   _____

5. YITNILDAIUVDI

   _____

6. TECDENONESNSC

   _____

7. ITNAGD SSTCPIR

   _____

8. TIRE FO SSAAGPE

   _____

9. ARLUILSPM

   _____

10. NIHTCE NTIETDYI

   _____

Key to Self-Test A

1.	b	LO 1	14.	c	LO 3	27.	d	LO 6
2.	c	LO 1	15.	d	LO 3	28.	c	LO 7
3.	d	LO 1	16.	c	LO 3	29.	a	LO 7
4.	a	LO 1	17.	d	LO 3	30.	d	LO 8
5.	b	LO 1	18.	c	LO 3	31.	a	LO 8
6.	c	LO 1	19.	a	LO 3	32.	d	LO 9
7.	d	LO 1	20.	b	LO 4	33.	c	LO 9
8.	b	LO 2	21.	d	LO 4	34.	b	LO 9
9.	a	LO 2	22.	a	LO 4	35.	b	LO 9
10.	c	LO 2	23.	a	LO 4	36.	b	LO 10
11.	d	LO 2	24.	b	LO 5	37.	b	LO 10
12.	b	LO 2	25.	a	LO 6	38.	c	LO 11
13.	a	LO 2	26.	a	LO 6			

Key to Self-Test B

1.	g		5.	c
2.	h		6.	b
3.	a		7.	d
4.	e		8.	f

Key to Essay Questions

1. Included in your answer should be a discussion of Erikson's and Marcia's ideas about the identity crisis and the different statuses an adolescent may be in with respect to different areas of her or his life; also critically important to this are Elkind's notion of adolescent egocentrism discussed in Chapter 12 and the extension of Baumrind's work on parenting styles. For the latter, note that within the culture of the United States, adolescents whose parents use an authoritative parenting style are more socially competent, socially responsible, and cognitively competent than adolescents whose parents use other parenting styles (the authoritative parenting style encourages children to make choices and understand the consequences of their choices, an important issue in terms of engaging in potentially harmful activities). Chapter 13 presents a great deal of information about various activities (e.g., peer-tutoring) that have been effective for increasing adolescents' self-esteem and keeping them engaged in prosocial activities. You might note, however, that some behaviors (such as drinking alcohol) may be both illegal and detrimental, but they are not outside the norm in terms of exploring the adolescent's identity.

2. Explore the notions of ethnicity and socioeconomic status to understand whether they are dealing with one or both of these issues, so they know how to proceed. It is important to discuss the stigmas associated with minority status, as well as the cultural differences (e.g., different customs and different values) that may or may not exist, including parenting practices and how they affect the adolescents' behavior. Note Stanley Sue's contention that value conflicts are often involved when individuals respond to ethnic issues, thus it would be important to teach the students to conceptualize or redefine these conflicts in innovative ways. Also important here is the research (for example, by Phinney & Alipuria) concerning the outcome of students' explorations of their ethnic identity and the finding that students who do explore their ethnic identity tend to have higher self-esteem. Based on the research, make your suggestions for ways to reduce the conflict that is becoming a problem as "requested" by your former principal and high school counselor.

Key to Scramblers

1. Joy Dryfoos: Described common components of programs successful in reducing adolescent problems
2. Jean Phinney: Researches ethnic identity among college students, including its relationship to self-esteem
3. Crisis: Period of identity development during which adolescents choose among meaningful alternatives
4. Identity diffusion: Term for adolescents who have not experienced crisis or made a commitment
5. Individuality: The part of identity that is comprised of self-assertion and separateness
6. Connectedness: The part of identity that is comprised of mutuality and permeability
7. Dating scripts: Cognitive models used to guide and evaluate dating interactions
8. Rite of passage: A ceremony or ritual that marks an individual's transition from one status to another
9. Pluralism: The coexistence of distinct ethnic and cultural groups in the same society
10. Ethnic identity: Enduring aspect of the self that includes a sense of membership in an ethnic group

Research Project 1: Observing Developmental Periods

In several places throughout this chapter the author discusses various prosocial activities such as peer-tutoring and mentoring. Organize your classmates into a peer-tutoring group. Decide which topics each of you will tutor, then approach the appropriate person at your college (e.g., dean of students, learning resources center, etc.) or at local high schools (e.g., principal, counselor, etc.) and offer your services. Before beginning the tutoring it is helpful to get assistance on effective ways to teach both your peers and younger students; also, at the beginning of this project, chart each group member's grades to use for comparison purposes after you have begun tutoring. Keep track of grades (e.g., midterms and papers throughout the term or, if you continue to tutor throughout your college career, each term) to see if they are going up. For most of you they probably will. Also, see which grades in particular are improving—are they related to the topics you are teaching to someone else? Is this consistent with what you have learned about peer tutoring? Explain.

Tutor (Name):			
Course	Grade	Grade Point Average	Comments
Introductory Psychology			
Life-Span Development			

Research Project 2: The Bridge to Youth Development

After reading the Sociocultural Worlds of Development box titled "El Puente and Quantum," consider the areas targeted for change and the methods used to achieve the targeted goals. Conduct a search (checking out your library, the Internet, local government, etc.) to assess other similar programs and to determine if your community has any programs like these to help disadvantaged youth reduce problem behaviors while developing the skills that will help them succeed in life.

1. Describe the programs that you believe are most useful in achieving their goals, explaining the specific goals and outcomes.
2. Discuss the specific outcome measures that demonstrate how effective these programs are (e.g., in numbers state reduced levels of school dropouts, homicides, suicides, teen pregnancies; increased success rate for college graduation; etc.).
3. How are these programs funded?
4. What can you do to establish a similar program in your community?

Personal Application Project 1: Reflecting on What You Learned

Consider what you read in Chapter 13, then answer the following questions:

1. What information in this chapter did you already know?
2. How can/do you use that information in your own life?
3. What information in this chapter was totally new to you?
4. How can you use that new information in your own life?
5. What information in this chapter was different from what you previously believed?
6. How was this information different?
7. How do you account for the differences between what you believed and what you learned in the chapter?
8. What is the most important thing you learned from reading this chapter?

Personal Application Project 2: Exploring Your Identity

Note the author's Adventures for the Mind concerning "Exploring Your Identity." Note that he asks you to think about your exploration and commitment in the eleven areas listed. Consider the experiences you have had that stimulated you to think about your identity. Have your classmates, friends, or instructors challenged your view of yourself? Consider your identity in the many domains of your life indicated on the charts and consider your identity status (achieved, moratorium, foreclosed, or diffused) in each of these different areas. If you are identity diffused or foreclosed, take some time to think about how you might move into a moratorium or achieved status—or consider if that is exactly where you want to be at this time.

Using the chart below (or, if you prefer, use the chart in the text), explore your identity status in each of the areas mentioned, explaining how you determined you are in that status; then state how you might move to moratorium or achieved status if you are not there.

Area	Status	Explanation	Plans for Changing Status
Career			
Political			
Religious			
Relationship			
Achievement			
Sexual			
Gender			
Ethnic/Cultural			
Interests			
Personality			
Physical			

1. As you look over the chart, are you in different statuses for different areas of your life? What does this tell you about yourself? What does it tell you about how Erikson's and Marcia's theories fit into adolescent development?
2. Santrock suggests that you work on moving from diffused or foreclosed to moratorium or identity achieved. Do you believe this is appropriate for you? Is there some reason why it may be more appropriate for you to be in any particular status at this point in your life? Explain your reasons.

Internet Projects

Check out the McGraw-Hill web site for this text (http://www.mhhe.com/santrockld8). You'll find numerous activities there, in particular various quizzes, flash cards of key terms, and a challenging and fun crossword puzzle. Please note that all website addresses in this Study Guide have been checked and are correct at the time of publication, however, websites may be discontinued or addresses may change so when you search a given site it may no longer be viable. If that occurs, I apologize for the inconvenience, and would appreciate you notifying me so I could make appropriate revisions in future editions of this Study Guide.

Internet Project 1: Being Proactive in Your Own
Socioemotional Development

An interesting website that offers a wide (as in very wide) range of socioemotional topics is http://www.psybersquare.com. Check out this site, including the topics covered, the advisory board, and the services offered, feeling free to go to "Ask an Expert" or any other link you might find interesting or helpful. (I found it rather intriguing that the advisory board is comprised of impressive professionals, and most of the topics seem academically sound, yet one link is to "Consult the Stars" for your weekly horoscope—what do you think about that?) Once you are at the site, go to the link for depression, then check out the articles on suicide, particularly one titled "Suicide: What if Someone You Care about Is Suicidal?" Have you ever had to deal with such an experience? If so, what did you do? How might you handle such a situation now? How can you use the information to help the people close to you (including yourself)?

Internet Project 2: Rites of Passage

The text discusses rites of passage, ceremonies or rituals that mark an individual's transition from one status to another, noting how in some cultures they are the avenue through which adolescents gain access to adulthood, while they seem to be much more nebulous for American adolescents. An interesting site presented by the Balch Institute of Ethnic Studies in Pennsylvania sponsors "Rites of Passage in America" at the web address: http://www.balchinstitute.org/rites/rites.html. The site offers information about rites of passage, as well as three essays on rites of passage (including one titled "Reviving Rites of Passage in America"), then presents more specifically several case studies. One essay, "Art and Rites of Passage," is particularly fascinating. After exploring this site, consider what our author says about rites of passage generally, and more specifically what he says about rites of passage in the United States.

1. Do you agree that rites of passage in the United States are more subtle than those in "primitive" cultures? Explain your response.
2. What ceremonies are common in the United States that would fall within the realm of rites of passage?
3. What purpose do these ceremonies serve?
4. What informal events do you think might serve as rites of passage for American youth? Explain.
5. Have you personally experienced a rite of passage (e.g., bar or bat mitzvah, quinceañera)? How does that compare with what you have learned from the chapter and from this website?
6. Before reading this chapter, had you ever thought about any of your experiences as being rites of passage?
7. After reading this chapter and viewing the website, do you now consider any of your experiences as rites of passage? Explain.

Other Relevant Sites on the Internet

APA site
http://www.apa.org

APS site
http://www.psychologicalscience.org/

Intelihealth
http://www.intelihealth.com/IH/ihtIH offers health information from a variety of sources, including Harvard Medical School. Feel free to search the site for any of the topics covered in this chapter (and others).

The National Institute of Child Health
http://www.nichd.nih.gov is one of the many information sites of the National Institutes of Health. This one is devoted to all aspects of children's and adolescents' health.

Society for Research in Child Development (SRCD)
http://srcd.org is the web site for SRCD, an organization whose purposes are to promote multidisciplinary research in the field of human development, to foster the exchange of information among scientists and other professionals of various disciplines, and to encourage applications of research findings.

Web MD
http://www.webmd.com offers a wide variety of information for the medical profession and for consumers.

Chapter 14: Physical and Cognitive Development in Early Adulthood

Learning Objectives

1. Discuss the criteria for becoming an adult.
2. Elaborate on the transition from high school to college.
2. Explain the changes in physical development that occur during early adulthood.
3. Explain the causes of and concerns about obesity, and then discuss the issues surrounding dieting and exercise.
4. Explore the issue of substance abuse in the college population.
5. Define addiction and explain the two models of addiction.
6. Examine heterosexual attitudes and behaviors during early adulthood.
7. Examine homosexual attitudes and behaviors during early adulthood.
8. Describe the sexually transmitted diseases prevalent among young adults, and discuss ways to protect against them.
9. Elaborate on the factors associated with rape and sexual harassment.
10. Address the ways in which cognition changes during early adulthood.
11. Explain the changes that take place in creativity in early adulthood and ways to encourage it.
12. Indicate the development changes that take place in career choices, and describe Holland's career-related personality types.
13. Explain the process of choosing a career and what employers look for.
14. Discuss the importance of work and how it shapes the identity of the young adult.

Chapter Outline

THE TRANSITION FROM ADOLESCENCE TO ADULTHOOD
  The Criteria for Becoming an Adult
  The Transition from High School to College
PHYSICAL DEVELOPMENT
  The Peak and Slowdown in Physical Performance
  Eating and Weight
    Obesity
    Dieting
  Exercise
  Substance Abuse
    Alcohol
    Cigarette Smoking
    Addiction
SEXUALITY
  Sexual Orientation
    Heterosexual Attitudes and Behavior
    Homosexual Attitudes and Behavior
  Sexually Transmitted Diseases
    Gonorrhea
    Syphilis
    Chlamydia
    Genital Herpes
    HPV

Self-Test A: Multiple Choice

1. Jeffrey Arnett (2000) has termed the age range from 18 to 25:
   a. late adolescence.
   b. early adulthood.
   c. emerging adulthood.
   d. adulthood transitioning.

2. The most widely recognized marker of entry into adulthood is:
   a. getting a full-time job.
   b. moving out of your parents' home.
   c. graduating from college.
   d. getting married.

3. In what way does the move from high school to college differ from that of elementary school to junior high school?
   a. Junior high school students are more likely to experience the top-dog phenomenon than are college freshmen.
   b. College freshmen experience increased achievement pressure, but junior high school students do not.
   c. College freshmen have more opportunities to explore lifestyles than junior high school students.
   d. Junior high school students generally find their academic work more challenging than do college freshmen.

4. Compared to their 1980s counterparts, college students today indicate that they feel:
   a. more excited about their opportunities.
   b. more depressed.
   c. less prepared for college.
   d. more prepared for college.

176

5. Peak physical performance is typically reached:
   a. in early adolescence.
   b. in late adolescence.
   c. in early adulthood.
   d. at different times, depending on the activity.

6. How well do college students use their knowledge about health?
   a. They are well informed and a majority use the information to live healthy lifestyles.
   b. Surveys indicate that most of them are aware of what it takes to be healthy and almost 50% practice what they know.
   c. Those who are well-informed also tend to practice what they know.
   d. Although most of them know what it takes to be healthy, most don't apply it.

7. Now in her middle twenties, Harriet exercises rarely, skips breakfast to get to work early, and parties hard on weekends to compensate for the long hours of hard work she must put in to support her ambitious career plans. Late in life, when she has achieved success and retired, Harriet will be:
   a. relatively healthy, because in her youth peak resources protected her against the stress she experienced.
   b. in satisfactory health, because her stressful living provided her with early success.
   c. vigorous, because she has trained herself for the demands of a successful career.
   d. relatively less healthy and dissatisfied with her life, because of her poor lifestyle choices early in life.

8. Which of the following might be expected to occur when an individual reaches age 30?
   a. greater muscle tone and strength
   b. radical changes in the sensory systems
   c. sagging chins and protruding abdomens
   d. decrease in the body's fatty tissues

9. Which of the following is LEAST likely to play a role in obesity?
   a. heredity
   b. metabolism
   c. personality
   d. environmental factors

10. Approximately what percentage of the American population is sufficiently overweight to be at increased health risk?
    a. one-quarter
    b. one-third
    c. one-half
    d. two-thirds

11. With increasing age, basal metabolism rate:
    a. increases steadily.
    b. reaches a peak and levels off.
    c. declines steadily.
    d. does not change.

12. All of the following are environmental influences on body weight EXCEPT:
    a. basal metabolism rate.
    b. declining physical activity.
    c. energy saving devices.
    d. greater availability of food.

13. _____ are individuals who chronically restrict their food intake to control their weight.
    a. Dieters
    b. Restrained eaters
    c. Yo-yo dieters
    d. Bulimics

14. The main focus of research on the effects of exercise on health has involved:
    a. reducing weight.
    b. preventing cancer.
    c. staying young.
    d. preventing heart disease.

15. At age 30 you find you are a successful, hardworking executive, but you are also slightly overweight and have increasing difficulty coping with the tension in your life. What do the "experts" recommend you do to ensure good health?
    a. Lose weight.
    b. Start a weight lifting program in which you alternate exercise of muscle groups every day.
    c. Walk or jog at a brisk pace for 30 minutes every day.
    d. Push yourself to jog fast for 30 minutes three to five times a week.

16. Experts recommend that American adults engage in at least _____ minutes of exercise or more _____.
    a. 15/daily
    b. 30/daily
    c. 30/every other day
    d. 60/weekly

17. A longitudinal study by Jerald Bachman (1997) found all of the following EXCEPT:
    a. college students drink less than youths who end their education after high school.
    b. people who do not go to college smoke more.
    c. non-married people use marijuana more than married individuals.
    d. becoming engaged, married, or remarried brings down alcohol use.

18. _____, a behavior modification technique in which the smoker is sensitized to smoking cues, has been used effectively in getting some individuals to stop smoking.
    a. Stimulus control
    b. Systematic desensitization
    c. Cue sensitization
    d. Cognitive control

19. _____ is a pattern of behavior characterized by an overwhelming involvement with using a drug and securing its supply.
    a. Drug tolerance
    b. Addiction
    c. Drug withdrawal
    d. Substance abuse

20. All of the following predict a positive outcome and recovery from alcoholism EXCEPT:
    a. promising to change.
    b. finding a substitute dependency.
    c. having new social supports.
    d. joining an inspirational group.

21. A study of sexual activity by Michael et al. (1994) found all of the following EXCEPT:
    a. married couples have sex more than single people.
    b. the favorite sexual act was oral sex.
    c. adultery is the exception rather than the rule.
    d. men think about sex far more than women do.

22. Recent research exploring the biological bases of homosexuality has found:
    a. homosexuals and heterosexuals have different physiological responses during sexual arousal.
    b. if male homosexuals are given male sex hormones, their sexual orientation changes.
    c. exposure of the fetus to hormone levels characteristic of females might cause an individual to become attracted to males.
    d. an area of the hypothalamus that governs sexual behavior has been found to be twice as large in homosexual males as in heterosexual males.

23. Laura Brown (1989) has suggested that gays and lesbians can best adapt to a world in which they are a minority by:
    a. getting therapy to help them change their sexual orientation.
    b. getting therapy to help them adjust to the stigmatism of being homosexual.
    c. living in a primarily gay or lesbian world.
    d. developing an identity that balances the minority gay/lesbian culture and the majority heterosexual culture.

24. The most common of all sexually transmitted diseases is:
    a. syphilis.
    b. gonorrhea.
    c. chlamydia.
    d. genital herpes.

25. AIDS CANNOT be transmitted by:
    a. intimate sexual contact.
    b. sharing needles.
    c. blood transfusions.
    d. contact with urine.

26. Andrea and Tom are at a point in their relationship where they will soon become sexually intimate. They would be wise to protect themselves against STDs by taking which of the following precautions?
    a. ask about each other's previous sexual encounters
    b. obtain medical examinations
    c. apply petroleum jelly to condoms before using them
    d. promise to be monogamous

27. Which of the following is TRUE concerning rape?
    a. A man cannot rape his wife.
    b. Rape is a traumatic experience for the victim and those close to her.
    c. Men cannot be raped.
    d. Many women actually want to be raped.

28. Which of the following is NOT a characteristic of rapists?
    a. They use aggression to enhance their sense of power.
    b. They have an abnormal need for sexual pleasure.
    c. They are generally angry at women.
    d. They want to hurt and humiliate their victim.

29. Sexual harassment is:
    a. a manifestation of power and domination of one person over another.
    b. so blatant that it is hard to miss.
    c. becoming less prevalent because of awareness.
    d. less prevalent than the media would have us believe.

30. With respect to adult cognitive processes, psychologist K. Warner Schaie (1977) concluded that:
    a. adults now enter a post-formal operational stage involving more complex strategies.
    b. many adults revert back to a pragmatic concrete stage rather than using formal operational thought.
    c. adults do not go beyond formal operational thought, but they do progress in how they use their intellect.
    d. adults in certain careers (e.g., higher education) tend to go into a post-formal operational stage, but most others do not.

31. Life-span development students often complain, "Why do we have to learn all of these theories? Why don't you just teach us the right one?" According to William Perry, this complaint reflects _____ thinking.
    a. absolute, dualistic
    b. dualistic, reflective
    c. reflective, relativistic
    d. full relativistic

32. Recent research on creativity has shown that it:
    a. is highly correlated with intelligence.
    b. peaks in adolescence, then declines.
    c. peaks in adulthood, then declines.
    d. peaks somewhere in middle to late

33. Which of the following can help you develop the heightened state of pleasure we experience when engaged in absorbing challenges described as "flow" by Mihaly Csikszentmihalyi (1995)?
    a. Keep your life structured so you know what to expect.
    b. Wake up in the morning open to whatever will strike you as the "thing to do today."
    c. Take charge of your schedule.
    d. Set a specific time each month to pursue something interesting.

34. According to John Holland, the person with a conventional personality is most likely to be:
    a. a bank teller.
    b. an artist.
    c. a social worker.
    d. a carpenter.

35. If Habib wants to get a career in the occupation currently believed to have the fastest growth and highest pay in the next few years, he will find a position as:
    a. a computer systems analyst.
    b. an engineering, science, or computer systems manager.
    c. a college professor.
    d. a commercial artist.

36. In a recent survey by the Center for Survey Research at the University of Connecticut (2000), _____ percent of Americans worked 51 hours or more per week.
    a. 18
    b. 23
    c. 32
    d. 35

37. Faye Crosby (1991) has described the "jugglers," women who have multiple roles of career, home, and family. She has concluded that:
    a. the high stress levels will undoubtedly create major problems in at least one of the "juggled" areas.
    b. women with multiple roles provide a chance to fashion social worlds that promote healthy communities, families, and individuals.
    c. while juggling may be beneficial for communities, it is a hardship on families and the individual.
    d. working from home will allow women to handle multiple roles more easily.

Self-Test B: Matching

Match the following persons with the statement or theory that most closely reflects their perspective:

1. Jeffrey Arnett
2. Robert Michael
3. William Perry
4. John Holland
5. K. Warner Schaie
6. Laura Brown
7. Faye Crosby
8. Mihaly Csikszentmihalyi

a. Surveyed American sexual patterns in 1994
b. Our view of the world evolves from dualistic to relativistic
c. "Emerging adults" explore a variety of possible directions for their life
d. "Flow": intense state of pleasure when engaged in absorbing challenges
e. Proposed the personality type theory of career development
f. How adults use intellect, not how they acquire information, progresses
g. Homosexuals experience life as a minority in a majority culture
h. Described the advantages of multiple roles ("juggling") for women

Essay Questions

1. Imagine that you have been offered the position of a career counselor at your college, but have been told that you may also need to offer advice to young adults about other life choices in areas such as drug use and sexuality. What specific things will you need to know so you can help these students?

2. You have been asked to talk to a group of college students about sex. While you know many have probably been sexually active, you are advised that since you are their peer, they may be more open and honest with you in what they say and the questions they ask. You need to be prepared to discuss the whole range of topics including sexual orientation, physiological changes, sexually transmitted diseases and ways to prevent them, sexual harassment, and rape. How will you address each of these topics?

Scramblers

Unscramble the following people or terms, then describe what they are known for (people) or define them (terms):

1. HALIMY ITMNIHEZASLKYIISC

   _____

2. YAFE YCBRSO

   _____

3. DREENSITAR SERAET

   _____

4. ORBEIAC RCEIXSEE

   _____

5. CITDIDOAN

   _____

6. AGRORHENO

   _____

7. HPIYLSSI

   _____

8. TIANLEG SHEEPR

   _____

9. EDTA ERPA

_____

10. OSTP-LFAOMR UGHOHTT

_____

Key to Self-Test A

1.	c	LO 1	14.	d	LO 4	27.	b	LO 10
2.	a	LO 1	15.	c	LO 4	28.	b	LO 10
3.	c	LO 2	16.	b	LO 4	29.	a	LO 10
4.	b	LO 2	17.	a	LO 5	30.	c	LO 11
5.	c	LO 3	18.	a	LO 6	31.	a	LO 11
6.	d	LO 3	19.	b	LO 6	32.	c	LO 12
7.	d	LO 3	20.	a	LO 6	33.	c	LO 12
8.	c	LO 3	21.	b	LO 7	34.	a	LO 13
9.	c	LO 4	22.	c	LO 8	35.	a	LO 14
10.	b	LO 4	23.	d	LO 8	36.	a	LO 15
11.	c	LO 4	24.	c	LO 9	37.	b	LO 15
12.	a	LO 4	25.	d	LO 9			
13.	b	LO 4	26.	b	LO 9			

Key to Self-Test B

1.	c	5.	f	
2.	a	6.	g	
3.	b	7.	h	
4.	e	8.	d	

Key to Essay Questions

1. First you will need to discuss John Holland's personality type theory and the importance of personal values so you can help the students select careers that match well with their personality type and what is important to them in life. You will also need to look at occupational outlook, how to find the right match between student and career, how to interview, skills employers want, and women's issues in the work force (e.g., changing roles, dual-career marriages, juggling roles, etc.). Then you will need to look at the basic health issues of alcohol and other drug use and how that might affect the students' current school performance as well as their ability to find and hold a job. Oftentimes students will look to school counselors as someone to talk to about their sexuality, sexual practices, and sexual orientation; thus, you will need to be familiar with the information concerning these areas of sexuality, but do know when to send a troubled student to the college psychologist.

2. Here you will need to discuss the wide range of sexual orientation (from heterosexuality to homosexuality and all points in between), physiological changes that occur in young adulthood, sexually transmitted diseases and AIDS and ways to prevent each of them (e.g., abstinence, use of condoms, monogamy, etc.), sexual harassment (e.g., what behaviors would constitute harassment, what are the consequences of

harassment for victim and perpetrator), and rape (e.g., the definition of rape, understanding this is an issue of power and control not of sex, etc.).

Key to Scramblers

1. Mihaly Csikszentmihalyi: How adults **use** intellect, not how they acquire information, progresses
2. Faye Crosby: Described the advantages of multiple roles ("juggling") for women
3. Restrained eaters: Individuals who chronically restrict their food intake to control their weight
4. Aerobic exercise: Sustained exercise that stimulates heart and lung activity
5. Addiction: A pattern of behavior characterized by overwhelming involvement with using/securing drugs
6. Gonorrhea: One of the most common STDs; caused by bacterium gonococcus
7. Syphilis: A sexually transmitted disease caused by the bacterium *Treponema pallidum*
8. Genital herpes: A sexually transmitted disease caused by different strains of viruses
9. Date rape: Coercive sexual activity directed at someone with whom the perpetrator is acquainted
10. Post-formal thought: Understanding that the correct answer to a problem requires reflective thinking

Research Project 1: College Drinking Patterns

This project will assist you in understanding the drinking patterns of college students. You may wish to look at surveys that have been used by other researchers (see the Adventures for the Mind box, "Do You Abuse Drugs?" for useful questions), and you may need to have your research project approved by an Internal Review Board at any college where you administer the survey. Gather basic demographic data, such as students' sex, age, years of education, etc., then ask about the students' drinking patterns (e.g., how often they consume alcohol, how much they consume at any given time, when they consume it, when they first started drinking, etc.) and the problems they encounter from consuming alcohol (refer back to the text for common problems). Perform a statistical analysis of your data to see what patterns emerge. What is the prevalence of alcohol consumption on campus? Who is most likely to abstain from drinking? Who is most likely to engage in moderate or heavy drinking? Is alcohol consumption primarily a social activity, or are many students drinking alone? What specific problems do the students encounter from drinking alcohol? Prepare a chart that indicates who has the problems and specifically what types of problems they have.

1. What did you notice in terms of the specific problems that drinkers have?
2. What patterns of drinking did you notice?
3. Were your observations consistent with what you might expect from the research described? Explain your response.
4. Based on your observations, what might you conclude about drinking patterns on college campuses and the problems that may be incurred? You may wish to share your findings with the Dean of Students or the Head of the Campus Counseling Center after you have completed your analysis.

Research Project 2: Avoiding Sexually Risky Behaviors

Consider the risk factors that young adults face when engaging in sexual activities. Design a public awareness campaign for your class, your campus, or your community that will assist young adults in viewing their sexual behaviors realistically. Be specific in stating the potential consequences of various forms of sexual interactions, ranging from kissing (minimal risk) to engaging in vaginal or anal intercourse without a condom (high risk). Include in your presentation a discussion of the range of sexual orientations (heterosexual to homosexual— you may wish to use Figure 14.4); rape (e.g., it is a matter of power and control, not sexual gratification; talk about marital rape and date rape, and concerns about whether a person has the mental capacity to consent); and sexual harassment. Relying on the text and the professional literature, provide a good outline of ways to reduce the risks involved in engaging in sexual activities. It's important to remember to keep one's own value judgments out of such a presentation, and rely instead on the heavy body of research in this field; however, the members of your audience will be sure to have strong emotional responses to what you say. (Note that if you get asked a question for which you don't have an answer, you can always respond with something like: "That's an excellent/interesting question. I don't have the answer right now, but if you'd like, I'll research it and get back to you." Or, "That's an interesting question. What do you think?") (By the way, you might also note a couple of concerns with regard to use of contraceptives: first, **do not** use Vaseline or any other petroleum product on condoms because it will destroy the latex; and second, birth control pills lose their effectiveness in preventing pregnancy when a woman is also taking antibiotics. You might want to throw those facts into any discussion on "safe sex.")

Allow for a question-and-answer period, keeping track of the questions. What types of questions are asked? Are they consistent with the type of information provided in the text? Were questions raised that weren't discussed in the text that you think would be appropriate for inclusion? What were they? Were there questions you couldn't answer? What were they? What have you learned from sharing this knowledge with others?

Personal Application Project 1: Reflecting on What You Learned

Consider what you read in Chapter 14, then answer the following questions:

1. What information in this chapter did you already know?
2. How can/do you use that information in your own life?
3. What information in this chapter was totally new to you?
4. How can you use that new information in your own life?
5. What information in this chapter was different from what you previously believed?
6. How was this information different?
7. How do you account for the differences between what you believed and what you learned in the chapter?
8. What is the most important thing you learned from reading this chapter?

Personal Application Project 2: Consider Your Own Development

Chapter 14 provides a lot of information about the transition from adolescence to adulthood and issues inherent in making that shift. Using the chart below, consider some of the topics discussed in terms of your own life, summarizing what the text says, then indicating whether this has been (or currently is) an important issue for you and, if so, how you have dealt with it (or are currently dealing with it), and whether from your own experience you agree with the research presented. What can you conclude about the current state of research on this important period of development?

Aspect of Your Self	Summary of Text	Your Own Experience	Comments
Transition from High School to College			
Peak and Slowdown in Physical Performance			
Substance Use/Abuse			
Sexuality			
Cognitive Development			
Creativity			
Career Choices			
Other (describe)			

Internet Projects

Check out the McGraw-Hill web site for this text (http://www.mhhe.com/santrockld8). You'll find numerous activities there, in particular various quizzes, flash cards of key terms, and a challenging and fun crossword puzzle. Please note that all website addresses in this Study Guide have been checked and are correct at the time of publication, however, websites may be discontinued or addresses may change so when you search a given site it may no longer be viable. If that occurs, I apologize for the inconvenience, and would appreciate you notifying me so I could make appropriate revisions in future editions of this Study Guide.

Internet Project 1: Ensuring Your Health in Later Years

The text cautioned that bad health habits in early adulthood can lead to poor health and lack of satisfaction with life later on. The first section of the chapter makes suggestions for healthier living, and Figure 14.2 presents examples of moderate and vigorous physical activity. Check out the Mayo Clinic website, which can be located at http://www.mayoclinic.com. Link to the "Food & Nutrition Center" (on the left of the page) then check out all of the articles available, including those on nutrition as well as those on exercise. Then scroll down toward the end of the page to the section "Take Charge of Your Health." Go to all three links (noting you will need to register for the first one, "Personal Health Scorecard," but it's free and it's for your own health!).

1. How can you use what you have learned from these websites to improve your chances of having a long, healthy, satisfying life?
2. Are you willing to follow their suggestions?
3. Why do you think that so many of us can have this information and, despite wanting to have good health in later years, fail to follow through?
4. How do you think people could be encouraged to take the necessary steps to ensure optimal health throughout their lifetime?

Internet Project 2: The Job Search

Notice that the author states in the beginning of the chapter, "The most widely recognized marker of entry into adulthood is the occasion when an individual first takes a more or less permanent, full-time job." Then the last section of the chapter is devoted to Careers and Work. There are many "job sites" on the Internet, some of which offer some useful information, others that are purely devoted to helping connect people with prospective employers. Some have a broad focus, others are quite specialized. Two particularly good resources are JobsOnline at http://www.jobsonline.com, and FlipDog at http://www.flipdog.com. Visit these sites to check out their resources and different jobs that might interest you. Notice that the second category at JobsOnline under "Resources" (the links on the left side of the page) is "Company Research." What kind of information can you find there? How can that link help you find the particular job that you'd like? After "surfing" around the site, answer the following questions.

1. When you first started taking this course in life-span development, did you have a particular job or career path in mind that you wished to pursue?
2. As you've progressed through this course, have those plans stayed the same, become more clear, or changed? Explain.
3. After exploring jobsonline.com and flipdog.com, were you better able to clarify your plans? Explain.
4. What did you learn from exploring these sites that could help you in your own job search? (Even if you currently have a position that you plan to keep, what have you learned that could help you in the event you wish/need to change jobs?)
5. How helpful do you think these sites could be in helping you find your dream job?
6. What other information would you want from an online job site that would help you find your dream job? You might wish to forward those comments to the site administrators.

Other Relevant Sites on the Internet

APA site
http://www.apa.org

APS site
http://www.psychologicalscience.org

The Addictions Newsletter
http://www.kumc.edu/addictions_newsletter is sponsored by Division 50 of the American Psychological Association.

CBS HealthWatch by Medscape

http://healthwatch.medscape.com/medscape/p/gcommunity/ghome.asp provides information on a wide range of health topics, as well as many other resources, such as a drug directory, self-care and first aid tips, and a medical dictionary.

Cooper Wellness
http://www.cooperwellness.com is the website of Dr. Kenneth Cooper, who notes "It is easier to maintain good health through proper exercise, diet, and emotional balance than to regain it once it is lost."

Drug and Alcohol Treatment and Prevention Global Network
http://www.drugnet.net offers information on many aspects of drug treatment, research, assessment, and prevention, as well as online training.

The Gay and Lesbian Alliance Against Defamation
http://www.glaad.org is the website for this national organization and provides information, support, a listing of upcoming events, and current media releases.

JobDirect
http://www.jobdirect.com/interpage.html is a helpful site for students (and non-students) who are looking for employment.

Monster.Com
http://monster.com is another popular website for finding jobs and posting résumés.

National Institute on Drug Abuse
http://www.nida.nih.gov is the website for this government-sponsored organization involved in research and prevention of drug abuse. There are information sections for researchers and health professionals, parents and teachers, and for students. Link to the "About the New NIDA Web Site," then click on the animated movie link for a quick but interesting clip on the effects of drugs on the brain.

Rape and Sexual Assault
http://www.icfs.org/bluebook/si000008.htm offers links to "services providing crisis intervention, information, therapy, support groups and/or legal assistance to those dealing with rape or sexual assault."

Web MD
http://www.webmd.com offers a wide variety of information for the medical profession and for consumers.

Chapter 15: Socioemotional Development in Early Adulthood

Learning Objectives

1. Discuss continuity and discontinuity from childhood to adulthood.
2. Address how temperament and attachment influence adulthood.
3. Elaborate on the factors that motivate attraction.
4. Discuss Erik Erikson's sixth stage of cognitive development.
5. Define the three levels of relationship maturity.
6. Indicate ways in which adults balance intimacy and independence.
7. Differentiate between romantic love and affectionate love, then explain Sternberg's triangular theory of love.
8. Discuss friendship and related gender differences.
9. Define loneliness and ways to decrease it.
10. Describe the stages of the family life cycle.
11. Explain recent marital trends and how the view of marriage differs throughout the world.
12. Elaborate on marital myths, what makes marriages work, and the benefits of a good marriage.
13. Discuss gender differences in expectations for marital relationships.
14. Explain the expectations of parenting and common parenting myths.
15. Elaborate on the diversity of adult lifestyles.
16. Address how women develop during early adulthood.
17. Address how men develop during early adulthood.

Chapter Outline

CONTINUITY AND DISCONTINUITY FROM CHILDHOOD TO ADULTHOOD
    Temperament
    Attachment
ATTRACTION, LOVE, AND CLOSE RELATIONSHIPS
    Attraction
        Familiarity and Similarity
        Physical Attraction
    The Faces of Love
        Intimacy
        Romantic Love
        Affectionate Love
        Friendship
    Loneliness
MARRIAGE AND THE FAMILY
    The Family Life Cycle
        Leaving Home and Becoming a Single Adult
        The New Couple
        Becoming Parents
        Families with Adolescents
        Families at Midlife
        Families at Later Life
    Marriage
        Marriage Trends

Self-Test A: Multiple Choice

1. Personality characteristics:
   a. are formed during the first 5 years of life.
   b. are affected more by later life experiences than by early life experiences.
   c. appear to change more over long time intervals than over short intervals.
   d. show little stability over time.

2. According to research by Thomas and Chess children who had a(n) _____ temperament at 3-5 years of age were _____ to be well-adjusted as young adults.
   a. easy/likely
   b. difficult/likely
   c. shy /likely
   d. shy/not likely

3. Ilene readily talks about her relationships, but is rather incoherent when she does. When talking about her parents, she switches between expressing her anger at them and trying to impress you with how she continues trying to please them. Which category of attachment would characterize Ilene?
   a. securely attachment
   b. insecure-dismissing attachment
   c. insecure-clinging attachment
   d. insecure-preoccupied attachment

4. Which of the following statements is consistent with the research findings on close relationships?
   a. People who live in glass houses shouldn't throw stones.
   b. Birds of a feather flock together.
   c. Distance makes the heart grow fonder.
   d. A rose by any other name will smell as sweetly.

5. Consensual validation refers to:
   a. the adolescent's first experiences of sexual intercourse.
   b. support for one's attitudes and behavior through another person's similar attitudes and behavior
   c. parental acceptance of their offspring as independent adults.
   d. attraction among similar individuals.

6. Erik Erikson believed that the primary crisis of the early adult years is:
   a. autonomy versus shame and doubt.
   b. identity versus identity confusion.
   c. intimacy versus isolation.
   d. generativity versus stagnation.

7. Carl knows that acknowledging and respecting Joanna is part of being a good romantic partner, and he frequently talks about the importance of communication in relationships. However, he has not yet been able to make a commitment to marry Joanna. In terms of relationship maturity, Carl is at the _____ level.
   a. self-focused
   b. role-focused
   c. individuated-connected
   d. generalized-communication

8. Ellen Berscheid (2000) believes that _____ is the most important ingredient of romantic love.
   a. sexual desire
   b. commitment
   c. proximity
   d. respect

9. When unattached college students identified their closest relationship, most named:
   a. a friend.
   b. their parents.
   c. a close, but nonparent, relative.
   d. a romantic partner.

10. A desire to have a partner who is adored and will be near is the basis of:
    a. affectionate love.
    b. consummate love.
    c. friendship.
    d. romantic love.

11. In his triangular theory of love, Robert Sternberg describes all of the following types of love EXCEPT:
    a. passion.
    b. intimacy.
    c. commitment.
    d. romance.

12. If the only real attraction that Richard and Jamie feel toward each other is sexual, Robert Sternberg would argue that they are:
    a. experiencing infatuation.
    b. experiencing companionate love.
    c. experiencing fatuous love.
    d. not experiencing love.

13. In what way are friends different from romantic partners?
    a. Relationships with romantic partners are more likely to involve fascination and exclusiveness.
    b. Relationships with friends are more likely to involve fascination and exclusiveness.
    c. Relationships with romantic partners are more likely to involve trust and spontaneity.
    d. Relationships with romantic partners are more likely to involve acceptance and mutual assistance.

14. Research has shown that people feel lonely for all of the following reasons EXCEPT:
    a. society's emphasis on self-fulfillment.
    b. the importance attached to commitment in relationships.
    c. a decline in stable, close relationships.
    d. the rising divorce rate.

15. Which of the following statements regarding loneliness and college is MOST accurate?
    a. Loneliness is likely to develop during the social transition from high school to college.
    b. Loneliness remains of little concern for college students.
    c. A lonely high school student is likely to be a lonely college student.
    d. Males are more likely to be lonesome than females.

16. The textbook suggests that one way an individual may try to reduce loneliness is by:
    a. changing his or her social needs or desires.
    b. going to social gatherings.
    c. getting involved in an Internet dating service.
    d. becoming absorbed in your work.

17. Which process in the family life cycle is related to "launching"?
    a. birth
    b. leaving home and becoming a single adult
    c. taking one's first job and entering the workforce
    d. expecting that, upon reaching the age of 18, the teenager will leave home

18. Which phrase would many individuals begin to hear during the sixth stage of the family life cycle?
    a. "How come I have to clean my room? I'm almost in the fifth grade!"
    b. "I now pronounce you husband and wife."
    c. "Hi, Grandpa. Hi, Grandma."
    d. "Honey, I'm pregnant!"

19. Which of the following best reflects the changes that have occurred in marital relations over the past 60 years?
    a. They have become more fragile due to the changing norm of male-female equality.
    b. They have become more stable because women are now more satisfied with their lives.
    c. The proportion of women who never marry has increased dramatically.
    d. There have been no major changes in terms of stability, only in terms of structure.

20. In a cross-cultural study of marriage around the world, Buss et al. (1990) found which of the following countries considered chastity to be the most important factor in marital selection?
    a. China
    b. Ireland
    c. Germany
    d. the United States

21. In a study of beliefs in marriage myths among college students, Jeffrey Larson (1988) found that:
    a. college students' beliefs about marriage are surprisingly realistic.
    b. females tended to approach the subject of marriage more realistically than males.
    c. highly romantic students are likely to experience more marital stability.
    d. the low participation rate in the study indicates that low interest in the subject of marriage seems characteristic among college students generally.

22. Which of the following is a myth about marriage described by Gottman and Silver (1999)?
    a. The rate of extramarital affairs by women has increased dramatically.
    b. Affairs are often about seeking to find friendship and support.
    c. There is no one "best" way to work out conflict.
    d. Men are not biologically made for marriage.

23. Gottman describes seven main principles that will determine whether a marriage will work or not. These include all of the following EXCEPT:
    a. establishing love maps.
    b. suppressing negative feelings.
    c. letting your partner influence you.
    d. creating shared meaning.

24. When looking at gender differences and marital satisfaction, which of the following has NOT been found by researchers?
    a. Women are more expressive and affectionate than men.
    b. Men do not understand what their wives want from them.
    c. Women want more warmth and openness from their husbands.
    d. Women find their family work highly rewarding.

25. Which statement is NOT is myth about parenting?
    a. The birth of a child will save a failing marriage.
    b. Children will take care of parents in their old age.
    c. When children fail, the parent is not entirely to blame.
    d. Mothers are naturally better parents than fathers.

26. American women have fewer children than in the past. One repercussion of this is that:
    a. men are able to invest a greater amount of time in fathering.
    b. fewer women are entering the workforce.
    c. institutionalized day-care use is on the decline.
    d. women are able to invest more heavily in their children's development.

27. Which of the following is NOT one of the common problems of single adults noted in the text?
    a. intimate relationships with other adults
    b. increased risk for sexually transmitted diseases
    c. confronting loneliness
    d. finding a niche in a marriage-oriented society

28. Which of the following is a benefit of cohabitation?
    a. Relationships in cohabitation tend to last longer than marriages because there are fewer pressures.
    b. Relationships in cohabitation tend to be more equal than in marriage.
    c. Cohabitation improves an individual's chances for choosing a compatible marriage partner.
    d. Cohabitation leads to greater marital happiness and success.

29. Which of the following couples is most likely to get divorced?
    a. Elaine and Alan, whose marriage in their late forties was the first for both
    b. Ivana and Edward, whose joint annual income exceeds $1,000,000
    c. Linda and Phil, who got married their senior year of high school when they learned Linda was pregnant
    d. Jennifer and Burt, who both have Ph.D.s in the social sciences

30. Divorced men and women have higher rates of all of the following EXCEPT:
    a. clinical depression.
    b. alcoholism.
    c. sleep disorders.
    d. immunity to diseases.

31. On average, after getting divorced:
    a. women remarry within a year after their divorce if they have young children.
    b. divorced adults remarry within 4 years.
    c. men will wait longer than women to get remarried.
    d. most divorced adults will not remarry.

32. With respect to gay and lesbian relationships, researchers have found:
    a. these relationships are similar to heterosexual relationships in their satisfactions, loves, and conflicts.
    b. there are more conflicts in homosexual relationships than in heterosexual relationships.
    c. gay and lesbian partners are generally more open about expressing their love than their heterosexual counterparts.
    d. there is both more conflict and more satisfaction in homosexual relationships than in heterosexual relationships.

33. Jean Baker Miller (1986) believes that the study of women's psychological development:
    a. opens up paths to a better understanding of both male and female psychological development.
    b. will harm the inroads women have been making in terms of gaining equal status with men.
    c. will further the feminist movement.
    d. opens the door for women to gain a stronger foothold in the business world.

34. In her research on intimate relationships, Harriet Lerner (1989) has found that:
    a. many men distance themselves from their partner when the going gets rough, rather than work on the relationship.
    b. once a person has reached his or her early twenties, it is nearly impossible to learn to move differently in key relationships.
    c. it is important for women to bring a strong, assertive, independent, authentic self to their relationships.
    d. the future well-being of the world rests on women improving their relationships, and men improving their self-development.

35. In her book, *The Dance of Intimacy*, Lerner (1989) argues that competent relationships are those in which:
    a. separateness and connectedness strike a balance.
    b. the intimacy versus isolation conflict is resolved.
    c. self-determination is sacrificed for intimacy with others.
    d. individuality is sacrificed for the good of the relationship.

36. According to Deborah Tannen's (1990) analysis of the talk of women and men:
    a. lack of communication is high on men's list of reasons for divorce.
    b. men use talk for information, women use it for interaction.
    c. men are more likely to engage in rapport talk, whereas women are more likely to engage in report talk.
    d. it is extremely unlikely that men and women will be able to make the giant leap across the communication gap.

37. According to Joseph Pleck's (1981, 1995) role-strain view:
    a. men need to allow women into the workforce to alleviate men's burden.
    b. the male role is contradictory and inconsistent.
    c. men have become workaholics out of their macho need to provide for their families.
    d. nurturing and being sensitive to others is now being viewed as a way for men to improve their lives.

Self-Test B: Matching

Match the following persons with the statement or theory that most closely reflects their perspective:

1. Ellen Berscheid   a. Women need to be assertive, independent, and authentic in relationships
2. Robert Sternberg   b. Analyzed the talk of women and men; distinguished rapport talk from report talk
3. Jean Baker Miller   c. Believes that sexual desire is the most important ingredient of romantic love
4. Harriet Lerner   d. Proposed that love includes passion, intimacy, and commitment
5. Jeffrey Larson   e. Found college students were grossly misinformed about marriage
6. Joseph Pleck   f. Found seven main principles determine whether a marriage will work or not
7. John Gottman   g. Believes the contradictory, inconsistent male role creates role strain
8. Deborah Tannen   h. Studying women's psychological development helps understand male and female psychological development

Essay Questions

1. You have been asked to address your local community on developing meaningful relationships in young adulthood. Among the topics you have been asked to discuss are: developmental norms in young adulthood; ways to recognize healthy and unhealthy relationships; and how to create healthy relationships. What will you tell these people?

2. You have been caught in the middle of an on-going argument between the men and women in your family. Each group says the other is to blame for marital dissatisfaction. They have asked for your wise input to help them deal more effectively with each other. How can you help them?

Scramblers

Unscramble the following people or terms, then describe what they are known for (people) or define them (terms):

1. **ODOERHET HCASW**

   _____

2. **CIKZ BIUNR**

   _____

3. **NESSUNAOLC DATIILOAVN**

   _____

4. **LOER-DUECSOF VELEL**

   _____

5. CRIOTMNA EVLO

_____

6. GULNARAIRT YTRHOE FO VOEL

_____

7. DNSEHIRIPF

_____

8. NUAHCLNIG

_____

9. LFYAIM THIW ESLOCEDNTAS

_____

10. IMLAFY NI RLAET FILE

_____

Key to Self-Test A

Key to Self-Test B

Key to Essay Questions

1. You need to discuss the transition from identity versus identity confusion to intimacy versus isolation, as well as the interaction between independence and intimacy, for both men and women; also include at least the first two stages of the family life cycle. You will then need to discuss the different theories of relationships, marriage, and intimacy suggested by Berscheid, Hazan and Shaver, Sternberg, and Gottman and relate them to issues of health. While discussing health and relationships, also be sure to look at the single adult as well as adults who are cohabiting and those in homosexual unions. Finally, present what the research (e.g., Lerner, Baker, Pleck) has indicated about developing healthy relationships for both men and women, as well as the marital and parental myths that were discussed in the chapter.

2. You will need to explore the relationships among gender, gender and parental roles, intimacy, and family work; women's and men's development and gender issues (e.g., male role strain); suggestions by Gottman for determining whether a marriage will work; strategies suggested for remarried couples living in stepfamilies (having realistic expectations is useful **before** divorce, too); and how men and women understand the world and communicate differently (e.g., Lerner and Tannen). Then, note what Miller says about how by understanding women better we will also come to understand men better. Add your own thoughts on how to improve communication and interactions between men and women, and how to reduce the blaming that often comes from these disagreements.

Key to Scramblers

1. Theodore Wachs: Proposed ways that linkages between childhood temperament & adult personality vary
2. Zick Rubin: Argues that liking involves our sense that someone else is similar to us
3. Consensual validation: We are attracted to people similar to ourselves; our attitudes/behavior are validated
4. Role-focused level: 2nd level in White's model of relationship maturity; others seen in their own right
5. Romantic love: "Passionate love"; has strong sexual and infatuation components
6. Triangular theory of love: Sternberg's theory that love has 3 main forms: passion, intimacy, commitment
7. Friendship: Close relationship involving enjoyment, acceptance, trust, mutual assistance, understanding
8. Launching: The process in which youths move into adulthood and exit their family of origin
9. Family with adolescents: The 4th stage in family life cycle; adolescent children push for autonomy
10. Family in later life: The 6th/final stage in family life cycle; involves retirement and often grandparenting

Research Project 1: Checking Out the Myths

Interview other college students to assess their beliefs about marriage and parenting. Develop a questionnaire that first asks how they define "love," then reword the myths about marriage and parenting so you can assess how much they actually know about these two topics. Record your respondents' sex and age and any other demographic information you consider to be relevant (e.g., educational level, ethnicity). Classify each participant's definition of love using one of the systems discussed in the text (e.g., Berscheid, Sternberg), which will help you determine whether your respondents have a romantic view of love; then indicate which myths they believe.

1. Looking at the results of your interviews, what patterns did you notice?
2. Were your observations consistent with what you might expect from the research described? Explain your response.
3. Based on your observations, what might you conclude about the college students' beliefs and knowledge about marriage and parenting?

4. How do you think college students might gain more realistic perceptions of marriage and parenting **before** they "take the plunge" and get married?

Research Project 2: Improving Male/Female Relationships

Based on what you have learned in this chapter, make a chart to help you look at the differences that men and women have in terms of relating to each other, dealing with other relationships, dealing with family matters, dealing with work, etc. Then state ways that you believe would help them improve their relationships and their lives.

Personal Application Project 1: Reflecting on What You Learned

Consider what you read in Chapter 15, then answer the following questions:

1. What information in this chapter did you already know?
2. How can/do you use that information in your own life?
3. What information in this chapter was totally new to you?
4. How can you use that new information in your own life?
5. What information in this chapter was different from what you previously believed?
6. How was this information different?
7. How do you account for the differences between what you believed and what you learned in the chapter?
8. What is the most important thing you learned from reading this chapter?

Personal Application Project 2: Consider Your Own Development and Relationships

This project will assist you in understanding your own socioemotional development in terms of personality and relationships. First, determine your own temperament characteristics as a child (feel free to get input from the people who knew you growing up) and reflect on your own early attachment, then look at your current level of adjustment, personality outcomes and intervening contexts (see, for example, Figure 15.1), and your current attachments, including your relationship maturity (as described by Kathleen White). Next, observe your relationships (friendships and romantic) and describe them according to Berscheid's and Sternberg's classifications.

	Current Level of Adjustment	Personality Outcomes	Intervening Contexts	Current Attachments
Your Childhood Temperament				
Your Childhood Attachment Level				

	Berscheid's Classification	Sternberg's Classification	Other Relevant Classification(s)	Comments
Your Romantic Relationship(s)				
Your Friendship Relationships				

1. How consistent were your adult outcomes (current level of adjustment, personality outcomes, current attachments) with what might be predicted from the research cited in the text?
2. What intervening contexts may have modified the expected links between your childhood temperament or your attachment style and your later adult outcomes?
3. What issues seem particularly relevant to you in terms of the relationship between childhood temperament and attachment with later adult outcomes?
4. What similarities did you notice in terms of Berscheid's and Sternberg's classifications for each relationship?
5. What differences did you notice in terms of Berscheid's and Sternberg's classifications for each relationship?
6. What patterns did you notice when comparing relationships in terms of these different classifications?
7. Were your observations consistent with what you might expect from the research described? Explain your response.
8. What might you conclude about relationships and the development of relationships based on your observations?
9. What other conclusions might you make based on these observations?

Internet Projects

Check out the McGraw-Hill web site for this text (http://www.mhhe.com/santrockld8). You'll find numerous activities there, in particular various quizzes, flash cards of key terms, and a challenging and fun crossword puzzle. Please note that all website addresses in this Study Guide have been checked and are correct at the time of publication, however, websites may be discontinued or addresses may change so when you search a given site it may no longer be viable. If that occurs, I apologize for the inconvenience, and would appreciate you notifying me so I could make appropriate revisions in future editions of this Study Guide.

Internet Project 1: Marriage Myths

This chapter presents the recent work of Gottman and Silver (1999) on myths about marriage. Due to limited space, only a few myths could be included—there are many more. Two different perspectives on marriage myths can be found at the following websites: http://marriage.about.com/people/marriage/library/weekly/aa072699.htm, an article about marriage myths at the "about.com" site; and http://www.marriageequality.com/index.htm, a site that supports legally-recognized civil marriages for gay and lesbian couples. Explore both of these websites (check out several of the links at the about.com site and go to "get the facts" at the marriage equality site. Reflect on the many myths that are presented at each site and think about your own personal assumptions about marriage.

1. Were any of your own beliefs challenged?
2. How do we come to believe these "myths"?
3. How does gathering more information or a different perspective about an issue change the way you might think about that issue?
4. Were there some items that were suggested as myths that you believe are, in fact, true?
5. What do you think accounts for the difference in perspective in those instances?
6. How has learning about marriage myths from the text and from these websites affected the way you view marriage?

Internet Project 2: Parenting Myths

As noted in the text, "The needs and expectations of parents have stimulated many myths about parenting." The author then goes on to list ten different myths, from expecting that "the birth of a child will save a failing marriage" to "parenting is an instinct and requires no training" (you might want to check out the research on Harry Harlow's rhesus monkeys to see how false that one is!). While these myths look at parental expectations, there are other areas of parenting in which myths abound as well. One site, http://www.breakthroughparenting.com/sevenparentingmyths.htm presents seven myths about discipline versus punishment; and a second site, http://www.parentsplace.com/family/singleparent/gen/0,3375,10039,00.html (a subsite of iVillage.com) looks at myths of single parenting, confronting the stigma attached to being a single parent. Consider the myths presented in all three places (the text plus both websites) and think about which of them you thought to be true and which you understood to be myths.

1. Were any of your views challenged?
2. Did gaining new information or new insights change your views?
3. Are there any views you had that were stated to be myths that you choose to hold onto and still believe to be true? Which ones, and what is it about those issues that keep you from changing your position?
4. How has learning about parenting myths from the text and from these websites affected the way you view parenting?
5. Something I try to impress upon my students is that our parents did what they knew, and did the best they knew, oftentimes taking information from the experts of the time. However, today (after many more years of research), those techniques may not necessarily be considered the most effective forms of parenting. So, if psychologists and developmentalists suggest that young parents today use different methods than their parents used, this does not mean our parents were "bad people," merely that we know more today than they knew when they were raising a family. Bearing that in mind, are you willing to try some of the suggestions presented in the text and at the websites?

Other Relevant Sites on the Internet

APA site
http://www.apa.org

APS site
http://www.psychologicalscience.org/

BabyBagOnline
http://www.babybag.com provides a great deal of information on parenting.

Divorce Source
http://www.divorcesource.com offers information on family law, custody, alimony and support, visitation, and includes specific information for all fifty states.

The Divorce Support Page
http://www.divorcesupport.com is "devoted to connecting you to the most valuable and comprehensive divorce related information on the Iternet." It includes resources for anything relating to divorce from lawyers, mediators, and arbitrators to state specific guidebooks and divorce forms, to child support calculation reports.

Flying Solo: The Life Management Resource for Divorce and Aging Issues
http://www.flyingsolo.com combines links to information on divorce and separation (including issues of cohabitation and stepfamilies) to matters affecting the elderly and disabled. Loads of useful information.

The Gay and Lesbian Alliance Against Defamation
http://www.glaad.org is the website for this national organization and provides information, support, a listing of upcoming events, and current media releases.

How to Divorce as Friends
http://www.divorceasfriends.com is the website of Bill Ferguson, a former divorce attorney, who walks you through the steps to "change both your relationship and your life." Ferguson notes that 15 percent of his clients chose not to divorce, and the remaining 85 percent "were able to part as friends." Sounds look good, sound advice, especially if children are involved.

Web MD
http://www.webmd.com offers a wide variety of information for the medical profession and for consumers.

Chapter 16: Physical and Cognitive Development in Middle Adulthood

Learning Objectives

1. Discuss changing middle age and the physical changes that take place during middle adulthood.
2. Elaborate on prominent health issues and chronic disorders that individuals face in middle adulthood.
3. Explain how culture, personality, and relationships are related to health.
4. Indicate the way in which mortality rates changed during the twentieth century.
5. Discuss the changes that characterize the sexuality of men and women as they go through middle adulthood.
6. Describe the cognitive changes in intelligence that take place during middle adulthood.
7. Discuss how speed of processing, memory, expertise, and problem solving are impacted by the aging process.
8. Examine how career, work, and leisure change from early adulthood.
9. Discuss the role that religion, spirituality, and meaning play during this stage of life.

Chapter Outline

CHANGING MIDDLE AGE
PHYSICAL DEVELOPMENT
    Physical Changes
    Health and Disease
    Culture, Personality, Relationships, and Health
        Culture and Cardiovascular Disease
        Type A/Type B Behavior Patterns
        Hardiness
        Health and Social Relationships
    Mortality Rates
    Sexuality
        Menopause
        Hormone Replacement Therapy
        Hormonal Changes in Men
        Sexual Attitudes and Behavior
COGNITIVE DEVELOPMENT
    Intelligence
        Fluid and Crystallized Intelligence
        Seattle Longitudinal Study
    Information Processing
        Speed
        Memory
        Expertise
        Practical Problem Solving
CAREERS, WORK, AND LEISURE
    Job Satisfaction
    Career Challenges and Changes
    Leisure
RELIGION AND MEANING IN LIFE

Self-Test A: Multiple Choice

1. According to our author, and as reflected in Jim Croce's song, "Time in a Bottle," our perception of time depends on:
   a. how full our lives are.
   b. where we are in the life span.
   c. our personal experiences.
   d. how many deadlines we have to meet.

2. Compared to the time that Freud and Jung studied midlife transitions, around 1900, and now, the boundaries of middle age have:
   a. moved downward.
   b. moved upward.
   c. become relatively indistinct.
   d. stayed the same, but apply to more people.

3. Which of the following is NOT a noticeable visible sign of aging?
   a. the skin begins to wrinkle and sag.
   b. small, localized areas of pigmentation in the skin produce aging spots.
   c. hair becomes thinner and grayer.
   d. fingernails and toenails become thinner.

4. Which of the following is most accurate concerning perceptions of gender differences in aging in the United States?
   a. Some aspects of aging in middle adulthood are taken as signs of attractiveness in men, but similar signs may be perceived as unattractive in women.
   b. Some aspects of aging in middle adulthood are taken as signs of attractiveness in women, but similar signs may be perceived as unattractive in men.
   c. Signs of aging in men and women are perceived as unattractive in our culture.
   d. Signs of aging in men and women typically elicit greater respect from people in our culture.

5. What changes are noticed in an adult's height as that person ages?
   a. It increases.
   b. It decreases.
   c. Unless there is illness, there is no noticeable change.
   d. The findings are contradictory—some people get taller, others get shorter.

6. Obesity has been linked to:
   a. hypertension and digestive disorders.
   b. cancer.
   c. early visible signs of aging.
   d. prostate disorders in men.

7. A person between the ages of 40 and 59 is going to have most difficulty:
   a. reading a wall chart at the eye-care professional's office.
   b. reading street signs.
   c. reading a newspaper.
   d. watching television at a distance.

8. Considering normal aging processes, whose blood pressure would be expected to be highest?
   a. Sally, a 60-year-old woman who is post-menopausal
   b. Cindy, a 40-year-old woman who is pre-menopausal
   c. Carl, a 60-year-old male whose prostate was removed
   d. Sam, a 40-year-old man whose prostate is still intact

9. In the Ni-Hon-San Study of Japanese men, those living in _____ had the highest rate of coronary heart disease.
   a. Hiroshima
   b. Nagasaki
   c. Honolulu
   d. San Francisco

10. Japanese men living in California have much lower rates of cerebrovascular disease (stroke) than Japanese men living in Japan, because:
    a. the diets of those living in California are more well-rounded.
    b. the Japanese men living in California have a more relaxed lifestyle.
    c. businessmen in Japan tend to drink a lot of alcohol and to chain-smoke.
    d. of the residual effects from the bombing of Hiroshima and Nagasaki during World War II.

11. One way to promote access to health care for many Latino Americans would be to:
    a. speak slowly and articulate clearly so they understand what the medical practitioner is saying.
    b. desegregate clinics for ethnic minorities.
    c. teach Latino Americans not to use medical care as a "quick fix."
    d. integrate Latino Americans' belief in the supernatural into their treatment.

12. Which factor of the Type A personality is most related to coronary heart disease?
    a. excessive competition
    b. being hard-driven
    c. impatience
    d. hostility

13. Marjorie is controlled, committed, and sees problems as challenges. She will most likely:
    a. remain healthy.
    b. develop heart disease.
    c. develop breast cancer.
    d. develop ulcers.

14. The main cause of death for individuals in middle adulthood is:
    a. heart disease.
    b. diabetes.
    c. cancer.
    d. cerebrovascular disease.

15. In a large-scale study of Americans in midlife, Brim (1999) found that for women who had experienced menopause, most reported that menopause was a _____ experience.
    a. positive
    b. negative
    c. neutral tending toward positive
    d. neutral tending toward negative

16. What is the basis of erroneous beliefs about menopause?
    a. A majority of women experience them.
    b. The beliefs conform well with gender-typed beliefs about middle-age women.
    c. The research is based on small, select samples of women.
    d. Drug companies promote them to sell their products.

17. The American Geriatric Association recommends that:
    a. post-menopausal women should consider hormone replacement therapy.
    b. women who have had hysterectomies should avoid estrogen replacement therapy.
    c. the benefits of hormone replacement therapy outweigh the risks in women who are at increased risk for breast cancer.
    d. women need to rely heavily on their doctor's advice when deciding whether they should use hormone replacement therapy.

18. What type of hormonal changes do middle-aged men experience?
    a. loss of their capacity to father children
    b. modest increase in sexual activity
    c. psychological adjustment to declining physical energy
    d. a dramatic drop in testosterone levels

19. When compared to that in early adulthood, sexual activity during middle adulthood is:
    a. more frequent.
    b. less frequent.
    c. about the same.
    d. more dependent on physical activity.

20. According to John Horn, in middle age:
    a. crystallized intelligence increases, while fluid intelligence begins to decline.
    b. fluid intelligence increases, while crystallized intelligence begins to decline.
    c. both crystallized and fluid intelligence increase.
    d. both crystallized and fluid intelligence begin to decline.

21. Data from the Seattle Longitudinal Study have shown that the highest level of functioning for four of the six intellectual abilities tested occurred in:
    a. late adolescence.
    b. early adulthood.
    c. middle adulthood.
    d. late adulthood.

22. A review of research methods that assess changes in the adult years suggests that:
    a. longitudinal and cross-sectional studies produce similar results.
    b. longitudinal studies are more likely than cross-sectional studies to show declining abilities with age.
    c. cross-sectional studies are more likely than longitudinal studies to show declining abilities with age.
    d. some abilities seem to show a decline in cross-sectional studies, while others show a decline using longitudinal studies.

23. Memory decline is more likely to occur when individuals:
    a. must remember numbers.
    b. try too hard to organize it in their minds.
    c. don't use effective memory strategies.
    d. enter middle adulthood.

24. We could distinguish Stephen, an expert chess player, from Darrell, who is a novice, because Darrell is more likely than Stephen to _____ when determining his moves.
    a. use his accumulated experience
    b. process information automatically
    c. have better strategies and short-cuts
    d. use set patterns

25. Job satisfaction increases with age for all of the following reasons EXCEPT:
    a. higher pay.
    b. job security.
    c. higher positions within the company.
    d. less need for intense commitment.

26. Aristotle viewed leisure as:
    a. a waste of time.
    b. harmful.
    c. unnecessary.
    d. important in life.

27. Leisure is particularly important during middle adulthood because it:
    a. improves the nation's economy.
    b. helps adults narrow their interests.
    c. eases the transition from work to retirement.
    d. gives grandparents something to talk about with their grandchildren.

28. The percentage of Americans who believe in God is _____ the percentage who attend religious services.
    a. less than
    b. greater than
    c. equal to
    d. changing in comparison to

29. While Americans generally show a strong interest in religion and believe in God, they also reveal:
    a. a declining faith in mainstream religious institutions.
    b. an increasing faith in mainstream religious institutions.
    c. less faith in mainstream religious institutions, but increased faith in religious leaders.
    d. no change in terms of their faith in mainstream religious institutions, but great disappointment with religious leaders.

30. What is the relation between religion and the ability to cope with stress?
    a. Religiousness has been shown to be an ineffective strategy for coping with stress.
    b. Religiousness can help some individuals cope more effectively with their lives.
    c. Religiousness often promotes anxiety, thus inducing stress.
    d. There appears to be little if any relationship between religiousness and the ability to cope with stress.

31. Research seems to indicate which of the following relationships between religion and happiness?
    a. Involvement in religion causes people to be happy.
    b. Happiness leads people to become involved in religion.
    c. There is no meaningful relationship between religion and happiness.
    d. People who are involved in religion tend to be happy.

32. Viktor Frankl believed that all of the following are distinct human qualities EXCEPT:
    a. spirituality.
    b. freedom.
    c. responsibility.
    d. altruism.

Self-Test B: Matching

Match the following persons with the statement or theory that most closely reflects their perspective:

1. Meyer Friedman   a.   Middle age: a mix of new opportunities, expanding resources, & physical decline
2. Gail Sheehy   b.   Believes some abilities decline in middle age while others increase
3. John Horn   c.   One of a pair of researchers who described the Type A personality
4. Nancy Denney   d.   Is conducting an extensive study of intellectual abilities in the adult years
5. K. Warner Schaie   e.   Commitment to/balance of work, family, & leisure shifts as we age
6. John Clausen   f.   Emphasized each person's uniqueness & the finiteness of life
7. Victor Frankl   g.   Wrote about the stigma attached to menopause
8. Lois Verbrugge   h.   Assessed practical problem solving abilities in adults

Essay Questions

1. Your next-door neighbors are a lovely couple whom you like very much. One day they both confide in you that they are fast approaching middle age and are really dreading it. They have heard that once you turn 40, everything begins to fall apart, including your sex life. What would you tell them to help them through this crisis?

2. One of your friends has come to you for advice about his aunt. She was widowed about a year ago, and since then she has become increasingly involved with the church she was brought up in, although neither she nor her husband (nor anyone in your friend's family) ever did much more than celebrate Christmas and Easter. Your friend is worried that this is a sign of her inability to cope with the untimely death of her husband, although she's never before shown any other indications of instability. In fact, he tells you that she worked full-time in the fashion industry for many years, has never smoked, drinks only socially, and has had no serious physical illnesses. Your friend asks for your thoughts on how to ensure his aunt's well-being. What do you tell him?

Scramblers

Unscramble the following people or terms, then describe what they are known for (people) or define them (terms):

1. CTROVI LFRNAK

_____

2. YAR RNOASMNE

_____

3. NOIRCHC SDRIESDOR

_____

4. ACTMIERLCIC

_____

5. IDNREASHS

_____

6. ILALZETSDYRC LELITNEGINCE

_____

7. IULFD IENCTEEGLILN

_____

8. POANUESME

_____

9. RETEPIXSE

_____

10. SUIRELE

_____

Key to Self-Test A

1.	b	LO 1	12.	d	LO 3	23. c	LO 7
2.	b	LO 1	13.	a	LO 3	24. d	LO 7
3.	d	LO 1	14.	a	LO 4	25. d	LO 8
4.	a	LO 1	15.	a	LO 4	26. d	LO 8
5.	b	LO 1	16.	c	LO 5	27. c	LO 8
6.	a	LO 2	17.	a	LO 5	28. b	LO 9
7.	c	LO 2	18.	c	LO 5	29. a	LO 9
8.	a	LO 3	19.	b	LO 5	30. b	LO 9
9.	d	LO 3	20.	a	LO 6	31. d	LO 9
10.	c	LO 3	21.	c	LO 6	32. d	LO 9
11.	d	LO 3	22.	c	LO 6		

Key to Self-Test B

1.	c	5.	d	
2.	g	6.	e	
3.	b	7.	f	
4.	h	8.	a	

Key to Essay Questions

1. Describe the specific physical changes (e.g., vision, hearing, wrinkles) and the changes in sexuality, noting that most women actually have a positive attitude toward menopause, and providing the recent information about how Viagra is being used by men (as well as some women) to improve their sex life, so long as the desire is still there. Discuss, too, the role that cultural attitudes play in how we feel about aging physically, and the differences in perception between signs of aging in men and in women. Be sure to explain the health issues, and the health practices that will allow them to remain vital and active (e.g., don't smoke, stay cognitively active, balance work and leisure, eat a nutritious diet).

2. Here you will assure him that the research indicates religious involvement has been positively correlated with good health, life satisfaction, happiness, and effective coping. Do explore Victor Frankl's research on the meaning of life, and also go over the various health issues that he brought up to let him know that his aunt is on a healthy path.

Key to Scramblers

1. Victor Frankl: Emphasized each person's uniqueness & the finiteness of life
2. Ray Rosenman: One of a pair of researchers who described the Type A personality
3. Chronic disorders: Characterized by slow onset & long duration increase from middle adulthood on
4. Climacteric: Term used to describe the midlife transition in which fertility declines
5. Hardiness: Personality style characterized by sense of commitment, control, seeing problems as challenges
6. Crystallized intelliigence: Accumulated information & verbal skills; Horn says it increases with age
7. Fluid intelligence: Ability to reason abstractly; Horn says it steadily declines from middle adulthood on
8. Menopause: Complete cessation of a woman's menstruation; usually occurs in late 40s or early 50s
9. Expertise: Having an extensive, highly organized knowledge & understanding of a particular domain
10. Leisure: Pleasant times after work when individuals are free to pursue activities & interest of their choosing

Research Project 1: Balancing Work, Family, Leisure, and School

The author states that "Most of us would like to balance work, family, and leisure activities in some fashion. Clearly, though, some individuals give priority to one or two of these to the exclusion of the other or others." He suggests you think about how balanced or unbalanced these factors are in your own life, and asks if (and how) you think your commitment to each of these areas of your life will change. Using the chart below, indicate whether each has a high, low, or medium priority in your life right now, and the priority you anticipate each will have in the future (state the approximate date). (I have added school, since that is also an important factor in your life at this time.) Then, consider how the priority you place on each of these factors is currently affecting your life.

Factor	Current Priority	Future Priority (Date:)	How It's Affecting My Life
Work			
Family			
Leisure			
School			

1. What did you notice concerning the balance of these priorities in your life?
2. What did you notice about how these priorities may affect your life?
3. How do your current priorities differ from your future priorities? What effect do you think that will have on your life?
4. What patterns did you notice when looking at these four factors in terms of the material discussed in this chapter?
5. Were your observations consistent with what you might expect from the research described? Explain your response.
6. What might you conclude about your own personal development based on these observations?
7. What plan might you make for balancing each of these factors in your life to ensure you stay as healthy as possible?

Research Project 2: Community Health Project

Conduct a needs assessment evaluation in your community to see what types of health issues are important (both to the community members and the health professionals in your area) and to determine the nature of ethnic/racial/religious diversity that exists. Considering the information in this chapter, work together with local health officials to plan an intervention that would promote healthy behaviors (e.g., strategies for lowering blood pressure, getting people to stop smoking, etc.). In terms of the diversity that does or does not exist in your community, what types of issues must you consider in addition to the physical and psychological health concerns?

Personal Application Project 1: Reflecting on What You Learned

Consider what you read in Chapter 16, then answer the following questions:

1. What information in this chapter did you already know?
2. How can/do you use that information in your own life?
3. What information in this chapter was totally new to you?
4. How can you use that new information in your own life?
5. What information in this chapter was different from what you previously believed?
6. How was this information different?
7. How do you account for the differences between what you believed and what you learned in the chapter?
8. What is the most important thing you learned from reading this chapter?

Personal Application Project 2: Consider Your Own Development

Depending on your age, either consider the issues of physical and cognitive aging with respect to yourself or interview a middle-aged relative or friend to assess the changes that person has experienced. Refer back to the text to see what changes typically take place in each of the systems described in the chart below, then indicate your own (or your relative's/friend's) experience in that regard. Comment on consistencies or inconsistencies between what is expected based on the text and what has been experienced in real life (e.g., state reasons why you believe there is an inconsistency).

Aspect of Your Self/Relative/Friend	Expected (based on text)	Actual (based on experience)	Comments
Visible Signs of Aging			
Height & Weight			
Strength, Joints, Bones			
Vision & Hearing			
Cardiovascular System			
Sleep			
Health			
Sexuality			
Fluid Intelligence			
Crystallized Intelligence			
Speed of Information Processing			
Memory			
Expertise			
Problem Solving			
Other (describe)			

Internet Projects

Check out the McGraw-Hill web site for this text (http://www.mhhe.com/santrockld8). You'll find numerous activities there, in particular various quizzes, flash cards of key terms, and a challenging and fun crossword puzzle. Please note that all website addresses in this Study Guide have been checked and are correct at the time of publication, however, websites may be discontinued or addresses may change so when you search a given site it may no longer be viable. If that occurs, I apologize for the inconvenience, and would appreciate you notifying me so I could make appropriate revisions in future editions of this Study Guide.

Internet Project 1: Life Coaching

Chapter 16 talks about such issues as retirement, health, and balancing your life. Oftentimes people would like to find balance, but don't really know where or how to get started—they aren't physically ill and they don't have the types of problems that would send them to a therapist, yet they would like "something more" out of life. A relatively new service area is life (or personal) coaching. Although not related to sports, it has the same kind of active movement and feedback to help people get the most out of their own innate abilities. This type of guidance is undoubtedly not financially feasible for most students, but to get some idea of the kinds of help that are offered (and just for the fun of it), check out some of the sites. Here are a few that I found interesting (although not all are equally as attractive): http://www.reallifecoach.com, http://www.coachdt.com, http://www.lifecoach.uk.net, and http://www.benchmarkcoaching.com. And, by the time this Study Guide is published, my own coaching website should be up and running, so come pay me a visit: http://www.ThePACE.org. After checking out these sites, consider how something like coaching can help people balance their lives, or reach goals they've put off to raise a family, or guide them toward achieving a sense of fulfillment in life. How would coaching be consistent with what you read in this chapter?

By the way, if coaching sounds like a good thing to do, there are many schools where you can be trained to become a coach (note, too, that one of the largest areas in this field is executive coaching where the coach works with companies and their employees). If you're interested, you can check some of them out, too: http://www.executivecoachcollege.com, http://www.coachu.com, and http://www.hudsoninstitute.com.

Here's to the most fulfilling life possible!

Internet Project 2: Staying Healthy

As stated in Chapter 16, the major cause of death in middle adulthood is chronic illness. This makes it especially important to remain as healthy as possible. Go to http://www.nhlbi.nih.gov/, which is one of the websites for the federally subsidized National Institutes of Health. Check out the links for healthy aging, women's health, and men's health.

1. How does this information supplement what you learned from the text?
2. What do you have to do to ensure that you remain healthy throughout your lifetime?
3. What additional information could you find on these sites about adults' changing hormonal processes and sexual activity? Based on what you learned, are these changes primarily positive, negative, or neutral?
4. How can you encourage your friends and family members to engage in a healthy lifestyle?
5. What resources are available to promote health?
6. What resources are available to answer your questions on health topics?
7. What resources are available for individuals who have chronic illnesses or any of the other illnesses mentioned in the chapter?

Other Relevant Sites on the Internet

APA site
http://www.apa.org

APS site
http://www.psychologicalscience.org/

American Association for Retired Persons (AARP)
http://www.aarp.org is the web site for AARP, an especially powerful organization that educates, lobbies, and provides services about and for persons age 50 and above.

CBS Healthwatch
http://healthwatch.medscape.com/medscape/p/gcommunity/ghome.asp provides information on a wide range of health topics, as well as many other resources, such as a drug directory, self-care and first aid tips, and a medical dictionary.

Cooper Wellness
http://www.cooperwellness.com is the website of Dr. Kenneth Cooper, who notes "It is easier to maintain good health through proper exercise, diet, and emotional balance than to regain it once it is lost."

Dr.Koop
http://www.drkoop.com is the website of former Surgeon General, C. Everett Koop. It offers a wealth of information on health.

Intelihealth
http://www.intelihealth.com/IH/ihtIH offers health information from a variety of sources, including Harvard Medical School.

Web MD
http://www.webmd.com offers a wide variety of information for the medical profession and for consumers.

Chapter 17: Socioemotional Development in Middle Adulthood

Learning Objectives

1. Discuss Erik Erikson's seventh stage of development.
2. Elaborate on Levinson's research on life-span transitions.
3. Describe the research conducted on the midlife crisis.
4. Examine the contemporary life-events approach to development.
5. Explain how historical context, gender, and culture impact development.
6. Discuss the longitudinal studies conducted to examine the issue of stability versus change in middle adulthood.
7. Examine how love and marriage change as people grow older.
8. Discuss the causes for and results of divorce in middle age.
9. Explain the empty nest syndrome and the reasons adult children return home.
10. Examine how sibling relationships and friendships change during middle adulthood.
11. Describe the nature of intergenerational relationships during middle adulthood, including the role that gender and culture play.

Chapter Outline

PERSONALITY THEORIES AND DEVELOPMENT IN MIDDLE ADULTHOOD
> Adult Stage Theories
>> Erikson's Stage of Generativity Versus Stagnation
>> Levinson's Seasons of a Man's Life
>> How Pervasive Are Mid-Life Crises?
>> Individual Variations
> Life-Events Approach
> Contexts
>> Historical Contexts (Cohort Effects)
>> Gender Contexts
>> Cultural Contexts

STABILITY AND CHANGE
> Longitudinal Studies
>> Neugarten's Kansas City Study
>> Costa and McCrae's Baltimore Study
>> Berkeley Longitudinal Study
>> Helson's Mills College Study
> Conclusions

CLOSE RELATIONSHIPS
> Love and Marriage at Midlife
>> Affectionate Love
>> Marriage and Divorce
> The Empty Nest and Its Refilling
> Parenting Conceptions
> Siblings and Friends
> Intergenerational Relationships

Self-Test A: Multiple Choice

1. Hyun-Joo experiences great satisfaction through nurturing, guiding, and teaching skills to her children. According to Erik Erikson, Hyun-Joo is dealing successfully with which psychological task?
   a. industry versus inferiority
   b. identity versus confusion
   c. intimacy versus isolation
   d. generativity versus stagnation

2. An adult who has successfully resolved the conflicts of the generativity versus stagnation psychosocial stage is most likely to:
   a. donate money to a scholarship fund.
   b. buy a piece of a football franchise.
   c. spend time and money on exercise programs.
   d. hire consultants to teach junior executives the finer points of business management.

3. According to Daniel Levinson, a major conflict that a middle-aged man must face is:
   a. mortality versus immortality.
   b. being young versus being old.
   c. empty nest syndrome.
   d. industry versus inferiority.

4. According to Daniel Levinson, the success of the midlife transition is dependent upon how effectively the individual:
   a. accepts polarities of the conflicts as an integral part of his or her being.
   b. chooses the most troublesome conflict and resolves it.
   c. learns to pay more attention to the needs of others than to his or her own needs.
   d. realizes the sense of urgency in his or her life and comes to terms with it.

5. According to George Vaillant:
   a. a majority of middle-aged adults go through a midlife crisis.
   b. the forties are a time for reassessing and recording the truth about the adolescent and adulthood years.
   c. there is a great deal of empirical research to support Gail Sheehy's observations.
   d. individuals between ages 40 and 60 are more nervous and worried than those under 40.

6. Stage theories of adult development have been criticized for all of the following reasons EXCEPT:
   a. stage theories place too much emphasis on crises in development.
   b. there often is considerable individual variation in the way people experience the stages.
   c. experts are virtually unanimous in their belief that midlife crises have been exaggerated.
   d. many of the studies have been flawed by the investigators' questionable research skills.

7. Evidence from an accumulation of studies indicates that the midlife crisis is:
   a. a universal phenomenon.
   b. present in a majority of individuals, but not all.
   c. dependent on the cohort that is currently middle-aged.
   d. exaggerated.

8. The contemporary life-events approach emphasizes that how life events influence the individual's development depends not only on the life event, but also on all of the following EXCEPT:
   a. the individual's cohort membership.
   b. the sociohistorical context.
   c. mediating factors such as physical health and family support.
   d. the individual's adaption to the life event.

216

9. In a study of daily hassles by Kanner and colleagues (1981), middle-aged adults were most concerned with:
   a. weight.
   b. rising prices of common goods.
   c. misplacing or losing things.
   d. crime.

10. The contemporary life-events approach is likely to place emphasis on:
    a. stability rather than change.
    b. change rather than stability.
    c. daily experiences.
    d. environmental rather than emotional change.

11. The "social clock," as described by Bernice Neugarten (1986), is a:
    a. timetable for accomplishing life's tasks.
    b. way to assess how extraverted or introverted an individual is.
    c. way to assess how extraverted or introverted a couple is.
    d. biological timetable that guides certain of life's tasks such as bearing children.

12. Stage theories of adult development have been criticized for:
    a. having a female bias.
    b. not adequately addressing women's concerns about relationships.
    c. placing too much importance on childbearing and child rearing.
    d. not adequately addressing how men balance career and family.

13. When women in nonindustrialized countries reach middle age, their status improves for all of the following reasons EXCEPT:
    a. they are freed from cumbersome restrictions placed on them when they were younger.
    b. they have authority over younger relatives.
    c. they have opportunities to gain status outside the home that younger women do not have.
    d. they are no longer able to bear children.

14. Regarding age changes in personality, Bernice Neugarten in the Kansas City Study found that:
    a. personality remains fairly constant, but age changes do exist.
    b. significant gender differences in personality were present, but mostly at younger ages.
    c. neurosis increases with age, but social inhibitions in personality decline.
    d. depression increases with age, but only in the personality of elderly who are widowed.

15. Paul Costa and Robert McCrae determined that the "big five" personality factors:
    a. showed different patterns of development during middle adulthood.
    b. became the "big three" as adults matured.
    c. go through a series of developmental stages.
    d. remain relatively stable during the middle adult years.

16. A cross-cultural study comparing adults from China and the United States found that:
    a. older adults in both countries became more extraverted and flexible than their younger adult counterparts.
    b. older adults in both countries became less extraverted and flexible than their younger adult counterparts.
    c. older adults in the United States became more extraverted, while the older Chinese became less extraverted.
    d. older adults in China became more flexible, while the older Americans became less flexible.

17. John Clausen (1993), a researcher in the Berkeley longitudinal studies, believes:
    a. not enough attention has been given to the role of discontinuity in adult development.
    b. the experience of recurrent crises and change is a universal factor in adult development.
    c. some people experience recurrent crises and change, while others have more stable, continuous lives.
    d. the overall pattern of development during the life course is one of stability rather than change.

18. Ravenna Helson described an awareness of limitations and death as a midlife:
    a. consciousness.
    b. stage.
    c. crisis.
    d. transformation.

19. During the middle years, _____ love increases.
    a. affectionate or companionate
    b. romantic or passionate
    c. intimate
    d. committed

20. Satisfying relationships in early, middle, and late adulthood share all of the following characteristics EXCEPT:
    a. emotional security.
    b. passion.
    c. respect.
    d. communication.

21. After 25 years of marriage, Andrew and Sarah have decided to divorce now that their daughters have left home. According to the research, we might expect their divorce to be more positive than a couple who divorces in early adulthood because:
    a. they have greater resources, so both will be able to take what they need to set up their separate household.
    b. their children no longer have any influence in what their parents decide.
    c. they may understand themselves better and may be searching for changes in their lives.
    d. they have fewer resources after paying for their daughters' college educations and weddings, so there are fewer resources to split up.

22. The empty nest syndrome predicts that parents experience decreased marital satisfaction when the children leave home. Research has found that:
    a. marital satisfaction does, in fact, decrease.
    b. marital satisfaction actually increases.
    c. conflict between parents and their children decreases.
    d. conflict between parents and their children increases.

23. When middle-aged parents mention disappointment regarding their adult children's development, they often say they wish:
    a. they could spend more time with their children now.
    b. their children had been more successful.
    c. they had spent more time with them.
    d. their children were more concerned about the parents' needs.

24. In terms of children's perceptions of their parents:
   a. adolescents and those over age 60 described their parents as providers of emotional and financial support.
   b. adolescents and those over age 60 described their parents' uniqueness.
   c. adolescents were more likely than the other individuals interviewed to be aware of the conditions that shaped their parents into the persons they were.
   d. middle-aged adults described their parents as continuing to be emotionally supportive.

25. The majority of sibling relationships in adulthood have been found to be:
   a. apathetic.
   b. close.
   c. rivalrous.
   d. antagonistic.

26. Anita and Larry were always very close as children. Now that they are in middle adulthood, we would expect that they would:
   a. still be very close.
   b. be less close, particularly if they live in different parts of the country.
   c. be less close no matter where they live.
   d. be able to count on each other in times of crisis, but otherwise not maintain much contact.

27. Parents and their adult children are most likely to DISAGREE about:
   a. political party.
   b. church attendance.
   c. choice of lifestyle.
   d. abortion.

28. Which of the following pairs is most likely to have the closest relationship?
   a. Margaret, age 65, and her son, Michael
   b. Mildred, age 65, and her daughter, Roberta
   c. Mort, age 65, and his son, Larry
   d. Milton, age 65, and his daughter, Sandy

29. Middle-aged adults have been described as the "sandwich" generation because:
   a. they are now responsible for taking care of grandchildren, including preparing their meals, while their adult children are at work.
   b. as retirees, they now spend more time at home and are able to eat together as a couple.
   c. they face the demands of caring for both their children and their elderly parents.
   d. it is now up to them to pass on family traditions to their children and grandchildren.

30. When three levels of acculturation are observed in Mexican American families, they are usually:
   a. children at beginning level, mothers at intermediate level, fathers at advanced level.
   b. fathers at beginning level, mothers at intermediate level, children at advanced level.
   c. mothers at beginning level, children at intermediate level, fathers at advanced level.
   d. mothers at beginning level, fathers at intermediate level, children at advanced level.

31. If the typical pattern is followed, which of the following middle-aged individuals is most likely to care for an aging parent?
   a. Arthur, a divorced man living alone
   b. Beatrice, whose children are now living on their own
   c. Candice, whose three teenagers are still living at home
   d. Derick, who lives with his wife and their teenage daughter

Self-Test B: Matching

Match the following persons with the statement or theory that most closely reflects their perspective:

1. Daniel Levinson
2. George Vaillant
3. Bernice Neugarten
4. Ravenna Helson
5. Paul Costa
6. Erik Erikson
7. John Clausen
8. Lilian Troll

a. Described the crisis of middle age as generativity versus stagnation
b. Believes that only a minority of adults experience a midlife crisis
c. Middle adulthood requires men to come to grips with four major conflicts
d. Returned to college at age 45 then began doing research on women's aging issues
e. Found evidence for stability in the "big five" personality factors
f. Too much attention is given to the role of discontinuity in adult development
g. Found midlife consciousness, rather than crisis, in Mills college alumnae
h. Believes an age group's social environment can alter its social clock

Essay Questions

1. You have found yourself stuck in the middle of an argument between your two best friends. One says that people never change, they're the same way they are at 50 as they were at 15; the other says that people are constantly changing—look at all the famous musicians who have moved on from folk to Rock'n'Roll to Rhythm & Blues to Country—even Pat Boone went from Bobby So music to Heavy Metal. How would you mediate between these two positions, based on what you have learned from this chapter?

2. Your cousin is about to turn 40, and has confided in you his concern about going through the midlife crisis. He is also concerned that his wife, who will be 40 next year, will have a similar crisis. He wants to know all that you know about what will and will not predict a crisis for both of them. What will you tell him, and what will you conclude in light of the research that has been conducted?

Scramblers

Unscramble the following people or terms, then describe what they are known for (people) or define them (terms):

1. BRETOR CRMEAC

   _____

2. NENVARA EOLSNH

   _____

3. RATEINVEIGYT

   _____

4. ANNSTTOAIG

   _____

5. IVNOCE EPSHA

_____

6. YCROANRTOEPM FILE-SETVNE AHPCPARO

_____

7. OHROTC

_____

8. ICAOLS OCKLC

_____

9. GIB EVIF SFRAOCT FO YPETIRSLANO

_____

10. PMETY SETN DNROYMSE

_____

Key to Self-Test A

1.	d	LO 1	12.	b	LO 4	23.	c	LO 9
2.	d	LO 1	13.	d	LO 5	24.	a	LO 9
3.	b	LO 2	14.	a	LO 6	25.	b	LO 10
4.	a	LO 2	15.	d	LO 6	26.	a	LO 10
5.	b	LO 3	16.	b	LO 6	27.	c	LO 11
6.	d	LO 3	17.	c	LO 6	28.	b	LO 11
7.	d	LO 3	18.	a	LO 6	29.	c	LO 11
8.	a	LO 4	19.	a	LO 7	30.	d	LO 11
9.	a	LO 4	20.	b	LO 7	31.	b	LO 11
10.	b	LO 4	21.	c	LO 8			
11.	a	LO 4	22.	b	LO 9			

Key to Self-Test B

1.	c		5.	e
2.	b		6.	a
3.	h		7.	f
4.	g		8.	d

Key to Essay Questions

1. Here you will need to examine all of the personality studies (e.g., Neugarten's Kansas City Study, Costa & McCrae's Baltimore study [remember the "big five"], the Berkeley longitudinal studies, and Helson's Mills College study). Indicate what each study says about what does and does not change, then, based on the evidence presented, come to a conclusion about change over the life span.

2. To answer this question, you will need to address all of the theories presented about adult development (e.g., Erikson's, Levinson's, the life-events approach) to discuss their different positions on whether a crisis is experienced by all, some, or no adults. Be sure to address gender differences and cultural differences in answering this question.

Key to Scramblers

1. Robert McCrae: The "big five" personality factors remain relatively stable during the middle adult years
2. Ravenna Helson: Described an awareness of limitations and death as a midlife consciousness
3. Generativity: Adults' desire to leave a legacy of themselves to the next generation
4. Stagnation: Develops when individuals sense they have done nothing for the next generation
5. Novice phase: A transition at end of adolescence from dependence to independence
6. Contemporary life-events approach: Influence on development of life events depends on event & other factors
7. Cohort: A group of people born within the same period of time
8. Social clock: Timetable according to which individuals are expected to accomplish life's tasks
9. Big five factors of personality: Emotional stability, extraversion, openness, agreeableness, conscientiousness
10. Empty nest syndrome: Decrease in marital satisfaction after children leave home

Research Project 1: Restructuring Perceptions of Parents

This project will assist you in understanding the relationship between parents and their children across the life span. Recall from Chapter 17 that parents and their children (at all ages) do not typically have the same perception of the parent-child relationship. Develop a questionnaire to assess respondents' perceptions of their parents (feel free to participate yourself, as well). Some questions are used to introduce this exploration, and you may gather others from looking at the research studies discussed (i.e., Berquist, Greenberg, & Klaum, 1993; Josselson, 1996 [also look at her book, *Finding Herself: Pathways to Identity Development in Women*, 1987]; Labouvie-Vief, 1995, 1996); of course, you may develop your own questions. Gather demographic data, such as age, sex, cultural background, and other information you think will be important to understand your findings. Create a chart to assist you in assessing the similarities and differences in the ways that adolescents, early adults, and middle adults view their parents and their relationships with their parents. On the basis of your findings, answer the following questions:

1. What similarities did you notice among adolescents, early adults, and middle adults in terms of how they perceive their parents and their relationships with their parents?
2. What differences did you notice among adolescents, early adults, and middle adults in terms of how they perceive their parents and their relationships with their parents?
3. What patterns of development did you notice when comparing the three groups in terms of the material discussed in this chapter?
4. Were your observations consistent with what you might expect from the research described? Explain.
5. What might you conclude about the development of relationships between children and their parents based on your observations?

Research Project 2: Assessing the Social Clock

Figure 17.5 in the text presents a comparison of "Individuals' Conceptions of the Right Age for Major Life Events and Achievements: Late 1950s and Late 1970s." Using the questions in that figure, survey college students as well as other members of your family and community, being sure to record age and gender. Calculate and chart the percentage of male and female respondents who agree with the suggested times for those activities/events (look at the ages of your respondents to determine if there is any major difference from one age category to another—if there is, use that as an additional variable in your chart). Compare the responses with those given in the late '50s and late '70s.

Activity/Event	Appropriate Age Range	% Agreeing (late '50s study)		% Agreeing (late '70s study)		% Agreeing (current study)	
		Men	Women	Men	Women	Men	Women
Best age for man to marry							
Best age for woman to marry							
When most people should become grandparents							
Best age to finish school & go to work							
When men should settle on a career							
When most men hold their top job							
When most people should be ready to retire							
When a man has the most responsibilities							
When a man accomplishes the most							
The prime of life for a man							
When a woman has the most responsibilities							
When a woman accomplishes the most							

1. What similarities did you notice across the different studies?
2. What differences did you notice across the different studies?
3. What gender similarities and differences did you notice in all three time periods? What might you conclude about how men and women view activities/events within the context of social clocks?
4. What patterns did you notice when comparing the three time periods in terms of the material discussed in this chapter?
5. Were your observations consistent with what you might expect from the research described? Explain your response.
6. What might you conclude about changes in attitudes about social clocks and the time frame within which society believes certain activities or events must take place, based on your observations?

Personal Application Project 1: Reflecting on What You Learned

Consider what you read in Chapter 17, then answer the following questions:

1. What information in this chapter did you already know?
2. How can/do you use that information in your own life?
3. What information in this chapter was totally new to you?
4. How can you use that new information in your own life?
5. What information in this chapter was different from what you previously believed?
6. How was this information different?
7. How do you account for the differences between what you believed and what you learned in the chapter?
8. What is the most important thing you learned from reading this chapter?

Personal Application Project 2: Looking at Your Own Personality

The first section of this chapter presents a debate about whether personality traits over time remain relatively stable or change. Consider the various elements involved in each of the theories (e.g., Erikson's crisis of generativity versus stagnation, Levinson's seasons of life [see if you can apply this to females as well], Costa & McCrae's "big five," etc.) and illustrate how they do or do not describe your own experience. You can use the chart below to organize your data.

Theory	Concepts	Do or Do Not Apply	Discussion
Erik Erikson			
Daniel Levinson			
George Vaillant			
Bernice Neugarten			
Paul Costa & Robert McCrae			
John Clausen			
Ravenna Helson			

Internet Projects

Check out the McGraw-Hill web site for this text (http://www.mhhe.com/santrockld8). You'll find numerous activities there, in particular various quizzes, flash cards of key terms, and a challenging and fun crossword puzzle. Please note that all website addresses in this Study Guide have been checked and are correct at the time of publication, however, websites may be discontinued or addresses may change so when you search a given site it may no longer be viable. If that occurs, I apologize for the inconvenience, and would appreciate you notifying me so I could make appropriate revisions in future editions of this Study Guide.

Internet Project 1: The Sandwich Generation

The chapter briefly discusses the "sandwich" generation, i.e., middle-aged adults who are "sandwiched" between caring for their adolescent or younger children and their aging parents. Check out an excellent article written by Herbert G. Lingren and Jayne Decker that is available at the University of Nebraska's website: http://www.ianr.unl.edu/pubs/family/g1117.htm. After reviewing this article, reflect on how it adds to the information provided in the text.

1. What are the expectations of middle age? What information did you gather from the article that added to what you learned in our text?
2. Look at Figure 1 to look at "what our kids want/need," "what we want/need," and "what our parents want/need," then explain whether you think the term "sandwich" generation is an appropriate one?

3. Compare the developmental tasks of middle years in this article with those presented in Chapter 16 of the text. How can this information help you deal more effectively with midlife (and, possibly, with the midlife crisis)?

4. The authors offer several "solutions" for adults caught in this situation. Which ones do you think would be most useful for you? If you are currently in this situation, have you tried any of these? Have they worked? Are there people you know who could benefit from this information? (If so, please feel free to share it with them!)

Internet Project 2: To Change or Not to Change, That Is the Question

A major debate in the first sections of Chapter 17 deals with the stability versus the continuity of personality as we go through adulthood. Two of the researchers whose work was cited in the chapter have particularly excellent websites for you to visit. First, go to MIDMAC at http://midmac.med.harvard.edu/. There you will find Midlife Research (note that the research of Orville Gilbert Brim was discussed in the chapter). This site summarizes the Research Network on Successful Midlife Development and offers links to research, publications, bulletins, and other useful information. The second site is the Laboratory of Personality & Cognition—http://lpcwww.grc.nia.nih.gov. This is an NIH (National Institutes of Health) program, and is headed up by Paul T. Costa, Jr., whose work (with co-investigator Robert McCrae) was discussed at length in Chapter 17. Here you are able to find a chapter on personality research as well as some recent papers, some of which also relate to research presented in Chapter 17. After exploring both of these sites and some of the papers they offer, state your conclusions about the stability-change/continuity-discontinuity debate on personality in adulthood, and discuss your reasons for those conclusions.

Other Relevant Sites on the Internet

APA site

http://www.apa.org Particularly, you might want to go to http://www.apa.org/journals/psp/psp7961007.html for an intersting article titled "The Age of Anxiety? Birth Cohort Change in Anxiety and Neuroticism, 1952-1993," by Jean M. Twenge.

APS site

http://www.psychologicalscience.org/

American Association for Retired Persons (AARP)

http://www.aarp.org is the web site for AARP, an especially powerful organization that educates, lobbies, and provides services about and for persons age 50 and above.

ThirdAge

http://www.thirdage.com is a forum for adults that presents a wide range of topics for the lay person.

Web MD

http://www.webmd.com offers a wide variety of information for the medical profession and for consumers.

Chapter 18: Physical Development in Late Adulthood

Learning Objectives

1. Distinguish between life expectancy and life span, including mention of cross-cultural differences.
2. Elaborate on the characteristics associated with being a centenarian.
3. Describe the sex differences in longevity and what may account for them.
4. Be able to determine differences between the young old, the old old, and the oldest old.
5. Discuss the biological theories of aging.
6. Elaborate on the course of physical development in late adulthood and the changes that take place in the brain as we age.
7. Indicate the physical and sensory changes that occur in the older adult.
8. Discuss how sexual performance is impacted by aging.
9. Describe common health problems in late adulthood, and expound on the causes of death in older adults.
10. Discuss arthritis and osteoporosis, including the symptoms, causes, and possible treatments for each.
11. Describe the robust oldest old.
12. Discuss the role of exercise, nutrition, and weigh in late adulthood, as well as the vitamin controversy.
13. Explain care options for the elderly and ways to improve their care in the nursing home.
14. Describe the relationship between health-care providers and the older adult.

Chapter Outline

LONGEVITY
    Life Expectancy and Life Span
        Centenarians
        Sex Difference in Longevity
    The Young Old, the Old Old, and the Oldest Old
    Biological Theories of Aging
        Cellular Clock Theory
        Free Radical Theory
        Hormonal Stress Theory
THE COURSE OF PHYSICAL DEVELOPMENT IN LATE ADULTHOOD
    The Aging Brain
    Physical Appearance
    Sensory Development
    The Circulatory System
    The Respiratory System
    Sexuality
HEALTH
    Health Problems
        Causes of Death
        Arthritis
        Osteoporosis
        Accidents
    The Robust Oldest Old
    Exercise, Nutrition, and Weight
    Health Treatment
        Care Options

Self-Test A: Multiple Choice

1. In the Images of Life-Span Development section, "Learning to Age Successfully," the author relates a story about 85-year-old Sadie Halperin. To what does Sadie attribute her increased vitality?
   a. better medical treatment
   b. her state of mind
   c. improved nutrition
   d. exercise

2. With improvements in medicine, nutrition, exercise, and lifestyle, our:
   a. life span has increased.
   b. life expectancy has increased.
   c. life expectancy has stayed the same, but our lives are healthier.
   d. life expectancy has dropped, but the quality of life has improved.

3. Researchers in the New England Centenarian study have found _____ contributes to living a long life.
   a. lack of stress
   b. good genes
   c. the ability to cope successfully with stress
   d. a healthy lifestyle

4. Women outlive men for all of the following reasons EXCEPT:
   a. financial status.
   b. health attitudes.
   c. occupations.
   d. lifestyle.

5. The second X chromosome that women have appears to give them a health advantage over men in that it may:
   a. counteract the negative effects of free radicals.
   b. be associated with production of more antibodies to fight disease.
   c. offer greater resistance for dealing with stress.
   d. protect women against lung cancer, a leading cause of death in men.

6. Who would be classified as the "oldest old"?
   a. Methuselah, who is 78
   b. Eve, who is 83
   c. Noah, who is 88
   d. All three are among the oldest old

7. As more information is gathered concerning the life and abilities of individuals over age 85, a more _____ picture is beginning to emerge.
   a. optimistic
   b. homogeneous
   c. depressing
   d. psychopathic

8. All of the following are biological theories of aging EXCEPT the _____ theory.
   a. life-span
   b. cellular clock
   c. free-radical
   d. hormonal stress

9. Leonard Hayflick believes that cells can divide a maximum of about _____ times and that as we age, our cells become increasingly less capable of dividing.
   a. 25 to 50
   b. 50 to 65
   c. 75 to 80
   d. 80 to 90

10. A recent extension to Hayflick's cellular clock theory suggests that cells die because:
   a. they disintegrate over time.
   b. they become too large and are no longer able to sustain themselves, thus they explore and leave harmful wastes.
   c. the telomeres, or DNA sequences that cap the chromosomes, become shorter over time.
   d. the RNA in our bodies is programmed to stop sending nutrients to the cells over time.

11. The _____ theory of aging states that people age because inside their cells normal metabolism produces unstable oxygen molecules that ricochet around the cells, damaging DNA and other cellular structures.
   a. free-radical
   b. cellular clock
   c. hormonal stress
   d. life-span

12. Jeremy has read that by taking testosterone supplements he will maintain muscle and increase his energy and sex drive, so he is willing to pay the $100 each month for a testosterone patch. If 70-year-old Jeremy is aging normally, without any illnesses or unhealthful habits, we might expect his reputable doctor to:
   a. encourage him to use the patch because it will make life happier for Jeremy and his wife.
   b. discourage him from using the patch because at his age he should be slowing down his sex drive to maintain his health.
   c. discourage him from using the patch because it's unnecessary in terms of normal sex drive and can put him at risk for heart attack, cancer, or stroke.
   d. suggest a penile implant instead.

13. Suzman's (1997) survey found all of the following account for decline in disability among the elderly EXCEPT:
   a. exercise.
   b. not smoking.
   c. socioeconomic status.
   d. improvements in medical care.

14. In the aging brain, at least through the seventies, it appears that:
   a. dendritic growth compensates for loss of neurons.
   b. neural efficiency is compensated for by neural size.
   c. neural cells will grow to compensate for loss of myelin.
   d. increased neural transmitter production compensates for loss of neurons.

15. The study of nuns in Mankato, Minnesota (Snowden, 1995, 1997) has found all of the following EXCEPT:
   a. the onset of Alzheimer's disease symptoms can be delayed for years.
   b. stimulating the brain with mental exercises can increase the number of neurons in the brain.
   c. more educated people are less likely to develop symptoms of Alzheimer's disease.
   d. when areas of the brain are damaged by stroke, new message routes can be created.

16. All of the following are normal declines in vision due to aging EXCEPT:
   a. diminished tolerance for glare that reduces night vision.
   b. slower dark adaptation, taking longer to recover vision when going from light to dark areas.
   c. lower ability to detect events in the center of the visual field.
   d. reduction in the quality or intensity of light reaching the retina.

17. Rozee's eyes have cloudy, opaque areas in the lens that prevent light from passing through, causing her to have blurred vision. The visual problem she has is:
    a. macular degeneration.
    b. cataracts.
    c. glaucoma.
    d. presbyopia.

18. To help hearing-impaired adults, the text suggests:
    a. surgery on the inner ear.
    b. wearing a hearing aid in the more impaired ear.
    c. wearing two hearing aids balanced to correct each ear separately.
    d. asking individuals who speak to the hearing impaired person to speak in a loud, clear voice.

19. Eighty-year-old Ethel noticed she cut her foot, although she didn't feel any pain when she did it. Since it is normal for older adults to be less sensitive to pain, Ethel:
    a. should consider herself lucky it didn't hurt.
    b. shouldn't worry about it one way or another, just bandage her foot.
    c. should be concerned that while it may be "normal," it may also indicate some other underlying disease process.
    d. needs to be aware of this because not feeling pain may mask injury or illness that needs treatment.

20. Which of the following is NOT a change that normally takes place in the respiratory system between ages 20 and 80?
    a. Lung capacity drops 40 percent.
    b. Lungs lose elasticity.
    c. The chest expands.
    d. The diaphragm weakens.

21. Physiological changes that affect sexual behavior:
    a. are more prevalent in men than in women.
    b. are more prevalent in women than in men.
    c. cannot be corrected in men and therefore limit their sexual activity.
    d. cannot be corrected in women and therefore limit their sexual activity.

22. A study by Matthias et al. (1997) of more than 1,200 adults with a mean age of 77 found:
    a. over half of them had participated in sexual activity in the past month.
    b. two-thirds were satisfied with their current level of sexual activity.
    c. almost 75 percent of them had discontinued having sex within the past 5 years.
    d. the men were more sexually active than the women.

23. The most common chronic disorder in late adulthood is:
    a. hypertension.
    b. heart condition.
    c. diabetes.
    d. arthritis.

24. The chronic illness that puts the greatest limitation on work is:
    a. asthma.
    b. arthritis.
    c. a heart condition.
    d. diabetes.

25. The leading cause of death among the elderly is:
    a. heart disease.
    b. cancer.
    c. influenza.
    d. diabetes.

26. An aging disorder associated with calcium and vitamin D deficiencies, estrogen depletion, and lack of exercise is:
   a. arthritis.
   b. osteoporosis.
   c. pernicious anemia.
   d. depression.

27. To prevent osteoporosis, young and middle-aged women should do all of the following EXCEPT:
   a. subscribe to estrogen replacement therapy.
   b. eat foods rich in calcium.
   c. avoid smoking.
   d. avoid weight-lifting exercises.

28. Compared to younger persons, elderly adult accident victims are likely to spend more time in the hospital because:
   a. recovery is often complicated by mental depression.
   b. Medicare focuses mainly on long-term treatments.
   c. healing rates are slower in older adults.
   d. family members feel the older adult is safer in the hospital.

29. Edith is 82 years old. She walks a mile a day, exercises with 10-lb weights, can stoop, crouch, and kneel, and walks the two flights of stairs to her apartment rather than take the elevator. She would be considered among the _____ oldest old.
   a. majority of the
   b. robust
   c. exceptional
   d. typical

30. Blumenthal et al. (1989) found that older adults who were _____ experienced significant improvement in cardiovascular fitness.
   a. in a yoga class
   b. taught transcendental meditation
   c. on a weight-loss program
   d. in an aerobic exercise group

31. Older adults subscribing to a low-calorie diet:
   a. have been shown to live substantially longer than those who do not.
   b. are likely to die sooner than those who do not.
   c. should use caution, because not much is known about the long-term effects of low-calorie diets.
   d. should be on high-protein diets with vitamin supplements.

32. Vitamin supplements called antioxidants may affect health by counteracting effects of:
   a. white corpuscles.
   b. DNA changes.
   c. free radicals.
   d. cholesterol.

33. Approximately _____ % of adults 65 and over reside in nursing homes, compared with over _____ % of those over 85.
   a. 5/20
   b. 5/50
   c. 10/20
   d. 10/50

34. Alternatives to nursing homes include all of the following EXCEPT:
   a. home health care.
   b. day-care centers.
   c. long-term care facilities.
   d. preventive medicine clinics.

35. Rodin and Langer found that nursing home patients who were given some responsibility and control over their lives became:
   a. more difficult to manage.
   b. more likely to want to return home.
   c. healthier.
   d. happier, but lived no longer than those given no responsibility or self-control.

36. Researchers have found physicians are:
   a. more responsive to older patients.
   b. more responsive to younger patients.
   c. equally responsive to patients of both age groups.
   d. more responsive to those with more severe illnesses, despite their age.

231

Self-Test B: Matching

Match the following persons with the statement or theory that most closely reflects their perspective:

1.	Leonard Hayflick	a.	Showed that nursing home residents who controlled visits were healthier
2.	Judith Rodin	b.	Geriatric nurse says solutions to patient problems require expertise & patience
3.	Ellen Langer	c.	Says that perception of control may reduce stress & related hormones
4.	Richard Schultz	d.	First author to recommend scientific evaluation of diet & longevity
5.	Stanley Rapaport	e.	Believes there are biological clocks in our cells that cause us to age
6.	Francis Bacon	f.	Found that old brains rewired themselves to compensate for losses
7.	Rita Young	g.	Argues that it is important for the aged to understand that they can **choose** the way they think

Essay Questions

1. Your next door neighbor is an 87-year-old woman who knows you have been taking this class in life-span development. She confides in you that she feels she is slowing down and can't quite do the things she used to do. Also, she feels that none of her doctors takes the time to listen to her, they just say, "Rose, you're in great shape for a woman your age." Knowing she's an intelligent woman who has been a writer her entire life, what would you tell her about the aging process, how to keep healthy, and how to get the best possible medical assistance?

2. You have been asked by your local Rotary Club to design a program for their older members to help them stay in optimum health. What areas would you focus on, and what kinds of activities would you suggest for them?

Scramblers

Unscramble the following people or terms, then describe what they are known for (people) or define them (terms):

1. LNLEE GNEARL

_____

2. IDTUJH DINOR

_____

3. ILFE NPAS

_____

4. FIEL TCEANPXCYE

_____

5. LULLAERC LOKCC REOYHT

_____

6. ERFE-CIDALAR YTRHOE

_____

7. MONRAOLH SESTRS YRHTOE

_____

8. HRITRTIAS

_____

9. POOREOTSSISO

_____

10. ATRIRICESG

_____

Key to Self-Test A

1.	d	LO 1	13.	c	LO 6	25.	a	LO 9
2.	b	LO 1	14.	a	LO 6	26.	b	LO 10
3.	c	LO 2	15.	b	LO 6	27.	d	LO 10
4.	a	LO 3	16.	c	LO 7	28.	c	LO 10
5.	b	LO 3	17.	b	LO 7	29.	b	LO 11
6.	c	LO 4	18.	c	LO 7	30.	d	LO 12
7.	a	LO 4	19.	d	LO 7	31.	c	LO 12
8.	a	LO 5	20.	c	LO 7	32.	c	LO 12
9.	c	LO 5	21.	a	LO 8	33.	a	LO 13
10.	c	LO 5	22.	b	LO 8	34.	c	LO 13
11.	a	LO 5	23.	d	LO 9	35.	c	LO 13
12.	c	LO 6	24.	c	LO 9	36.	b	LO 14

Key to Self-Test B

1.	e	5.	f
2.	c	6.	d
3.	g	7.	b
4.	a		

Key to Essay Questions

1. To answer this question you would need to summarize everything in this chapter, including age changes in the brain, and in the sensory, circulatory, and respiratory systems, and you might also let her know there is no need to expect a reduction in her sexual activity; then let her know about the various health issues including the diseases that are common and what she can do to reduce her risk factors (e.g., estrogen replacement therapy, taking calcium, exercising), while letting her know what has and has not yet been determined about the use of supplements ("yes" on calcium and antioxidants, but either too little is known about some of the others or they pose potential risks). Finally, help her develop techniques to talk effectively with her physicians, pharmacist, and family members about her health needs and how to find the types of information and health care that are appropriate for her. Do be sure to let her know about the research by Langer, Rodin, and Schultz about the importance of maintaining control (or, at least, the perception of control) for living a longer, healthier life.

2. Here you would first need to address the basic issues of aging—what can be expected to change (e.g., vision, hearing) and what can be done to avoid problems (e.g., don't smoke, do exercise). Then discuss what kinds of things you believe (in light of this chapter) would be appropriate for helping seniors maintain a long, healthy life. Be sure to include exercise and nutrition as well as assertiveness training.

Key to Scramblers

1. Ellen Langer: Argues that it is important for elderly to understand they can **choose** the way they think
2. Judith Rodin: Believes that the perception of control can have a direct effect on the body
3. Life span: The maximum number of years an individual can live (120 for humans)
4. Life expectancy: The number of years that will probably be lived by the average person born in a given year
5. Cellular clock theory: Theory that the maximum number of times human cells can divide is about 70-80
6. Free-radical theory: States that people age because normal metabolism produces unstable oxygen molecules
7. Hormonal stress theory: Aging in the body's hormonal system may lower resilience to stress
8. Arthritis: Inflammation of the joints accompanied by pain, stiffness, & movement problems
9. Osteoporosis: Aging disorder involving extensive loss of bone tissue
10. Geriatrics: The branch of medicine dealing with the health problems of the aged

Research Project 1: The Nuns' Study

As our author notes, the Nuns' study is an intriguing investigation of Alzheimer's disease; it is one that I discuss with my students that offers great potential for understanding the disease and learning about its precursors and how to forestall its onset. Although space did not allow for a greater discussion of this study, you may wish to pursue it further because of the implications it may have in terms of prolonging mental acuity. To do so, you may wish to explore the research further by reading what David Snowden and others have written about his investigation so far—you can find articles in the library (see the Reference section of the text); check out the Internet; or even write to Professor Snowden at the University of Kentucky. Also, there are videotapes about this research—the one I use in my classes was from *Nightline* with Ted Koppel a few years back and is obtainable from ABC News (*Beating Alzheimer's—The Nuns' Gift*). One thing you will note as you delve further into this topic is that remaining active does not necessary **prevent** Alzheimer's, but it does appear to delay the onset of symptoms. What advantage do you see to that? Another thing you'll find is that early life experiences and abilities seem to be connected to later life lucidity, on the one hand, but on the other hand, keeping your mind and body challenged acts as a buffer. As you read more about this topic, consider what you have read in Chapter 18.

1. What did you notice in your reading about the Nuns' study that was consistent with what you read in the chapter?
2. What differences did you notice between your reading about the Nuns' study and what you read in the chapter? How would you explain those differences (if there were any)?
3. What patterns of development did you notice when learning more about the research on Alzheimer's in terms of the material discussed in this chapter?
4. What might you conclude about cognitive changes with age based on your reading?

Research Project 2: Issues in the Media

Consider the thoughts of the centenarians presented in the first section of this chapter. While you may not know anyone who is 100 years old or older, do your own interviews of elderly people you do know and compare them with the comments made by the five representatives of Segerberg's (1982) sample (i.e., Mary Butler, Elza Wynn, Anna Marie Robertson, Billy Red Fox, and Duran Baez).

1. What similarities did you notice when comparing the comments of the five people in Segerberg's sample? What similarities did you notice when comparing the comments of the people you interviewed with those from Segerberg's sample?
2. What differences did you notice when comparing the comments of the five people in Segerberg's sample? What differences did you notice when comparing the comments of the people you interviewed with those from Segerberg's sample?
3. What patterns of development did you notice when looking at the comments, both from Segerberg's study and from your own interviews, in terms of the material discussed in this chapter?
4. Were your observations consistent with what you might expect from the research described? Explain your response.
5. What might you conclude about development in old age based on your observations?

Personal Application Project 1: Reflecting on What You Learned

Consider what you read in Chapter 18, then answer the following questions:

1. What information in this chapter did you already know?
2. How can/do you use that information in your own life?
3. What information in this chapter was totally new to you?
4. How can you use that new information in your own life?
5. What information in this chapter was different from what you previously believed?
6. How was this information different?
7. How do you account for the differences between what you believed and what you learned in the chapter?
8. What is the most important thing you learned from reading this chapter?

Personal Application Project 2: Can You Live to Be 100?

Take the test in Figure 18.1 for predicting your longevity, noting the additional instructions in the introductory paragraph (e.g., if you are in your 50s or 60s add 10 years). Adding and subtracting the points in each category, determine your life expectancy total and compare it with the basic life expectancy (74 for males, 80 for females). Where do you rank? Give the test to family members and friends to see where they rank. How does your score compare with theirs and with the scores of your classmates? What steps could you take at this point in your life to extend your life expectancy?

Internet Projects

Check out the McGraw-Hill web site for this text (http://www.mhhe.com/santrockld8). You'll find numerous activities there, in particular various quizzes, flash cards of key terms, and a challenging and fun crossword puzzle. Please note that all website addresses in this Study Guide have been checked and are correct at the time of publication, however, websites may be discontinued or addresses may change so when you search a given site it may no longer be viable. If that occurs, I apologize for the inconvenience, and would appreciate you notifying me so I could make appropriate revisions in future editions of this Study Guide.

Internet Project 1: Check Out the Biological Theories of Aging

There are a host of websites that deal with aging. One that offers particularly useful and up-to-date information can be found at http://www.healthandage.com/positivelifestyles/afar/index.htm. Here you can find the American Federation for Aging Research. This site asks questions such as, "How and why do we age?" "Are the answers in our genes?" "Can antioxidants prevent cell damage, disease, and aging?" "How do we age?" and "Can cutting calories increase longevity?" Explore the many links at this site, then answer the questions posed.

1. What did you learn that supplemented the information in Chapter 18?
2. Was there anything you learned that was different from the information contained in the text? How would you explain the differences (if any)?
3. What were your feelings about aging before you read the chapter? What were your feelings about aging before you checked out this website?
4. Did your exploration of these links make you more or less concerned about your own aging or the aging of your loved ones? Or did this information not change your feelings?
5. Having read Chapter 18 and explored the links on this site, how might you change your own lifestyle to reduce risk factors for poor health and shortened longevity? What is the first step you might take?
6. Do you think it would be worth changing your lifestyle to live a longer, healthier life? Explain your response.

Internet Project 2: Research on Aging

Perhaps one of the best sites on the web to find information about aging is the National Institute of Aging, which is one of the NIH (National Institutes of Health) programs sponsored by the federal government. Go to the NIA website at http://www.nih.gov.nia and do a search for "anti-aging." Three areas of particular interest with respect to Chapter 18 cover the use of supplements to prevent aging (the caution here is to use caution!), searching for the secrets of aging (which addresses topics in the first part of the chapter), and promoting longer, healthier lives. Check out these topics (and any others you find of particular interest) and compare what you read with the briefer versions in the text. Personally, I find these articles exciting and positive about our future as we get older—how did you react?

Other Relevant Sites on the Internet

APA site
http://www.apa.org

APS site
http://www.psychologicalscience.org/

American Academy of Anti-Aging Medicine (A4M)
http://www.aaaam.com is (will be?) the website for the physicians and scientists of the A4M, who "are committed to the belief that aging is not inevitable." Unfortunately, at the time of writing this Study Guide the site is not yet working—hopefully it will be up and running by the time of publication (or at least by the time you get to Chapter 18!).

American Association for Retired Persons (AARP)
http://www.aarp.org is the web site for AARP, an especially powerful organization that educates, lobbies, and provides services about and for persons age 50 and above.

Intelihealth
http://www.intelihealth.com/IH/ihtIH offers health information from a variety of sources, including Harvard Medical School. Feel free to search the site for any of the topics covered in this chapter (and others).

ThirdAge
http://www.thirdage.com is a forum for adults that presents a wide range of topics for the lay person.

Web MD
http://www.webmd.com offers a wide variety of information for the medical profession and for consumers.

Chapter 19: Cognitive Development in Late Adulthood

Learning Objectives

1. Explain the multidimensional, multidirectional nature of change in cognitive functioning.
2. Discuss the different types of memory, memory changes, and wisdom.
3. Explain the relationship to cognitive functioning of education, work, and health.
4. Elaborate on the training of cognitive skills.
5. Explain the work trends among older adults.
6. Discuss retirement in the United States and in other countries, including factors that aid adjustment to retirement.
7. Describe the nature of mental disorders in older adults, being sure to mention the predictors of and treatment for depression.
8. Discuss the different types of dementia, including their causes, symptoms, and treatments.
9. Identify the effects of fear of victimization, crime, and elder maltreatment on older adults.
10. Expound on ways in which society can meet the mental health needs of older adults.
11. Discuss the role of religion in late adulthood.

Chapter Outline

COGNITIVE FUNCTIONING IN OLDER ADULTS
>   The Multidimentional, Multidirectional Nature of Cognition
>>   Cognitive Mechanics and Cognitive Pragmatics
>>   Sensory/Motor and Speed-of-Processing Dimensions
>>   Memory
>>   Wisdom
>   Education, Work, and Health: Links to Cognitive Functioning
>   Use It or Lose It
>   Training Cognitive Skills

WORK AND RETIREMENT
>   Work
>   Retirement in the United States and Other Countries
>   Adjustment to Retirement

THE MENTAL HEALTH OF OLDER ADULTS
>   The Nature of Mental Health in Older Adults
>   Depression
>   Dementia and Alzheimer's Disease
>   Fear of Victimization, Crime, and Elder Maltreatment
>   Meeting the Mental Health Needs of Older Adults

RELIGION IN LATE ADULTHOOD

Self-Test A: Multiple Choice

1. According to Paul Baltes, cognitive _____ are the culture-based software programs of the mind.
   a. mechanics
   b. pragmatics
   c. functionings
   d. structures

2. In older adulthood:
   a. cognitive pragmatics are likely to improve with aging.
   b. cognitive mechanics are likely to improve with aging.
   c. cognitive pragmatics and cognitive mechanics are both likely to improve with aging.
   d. cognitive pragmatics and cognitive mechanics are both likely to decline with aging.

3. In the Berlin study of aging, the key factors accounting for age differences in intelligence were:
   a. visual and auditory acuity.
   b. amount of early education.
   c. quality of early education.
   d. experience with taking tests.

4. In a study of younger and older typists, Salthouse (1984) found that:
   a. younger typists consistently outperformed the older typists.
   b. older typists consistently outperformed the younger typists.
   c. when older typists could look ahead, they typed as fast as younger typists.
   d. when the number of characters that the typists could look ahead at was limited, the younger typists slowed considerably.

5. The noncognitive factors that have been studied in relation to memory and aging include all of the following EXCEPT:
   a. health.
   b. intelligence.
   c. education.
   d. socioeconomic factors.

6. Evelyn, who is 105 years old, is active in her community and continues to play the piano at social gatherings. She loves to tell stories about when she was a little girl. Based on the research on memory and aging, we could expect that:
   a. she believes her memory to be accurate, but in reality it has become increasingly inaccurate as she has aged.
   b. her memory of the events is accurate, and she is telling the stories as they happened.
   c. her memory of the events is accurate, but she is probably adding a lot to her stories that didn't happen.
   d. she can no longer remember these events very well, but she wants to entertain her audience, so she pretends her memory is good.

7. As we proceed into late adulthood, we can normally expect the LEAST amount of decline in which aspect of memory?
   a. episodic memory
   b. working memory
   c. semantic memory
   d. perceptual speed

8. Older adults are most likely to forget:
   a. the bottom items on a written list of items they need from the hardware store.
   b. how to drive a car.
   c. what items they wanted to buy at a grocery store.
   d. how to play golf.

9. Which of the following statements about memory and aging is FALSE?
   a. Positive or negative beliefs about one's memory skills are related to actual memory performance.
   b. Health, education, and socioeconomic status can influence an older adult's performance on memory tasks.
   c. Research has found that maintaining good health can eliminate memory decline.
   d. Using familiar tasks in research reduces age decrements in memory.

10. Which task would require wisdom?
    a. remembering a grocery list
    b. braking when a pedestrian steps out in front of your car
    c. helping a son keep his marriage from falling apart
    d. helping a granddaughter with her algebra homework

11. The research on wisdom suggests:
    a. wisdom involves the ability to use abstract ideas.
    b. although not all old people are wise, generally speaking wisdom comes with age.
    c. older adults who demonstrate wisdom are faster at processing ideas than those who are less wise.
    d. recent research suggests that there are no age differences in wisdom.

12. Which of the following characteristics is positively correlated with scores on intelligence tests?
    a. introversion
    b. well-rounded personality
    c. job experience
    d. educational experience

13. The text has noted that older adults return to school because they:
    a. become obsolete due to technological changes.
    b. want to learn more about aging.
    c. have a desire to learn more effective cognitive and social-coping skills.
    d. all of the above.

14. Recent research found substantive complex work to be linked with _____ older adults.
    a. higher intellectual functioning in
    b. more accidents in the workplace for
    c. forced retirement of
    d. frustration and inability to cope in

15. The cognitive dropoffs that are linked to poor health in the elderly:
    a. are the causative factors of the poor health.
    b. appear to be the direct result of the poor health.
    c. are probably the result of lifestyle behaviors such as inactivity and stress.
    d. appear to be caused by genetic factors.

16. Clarkson-Smith and Hartley (1989), in their study of the effects of exercise on cognitive functioning, found that:
    a. aerobic exercise is related to improved cognitive functioning.
    b. yoga is related to improved cognitive functioning.
    c. stretching exercises are related to improved cognitive functioning.
    d. any type of exercise (i.e., aerobic, yoga, stretching) shows greater cognitive benefits for older people than for those who are younger.

17. The terminal drop hypothesis claims that death is preceded by a decrease in:
    a. physical functioning.
    b. cognitive functioning.
    c. social interaction.
    d. emotional attachment.

18. The mnemonic technique being used when an item to be remembered is paired with a location is:
    a. chunking.
    b. story-telling.
    c. rehearsing.
    d. the method of loci.

19. Which statement is most accurate concerning cognitive skills in the elderly?
    a. Training has little effect on slowing declines.
    b. An increasing number of developmentalists have found the elderly can be retrained.
    c. Memory is the only cognitive skill that can be improved by training.
    d. A shift from factual knowledge to wisdom occurs in most elderly adults.

20. Which of the following is NOT true when older workers are compared with younger workers?
    a. Older workers have better attendance records.
    b. Older workers have fewer accidents.
    c. Older workers have more disabling injuries.
    d. Older workers are more productive.

21. The main reason given in a recent survey of "baby boomers" for why they expect to work during the retirement years is:
    a. for interest or enjoyment.
    b. they need the income.
    c. they want to start a new business.
    d. they want to try a different field of work.

22. The 1986 United States ban on any type of age-related mandatory retirement would not apply to:
    a. Harpo, the president of a Fortune-500 company.
    b. Groucho, a college professor.
    c. Chico, a mail carrier.
    d. Zeppo, a fire fighter.

23. In Europe:
    a. many of the capitalist countries are attempting to encourage early retirement, while the former Communist countries are trying to encourage older adults to continue working.
    b. many of the former Communist countries are attempting to encourage early retirement, while the capitalist countries are trying to encourage older adults to continue working.
    c. many capitalist and former Communist countries are attempting to encourage early retirement.
    d. many capitalist and former Communist countries are attempting to encourage older adults to continue working.

24. Which retiree would be expected to have the POOREST adjustment to retirement?
    a. Zachary, a Ph.D. in sociology, who has been saving for retirement for the past 30 years
    b. Yoel, a widower who has worked in a minimum-wage construction job since high school graduation
    c. Xanath, an interior decorator who has decided to move to France to attend art school at the Sorbonne
    d. Wilma, a widow who volunteers as a guide at the art museum

25. All of the following individuals are exhibiting a symptom of major depression EXCEPT:
    a. Ariel, who is making self-derogatory comments.
    b. Belle, who has recurring nightmares.
    c. Cathy, who is not eating.
    d. Darlene, who is completely unmotivated.

26. Who is most likely to commit suicide?
    a. Gerard, a widower who lives alone and is in poor health
    b. Harriet, a widow who lives alone and is in poor health
    c. Isaac, who has been arguing with his wife for 50 years
    d. Judith, who has been arguing with her husband for 50 years

27. _____ is a progressive, irreversible disorder characterized by gradual deterioration of memory, reasoning, language, and eventually physical functioning.
    a. Cognitive dementia
    b. Alzheimer's disease
    c. Multi-infarct dementia
    d. Schizophrenia

28. In the 1970s, a deficiency of acetylcholine, which plays an important part in memory, was discovered to occur in:
    a. Parkinson's disease.
    b. Alzheimer's disease.
    c. arteriosclerosis.
    d. multi-infarct dementia.

29. Depression has been reported in _____ percent of family caregivers for Alzheimer's patients.
    a. 10
    b. 25
    c. 35
    d. 50

30. How is the clinical picture of multi-infarct dementia different from that of Alzheimer's?
    a. There is a faster decline with multi-infarct dementia.
    b. With treatment, some Alzheimer's patients have been able to slow or reverse their disease; this is not so with multi-infarct dementia.
    c. Individuals with multi-infarct dementia often recover, while those with Alzheimer's don't.
    d. A diagnosis can only be made after death when an autopsy of the brain shows either obstructed blood vessels in a patient with multi-infarct dementia or plaques and tangles in the Alzheimer's patient.

31. Parkinson's disease is triggered by a reduction in production of the neurotransmitter:
    a. L-dopa.
    b. serotonin.
    c. acetylcholine.
    d. dopamine.

32. Older adults may feel more vulnerable to crime due to:
    a. physical declines.
    b. inability to crime-proof their homes.
    c. the fact that most neighborhoods they live in have deteriorated and become high-crime areas.
    d. large amounts of cash kept at home due to their general distrust of banks.

33. Elder maltreatment is primarily carried out by:
    a. family members.
    b. residential care workers.
    c. unknown assailants.
    d. in-home health care workers.

34. When compared with younger adults, adults over the age of 65 receive _____ of psychological services.
    a. more than their share
    b. less than their share
    c. about the same amount
    d. substantially more than their share

35. Psychotherapists have been accused of failing to accept many older adult clients because:
    a. they believe the prognosis for the older adult is poor.
    b. fewer techniques for treating mental problems among older adults exist.
    c. older clients, compared to younger clients, are less likely to pay the therapists for services rendered.
    d. older clients typically forget their appointments.

36. Margaret Gatz suggests a step that should be taken in order for the current health-care system to meet the needs of older adults with mental disorders is to:
    a. allow physicians to provide prescriptions over the phone.
    b. consider limiting the types of psychological care covered by Medicare.
    c. create elder care centers in the workplace.
    d. provide better education for the elderly on how they can benefit from therapy.

37. As noted in the text, religion can provide important psychological needs in older adults, including all of the following EXCEPT:
    a. assistance in finding and maintaining a sense of meaningfulness and significance in life.
    b. the ability to accept impending death and the inevitable losses of old age.
    c. social activities and social support.
    d. assistance with psychological problems, such as depression.

38. Which of the following would be most consistent with the research on religion and aging?
    a. Rivka, an 87-year-old widow who considers her religious faith to be extremely significant in her life, expresses a sense of well-being.
    b. Avram, a 75-year-old man who practices his religion faithfully, lacks a sense of satisfaction with his life.
    c. Malka, an 88-year-old housewife who has begun to doubt whether there is a god, is satisfied with her life as it is.
    d. Mort, an 80-year-old retiree who no longer practices his faith, expresses a sense of satisfaction with his life.

Self-Test B: Matching

Match the following persons with the statement or theory that most closely reflects their perspective:

1. Paul Baltes
2. K. Warner Schaie
3. Sherry Willis
4. Alois Alzheimer
5. Margaret Gatz
6. Marilyn Albert
7. James House

a. Mental activities like reading & doing crossword puzzles benefit cognitive skills
b. First diagnosed a form of dementia characterized by tangles and plaques
c. Crusader for better mental health treatment of the elderly
d. Believes middle-aged workers want less paid work, older adults want more
e. Concluded that some diseases are linked to cognitive dropoff
f. Has shown that older adults can be trained to improve their memory
g. Distinguished aspects of aging mind that decline from those that stay stable

Essay Questions

1. Your parents have started worrying about getting older and the effect that will have on their ability to take care of themselves and retain their cognitive functioning. Already they notice that they are forgetting more than they did even a year or two ago. What can you tell them about cognitive changes in late adulthood and how best to hold onto their mental faculties?

2. Your mother is CEO of a large corporation that offers an excellent retirement package. However, after evaluating a survey conducted of the employees, she is now concerned that relatively few employees have made any plans for their retirement. Because you are taking this life-span development class, she has asked you to address her employees about retirement, their need to plan for the future (including both continuing work and retirement), and what they can expect once they do decide to retire. What will you tell them?

Scramblers

Unscramble the following people or terms, then describe what they are known for (people) or define them (terms):

1. DEDRAF NCHAALRBD-SFLEID

_____

2. RERHYS LILIWS

_____

3. NIGTIOVCE CHNAEMCIS

_____

4. OSDPICIE MOERYM

_____

5. NAMTEISC YMREOM

_____

6. DSOIMW

_____

7. MIRNEALT ORPD TOHYPSHEIS

_____

8. MOENIMCNS

_____

9. ILCPIXTE EMOYRM

_____

10. LPIMICTI YMREOM

_____

Key to Self-Test A

1.	b	LO 1	14.	a	LO 3	27.	b	LO 8
2.	a	LO 1	15.	c	LO 3	28.	b	LO 8
3.	a	LO 1	16.	a	LO 3	29.	d	LO 8
4.	c	LO 1	17.	b	LO 3	30.	c	LO 8
5.	b	LO 2	18.	d	LO 4	31.	d	LO 8
6.	a	LO 2	19.	b	LO 4	32.	a	LO 9
7.	c	LO 2	20.	c	LO 5	33.	a	LO 9
8.	c	LO 2	21.	a	LO 5	34.	b	LO 10
9.	c	LO 2	22.	d	LO 6	35.	a	LO 10
10.	c	LO 2	23.	c	LO 6	36.	d	LO 10
11.	d	LO 2	24.	b	LO 6	37.	d	LO 11
12.	d	LO 3	25.	b	LO 7	38.	a	LO 11
13.	d	LO 3	26.	a	LO 7			

Key to Self-Test B

1.	g		5.	c
2.	e		6.	a
3.	f		7.	d
4.	b			

Key to Essay Questions

1. To answer this question, you will need to discuss the types of decline that might be expected (e.g., Paul Baltes' research with cognitive mechanics versus cognitive pragmatics) and what would affect whether a decline is or is not seen. Also address the issues of sensory/motor and speed of processing, and what has been concluded about the various memory systems (e.g., declines are seen in episodic and working memory, less so in semantic memory); the relationship between health and cognitive aging; and look at the different factors involved in the terminal drop hypothesis. Be sure to underscore how teaching memory strategies (e.g., mnemonics) and retraining, as well as keeping mentally and physically active have a positive effect on cognitive processes. You might end with some discussion of the role that spirituality plays in life satisfaction and sense of well-being.

2. First you would need to address changes in work patterns since the turn of the century, and look at how many older adults are not continuing to work either full-time or part-time, noting that as the Age Discrimination Act now stands, unless there is an issue of safety (e.g., fire or police departments), employers are prohibited form firing older workers. Address the issue of who adjusts best to retirement, pointing out ways to retain their sense of control and self-determination, which are so important for their continued health and well-being—something they are sure to want when they finally have time to enjoy life.

Key to Scramblers

1. Fredda Blanchard-Fields: Concluded that older adults' competency is most evident in everyday situations
2. Sherry Willis: Has shown that older adults can be trained to improve their memory
3. Cognitive mechanics: The "hardware" of the mind; involve speed & accuracy of cognitive processes
4. Episodic memory: Retention of information about the where & when of life's happenings
5. Semantic memory: Knowledge about the world, e.g., fields of expertise, academic & everyday knowledge
6. Wisdom: Expert knowledge about life's practical aspects that permits excellent judgment
7. Terminal drop hypothesis: The hypothesis that death is preceded by a decrease in cognitive functioning
8. Mnemonics: Techniques designed to make memory more efficient
9. Explicit memory: Memory of facts & experiences that individuals consciously know & can state
10. Implicit memory: Memory without conscious recollections; automatic skills & routine procedures

Research Project 1: Retirement Planning

First, consider your own present situation with regard to career planning and retirement planning in light of the material presented in the text. Then, interview people of different ages, asking them about the type of job they currently hold or if they are currently retired, the type of career path they see for themselves or they followed while employed, the plans they have made for their retirement (whether still working or retired), and what they expect they will be doing or expected they would be doing upon retirement. For those who are already retired, ask what they are currently doing with their time and if that is consistent with what they anticipated. Look, too, at the factors that predict good adjustment to retirement (e.g., good health, adequate income, better education, support system, flexibility). Based on what you learn from these interviews, chart your findings in a way that would make it clear to understand the relevant factors and any progressive steps you've noticed for adjusting well to retirement. Were your findings consistent with what you might expect from the text (e.g., people who are further away from retirement have not yet begun to plan)? What have your learned in terms of your own retirement plans from doing this?

1. What similarities did you notice among your respondents in terms of how they have planned for retirement? Was age a predictive variable?
2. What differences did you notice among your respondents in terms of how they have planned for retirement? Was age a predictive variable?
3. What patterns of development did you notice when looking at people's retirement plans in terms of the material discussed in this chapter?
4. How did personal factors (e.g., personality traits, support system, health) affect people's retirement plans in terms of the material discussed in this chapter?
5. Were your observations consistent with what you might expect from the research described? Explain your response.
6. What might you conclude about retirement planning based on your observations?

Research Project 2: Maintaining a Challenging Life in Old Age

Visit local senior centers, including nursing homes, senior day care, and centers for active older adults. Notice the people who are active and involved as compared with those who seem isolated and withdrawn. Get permission to interview some of these elderly people—those who are active as well as those who are more isolated. Determine from them what it is that they believe keeps them active or withdrawn, involved or isolated, happy or unhappy, etc. Note what the text says about keeping mentally active, staying physically healthy, reducing cognitive decline, adapting to work and retirement, maintaining good mental health, and having an interest in religion or the meaning of life. Combining what you find from these observations and interviews with the information in the text, design two programs: (1) one to help younger adults develop the types of skills they will need to remain challenged and happy with their lives; and (2) one to help older adults maximize and enjoy their lives by remaining as active and involved as their health allows.

1. While interviewing your respondents, did you notice that some of the people who have a sense of well-being may have more physical handicaps and chronic health problems than some who seem unhappy? What would account for this?
2. What part does religion play in your respondents' sense of well-being and satisfaction with life?
3. Is what you learned from these interviews consistent with what you read in the text? Explain your response.
4. What might you conclude about maintaining a challenging life in old age based on your observations?

Personal Application Project 1: Reflecting on What You Learned

Consider what you read in Chapter 19, then answer the following questions:

1. What information in this chapter did you already know?
2. How can/do you use that information in your own life?
3. What information in this chapter was totally new to you?
4. How can you use that new information in your own life?
5. What information in this chapter was different from what you previously believed?
6. How was this information different?
7. How do you account for the differences between what you believed and what you learned in the chapter?
8. What is the most important thing you learned from reading this chapter?

Personal Application Project 2: Consider Your Own Development

Chapter 19 presents many factors relevant to healthy cognitive development in later years. Evaluate these factors in your own life to assess whether you are currently engaging in activities that are likely to promote a satisfying later life for you (and what you are doing), what aspect of your life would be affected, and if there are any changes you might consider making to offer the greatest opportunities for enjoying your later years.

Aspect of Your Self	Current Status & Current Activities	Aspect of Life Affected	Changes to Enhance Later Years
Education/Learning/Training			
Work			
Health (Exercise, Nutrition, etc.)			
Use/Disuse			
Retirement Plans (Financial, Social, etc.)			
Mental Health			
Safety Needs			
Spiritual Self			
Other (describe)			

1. After completing the chart, what aspects of your current life do you see as leading toward satisfying later years? Explain how these aspects will help.
2. After completing the chart, what aspects of your current life do you see as needing change in order to provide you with the optimum satisfaction in later years? What specific changes do you plan to make?
3. You may see that making some changes in your life right now would help promote a more satisfying life as you get older, but you choose not to make those changes. If that's the case, what is holding you back from making the changes? What might motivate you to make changes?
4. What have you learned about yourself by doing this project?

Internet Projects

Check out the McGraw-Hill web site for this text (http://www.mhhe.com/santrockld8). You'll find numerous activities there, in particular various quizzes, flash cards of key terms, and a challenging and fun crossword puzzle. Please note that all website addresses in this Study Guide have been checked and are correct at the time of publication, however, websites may be discontinued or addresses may change so when you search a given site it may no longer be viable. If that occurs, I apologize for the inconvenience, and would appreciate you notifying me so I could make appropriate revisions in future editions of this Study Guide.

Internet Project 1: Dealing with Alzheimer's Disease

There are many sites on the Internet that deal with the subject of Alzheimer's. One that presents a diverse spectrum of offerings is the Mayo Clinic site, http://mayoclinic.com. If you have someone close to you who is affected by this disease, you are likely to want to explore all of the links. From a researcher's point of view, though, two articles are of particular interest (hopefully these will still be up at time of publication of this Study Guide!): "The Genetics Behind Alzheimer's" and "Why Does It Take So Long? Clinical Trials."

1. Based on what you have read in these articles, how would you describe the current state of research on the origins, management, treatment, and possible cure of Alzheimer's disease (looking at some of the other articles might help here, too).
2. Why do you think researchers take so long to put a drug on the market? What are some of the obstacles they face?
3. When a disease is as devastating as Alzheimer's, do you think it's better to go ahead and put a promising drug on the market, or wait until it has been thoroughly tested? Explain your response.
4. Are there any steps a person could take to reduce the risk of getting Alzheimer's disease, or at least delaying the onset of symptoms?
5. By the time Alzheimer's might pose a problem for you personally, do you believe that there will be effective ways to treat this disease? To cure it? To prevent it? Explain your response.

Internet Project 2: Work and Retirement in the Later Years

Go to the Intelihealth website, http://www.intelihealth.com, then click on the Seniors Health link at the top menu bar. Look for articles on employment and retirement, such as "Age Discrimination: A Pervasive and Damaging Influence" by the National Institute on Aging, and "Adjusting to Retirement." Think about your own plans for continuing to work or deciding to retire.

1. What can you learn from articles such as these that would help you make that decision?
2. Do you think that age bias continues to exist despite passage in 1967 of the Age Discrimination in Employment Act (ADEA)? Whom does that act protect?
3. How easy do you think it is to bring an action against a current or potential employer for age discrimination?
4. In the event you decide to continue working as you get older, what plans would you need to make?
5. Should you decide to retire, what advice did you find that will help optimize your retirement so you can enjoy your later years? If you were going to give advice to a young person (adolescent or early adult), what would you tell them?

Other Relevant Sites on the Internet

APA site
http://www.apa.org

APS site
http://www.psychologicalscience.org/

American Academy of Anti-Aging Medicine (A4M)
http://www.aaaam.com is (will be?) the website for the physicians and scientists of the A4M, who "are committed to the belief that aging is not inevitable." Unfortunately, at the time of writing this Study Guide the site is not yet working–hopefully it will be up and running by the time of publication (or at least by the time you get to this chapter).

American Association for Retired Persons (AARP)
http://www.aarp.org is the web site for AARP, an especially powerful organization that educates, lobbies, and provides services about and for persons age 50 and above.

CBS Healthwatch
http://healthwatch.medscape.com/medscape/p/gcommunity/ghome.asp provides information on a wide range of health topics, as well as many other resources, such as a drug directory, self-care and first aid tips, and a medical dictionary.

Cooper Wellness
http://www.cooperwellness.com is the website of Dr. Kenneth Cooper, who notes "It is easier to maintain good health through proper exercise, diet, and emotional balance than to regain it once it is lost."

Intelihealth
http://www.intelihealth.com/IH/ihtIH offers health information from a variety of sources, including Harvard Medical School. Feel free to search the site for any of the topics covered in this chapter (and others). (Although this site is suggested in Internet Project 2 above, it is also an excellent resource for just about any other topic on senior health, not just on issues of employment, so check it out for other topics, such as depression, wellness, or any of the others discussed in this chapter.)

ThirdAge
http://www.thirdage.com is a forum for adults that presents a wide range of topics for the lay person.

Web MD
http://www.webmd.com offers a wide variety of information for the medical profession and for consumers.

Chapter 20: Socioemotional Development in Late Adulthood

Learning Objectives

1. Discuss Erikson's eighth stage of psychosocial development and Robert Peck's reworking of this final stage.
2. Explain the life review process.
3. Elaborate on the four theories of socioemotional development.
4. Discuss the stereotyping of older adults.
5. Indicate the policy issues we face in an aging society.
6. Discuss how income changes for the elderly.
7. Discuss the living arrangements of the elderly.
8. Describe the aging couple, including marriage, dating, and sexuality.
9. Explore aspects of grandparenting such as their satisfaction, their roles and styles, and changing characteristics.
10. Describe how friendship changes as we grow old.
11. Elaborate on the importance of social support and social integration for older adults.
12. Explain the roles of ethnicity, gender, and culture in aging.
13. Describe the factors associated with holding a high position in a culture.
14. Expound on the factors related to successful aging.

Chapter Outline

THEORIES OF SOCIOEMOTIONAL DEVELOPMENT
    Erikson's Theory
        Peck's Reworking of Erikson's Final Stage
        Life Review
    Disengagement Theory
    Activity Theory
    Socioemotional Selectivity Theory
    Selective Optimization with Compensation Theory
OLDER ADULTS IN SOCIETY
    Stereotyping Older Adults
    Policy Issues in an Aging Society
    Income
    Living Arrangements
FAMILIES AND SOCIAL RELATIONSHIPS
    The Aging Couple
    Grandparenting
        Satisfaction with Grandparenting
        Grandparenting Roles and Styles
        The Changing Profile of Grandparenting
    Friendship
    Social Support and Social Integration
ETHNICITY, GENDER, AND CULTURE
    Ethnicity and Gender
    Culture
SUCCESSFUL AGING

Self-Test A: Multiple Choice

1. Erik Erikson believed that which final life-cycle stage characterizes late adulthood?
   a. integrity versus despair
   b. trust versus mistrust
   c. generativity versus stagnation
   d. intimacy versus isolation

2. Older adults who have derived part of their identity from their physical appearance are going to have the most difficult time with Peck's _____ developmental stage.
   a. differentiation versus role preoccupation
   b. ego transcendence versus ego preoccupation
   c. keeping the meaning versus rigidity
   d. body transcendence versus body preoccupation

3. Which of the following developmental tasks, according to Robert Peck (1968), requires older adults to face and accept the reality of death and the value of their lives?
   a. life review versus life satisfaction
   b. differentiation versus role preoccupation
   c. body transcendence versus body preoccupation
   d. ego transcendence versus ego preoccupation

4. Which is the LEAST likely outcome of life review?
   a. increased fear of death
   b. the discovery of the meaning of one's life
   c. a new sense of self
   d. an opportunity to share insights with significant others

5. Those who adopt a disengagement theory of aging believe that:
   a. as older adults slow down, they gradually withdraw from society.
   b. the more active adults are, the less likely they will age.
   c. the more active adults are, the more satisfied they will be.
   d. reduced social interaction leads to decreased satisfaction with life.

6. When Rosaria sold her business and retired, she gradually became less active and began to withdraw from society. This is an example of the _____ theory of aging.
   a. activity
   b. life review
   c. life satisfaction
   d. disengagement

7. Omar, an older retired adult who maintains his interest in friends, gold, and the stock market, illustrates which theory of aging?
   a. engagement
   b. disengagement
   c. activity
   d. social construction

8. Activity theory holds that when one of an older person's roles is taken away, the individual should:
   a. withdraw from society.
   b. become self-preoccupied.
   c. lessen emotional ties with others.
   d. find a replacement role.

9. Socioemotional selectivity theory argues that older adults deliberately withdraw from social contact with:
   a. individuals peripheral to their lives.
   b. close friends.
   c. family members.
   d. all but a few close family members and health-care professionals.

10. According to socioemotional selectivity theory, older adults narrow their social circles:
    a. because they are preparing for death.
    b. to have social partners who satisfy their emotional needs.
    c. because it is more difficult for them to maintain large social networks.
    d. as they become increasingly depressed.

11. Research by Kasser and Ryan (1999) assessing the emotional well-being of older adults in nursing homes found that _____ is linked with overall well-being.
    a. emotional quality
    b. number of the residents' social contacts
    c. education
    d. activity level

12. According to the optimization component of the selective optimization with compensation model, a 70-year-old secretary who complains about her poor eyesight interfering with her proofreading skills should:
    a. use positive affirmations to remind herself of her excellent skills in the past.
    b. just accept the fact that she cannot perform the way she used to.
    c. practice grammar and spell-checking during her off-time.
    d. quit her job.

13. In a cross-sectional study of the personal life investments of adults, the most important personal investment for 85 to 105-year-olds was their:
    a. family.
    b. independence.
    c. friends.
    d. health.

14. _____ is a term that is defined as prejudice against others because of their age, especially prejudice against older adults.
    a. Scapegoating
    b. Ageism
    c. The generation gap
    d. Senility

15. All of the following are examples of ageism EXCEPT:
    a. not being hired for a new job.
    b. when older couples holding hands are labeled as "cute" and "adorable."
    c. when older adults are asked to serve as "grandparents" for teenage parents.
    d. being eased out of their jobs because they are perceived as feebleminded.

16. The increased number of adults living to an older age has led to active efforts to do all of the following EXCEPT:
    a. improve society's image of the elderly.
    b. obtain better living conditions for older adults.
    c. find suitable employment for older adults.
    d. gain political clout.

17. People over 65 make up about 12 percent of the population and account for _____ percent of the total health-care bill in the United States.
    a. about 12
    b. over 30
    c. over 40
    d. over 50

18. One special concern over the current medical system is that it is _____ oriented, while most elderly health problems are _____.
    a. care/chronic
    b. care/acute
    c. cure/chronic
    d. cure/acute

19. Due to the increase in chronic illnesses as people age, many older people are cared for in their homes. This necessitates:
    a. more Medicare assistance.
    b. cooperation among health-care professionals, patients, and family members.
    c. that doctors return to the practice of making house calls.
    d. improved facilities for placing elders so their adult children can live their lives.

20. Problems with eldercare include all of the following EXCEPT:
    a. age of the persons giving the care.
    b. the increasing number of women in the job market.
    c. lack of cooperation from medical professionals.
    d. costs.

21. A policy issue that focuses on the greater amount of resources received by the elderly compared to those received by younger adults is referred to as:
    a. generational inequity.
    b. eldercare.
    c. ageism.
    d. role preoccupation.

22. In stating that it is a disgrace to an affluent society such as ours that we have such large numbers of poor children, Bernice Neugarten (1988) stresses:
    a. we must reassess the sums of money going to the elderly, and reallocate some of those funds to children.
    b. the only way to meet the needs of both our youth and our elders is to reallocate funds from other social programs.
    c. the elderly have already lived their lives; it is the children who need the funds to have a better chance to succeed.
    d. the problem should not be viewed as one of generational equity, but a shortcoming in our economic and social policies.

23. Since the early 1980s, the percentage of older persons living in poverty has:
    a. increased slightly.
    b. increased dramatically.
    c. decreased dramatically.
    d. remained consistent.

24. The average income of retired Americans is:
    a. approximately 80 percent of what they earned at the time they retired.
    b. about half of what they earned when they were fully employed.
    c. greater than what they earned while working once we consider they have fewer work-related expenses such as meals, work clothes, etc.
    d. about the same as what they earned while working once we consider they have fewer work-related expenses such as meals, work clothes, etc.

25. Sixty-year-old Anna is a widowed African American woman living alone. If she is typical of single, elderly African-American females in the United States, it is most likely that Anna is:
    a. emotionally depressed.
    b. among the physically disabled.
    c. poor.
    d. more in control of her life.

26. Within the United States, which of the following groups of older people would be the poorest?
    a. African American females
    b. Latina females
    c. Asian American females
    d. ethnic American males who must depend on churches for assistance

27. The majority of elderly adults prefer to live:
    a. alone or with spouses.
    b. with an adult child or other relative.
    c. in a retirement community.
    d. in the Sunbelt.

28. Retirement seems to lead to greatest changes in a:
    a. "traditional" family with a working male and a homemaking female.
    b. family where both spouses work and retire at the same time.
    c. family in which both spouses work, but retire at different times.
    d. single-parent household.

29. The traditional older couple adjusts best to retirement when:
    a. the husband gets a part-time job.
    b. the wife gets a part-time job.
    c. both members of the couple become more expressive.
    d. both members of the couple become more independent.

30. Regarding their relationship with grandchildren, most grandparents report that:
    a. grandchildren these days show little respect for their elders.
    b. grandfathers are more satisfied than grandmothers.
    c. older grandparents, compared with younger grandparents, are more likely to be strict with their grandchildren.
    d. grandparenting is less difficult than parenting.

31. Which of the following facts about grandparents is TRUE?
    a. Grandfathers are more satisfied with the grandparenting role than grandmothers.
    b. Younger grandparents are less willing to care for grandchildren than older grandparents.
    c. Paternal grandparents spend less time with their grandchildren than maternal grandparents.
    d. About 50 percent of grandparents say they are happy with their relationship with their grandchildren.

32. In the _____ style of grandparenting, according to Neugarten and Weinstein (1964), grandchildren are a source of leisure activity, and mutual satisfaction is emphasized.
    a. formal
    b. fun-seeking
    c. distant figure
    d. nurturant

33. Which child is most likely to be raised by a single grandmother?
    a. Aisha, who is African American
    b. Greg, who is White
    c. Kim, who is Korean
    d. Maria, who is Latina

34. Laura, an elderly woman, will be most content if she:
    a. continues to make new friends.
    b. has at least one close person in her network.
    c. has several close people in her network.
    d. remarries after her divorce.

35. All of the following support systems help elderly ethnic minority individuals survive in the dominant White world EXCEPT:
    a. families.
    b. income from Social Security.
    c. churches.
    d. neighbors.

36. Who is the best example of the concept of "triple jeopardy"?
   a. Maximilian, who is 75 years old, White, and male
   b. Mattia, who is 75 years old, African American, and female
   c. Carlos, who is 15 years old, Latino, and male
   d. Yeh, who is 15 years old, Asian, and female

37. Eula is typical of elderly African American women in cities. Consequently, we would expect her to value all of the following EXCEPT:
   a. solitude.
   b. her family.
   c. the American work ethic.
   d. her religion.

38. Which 72-year-old has a characteristic that is NOT typically associated with elevating the status of elderly individuals within a culture?
   a. Uri, who like most people in his country, will live to be about 90
   b. Henry, who controls his family's wealth
   c. Haing, who possesses information valuable to the welfare of his country
   d. James, who is given promotions and more authority in his company based on performance and time on the job

39. The concept of _____ is often used to describe perceived control over the environment and the ability to produce positive outcomes.
   a. self-esteem
   b. self-control
   c. self-efficacy
   d. self-satisfaction

Self-Test B: Matching

Match the following persons with the statement or theory that most closely reflects their perspective:

1. Bernice Neugarten
2. Laura Carstensen
3. Erik Erikson
4. Robert Peck
5. Robert Butler
6. Paul Baltes
7. Lillian Troll
8. Mary Rose Oakar

a. Being embedded in a family is a positive aspect of life for older adults
b. Believes late adulthood is characterized by integrity versus despair
c. The top priority for middle-aged women should be economic security
d. Suggests thinking what a positive spirit of aging would mean to America
e. Said adults who have several close people in their network seem content
f. Believes older adults must pursue a set of value activities
g. Believes life review is set in motion by looking forward to death
h. Successful aging is related to selection, optimization, & compensation

Essay Questions

1. Your local senior citizens center has asked you to talk to its patrons about patterns of aging and how to "stay young longer." Of special concern are issues of ageism, retirement, relationships, and health. What would you tell them?

2. The City Council in your city has approached you because the population seems to be split between the young adults and the old adults. There is a concern that problems may arise as limited resources must be allocated that would affect each of these groups. What issues would you tell them to consider, and how would you suggest the matter be resolved?

Scramblers

Unscramble the following people or terms, then describe what they are known for (people) or define them (terms):

1. EBROTR CEPK

_____

2. URALA TSENRSAENC

_____

3. GERTINTYI SRUESV DPEAISR

_____

4. DOBY NECDESNNACRTE VSEURS ODBY NPORIETOACPCU

_____

5. TDNISEMEGEAGN YTRHOE

_____

6. VITITCAY OEHRYT

_____

7. EMOOTICINOOSLA CTIEVLIETSY ETRHOY

_____

8. SIEGMA

_____

9. RCEARDELE

_____

10. GLEANNEORIAT YITNIEUQ

_____

Key to Self-Test A

1.	a	LO 1	14.	b	LO 4	27.	a	LO 7
2.	d	LO 1	15.	c	LO 4	28.	a	LO 8
3.	d	LO 1	16.	c	LO 5	29.	c	LO 8
4.	a	LO 2	17.	b	LO 5	30.	d	LO 9
5.	a	LO 3	18.	c	LO 5	31.	c	LO 9
6.	d	LO 3	19.	b	LO 5	32.	b	LO 9
7.	c	LO 3	20.	c	LO 5	33.	a	LO 9
8.	d	LO 3	21.	a	LO 5	34.	c	LO 10
9.	a	LO 3	22.	d	LO 5	35.	b	LO 11
10.	b	LO 3	23.	d	LO 6	36.	b	LO 12
11.	a	LO 3	24.	b	LO 6	37.	a	LO 12
12.	c	LO 3	25.	c	LO 6	38.	a	LO 13
13.	d	LO 3	26.	a	LO 6	39.	c	LO 14

Key to Self-Test B

1.	d		5.	g
2.	e		6.	h
3.	b		7.	a
4.	f		8.	c

Key to Essay Questions

1. You should address the five theories of aging discussed in this chapter (i.e., Erikson's, disengagement, activity, socioemotional selectivity, and selective optimization with compensation), noting that older adults' active participation in society is beneficial; discuss ageism, its causes and consequences, and efforts to improve the status of the elderly, but don't neglect the issue of generational inequity; discuss the impact that health, income, gender, culture, and relationships have on an elderly person's well-being; then address the personality factors noted by Erikson and Peck. It would be appropriate for you to discuss the importance of a life review and the strategies presented for successful aging (e.g., Baltes' selective optimization with compensation model). Be sure to underscore the importance of relationships and support systems in maintaining optimum life satisfaction and well-being.

2. Perhaps the most important issue to discuss here is generational inequity—what it is, how it came to be, and what are its consequences; then present what Neugarten says about the problem (i.e., the real issue is one of shortcomings of our broad economic and social policies). Looking at the cultural factors associated with whether the elderly are accorded a position of high status, suggest how the younger and older people can work together for the common good of the whole community.

Key to Scramblers

1. Robert Peck: Believes older adults must pursue a set of value activities
2. Laura Carstensen: Believes adults who have several close people in their network seem content
3. Integrity versus despair: Reflect on the past, see it as a positive review or conclude life was not well spent
4. Body transcendence versus body preoccupation: Elderly cope with declining physical well-being
5. Disengagement theory: To cope effectively, older adults should gradually withdraw from society
6. Activity theory: The more active older adults are, the more likely they are to be satisfied with life
7. Socioemotional selectivity theory: Older adults become more selective about their social networks
8. Ageism: Prejudice against other people because of their age, especially prejudice against older adults
9. Eldercare: Physical & emotional caretaking for older members of the family
10. Generational inequity: An aging society being unfair to younger members as the elderly pile up advantages

Research Project 1: Dealing with Diversity

As pointed out throughout this chapter, and elsewhere throughout the text, being female, ethnic, and old places women at high risk for all of the problems associated with poverty and aging. Consider the various factors that may put these women at risk (e.g., low educational level, prejudice) and the potential consequences that each may have (e.g., inability to access services); then consider the strengths that have been noted that these women often have (e.g., family support) and the consequences that these may have (e.g., caregiving support). (You should gather ideas from throughout the entire chapter, especially the Sociocultural Worlds of Development box; also use your own observations and ideas.) Chart these factors and consequences, then answer the questions that follow:

Risk Factors	Potential Consequences
Women's Role Is Unimportant	
Low Income	

Strengths	Potential Consequences
Family Support	
Religious/Spiritual	

1. What did you notice about the risk factors and their potential consequences?
2. What did you notice about the strengths and their potential consequences?
3. What patterns did you notice when comparing these risk factors and strengths and the information discussed in this chapter?
4. Were these patterns consistent with what you might expect from the research described? Explain your response.
5. What might you conclude about the issues that older women (particularly minority women) face based on what you have observed?
6. Based on your observations here, what type of interventions (individual, community, federal, etc.) would you suggest for alleviating the problem of double- and/or triple-jeopardy that these women experience?

Research Project 2: Issues in the Media

In Chapter 1 it was suggested that you review the learning objectives for that chapter and notice the issues that Santrock discusses. Do it again for this chapter, and then monitor the media (newspapers, talk/news radio, television) for a week and keep track of when and in what context these issues are raised. Calculate how often each specific issue is discussed and note which issue was raised most often, how it was presented (did you notice biased reporting, was it presented in terms of the life-span perspective, was it fully covered, etc.), and what additional information you would need to understand the issue (or story presented in the media) better. Throughout the life span we are affected by stereotypes of the different age groups. Sometimes these stereotypes might be rather benign, but often they are the basis of discrimination, mistrust, and a whole host of other problems. This is especially true for two age groups: adolescence and older adulthood. To assess the extent of the stereotypes and myths that are perpetrated by the media, for one week keep a record of the television shows you watch and the print media (newspapers, magazines, books, etc.) that you read.

1. Describe the percentage of elderly people included in these media presentations, whether they play a major role or merely have supporting or minor roles, the traits used to characterize each, etc.
2. Describe examples of characteristics that demonstrate whether they are portrayed in a positive or negative manner, whether these traits are stereotypical, and how their portrayal can be either beneficial or detrimental to the well-being of the elderly as a group.
3. What ethnic and gender differences did you notice and how did they affect the portrayal of the elderly?
4. What social policy issues were raised, and how were they handled?
5. Discuss your findings in class.

Personal Application Project 1: Reflecting on What You Learned

Consider what you read in Chapter 20, then answer the following questions:

1. What information in this chapter did you already know?
2. How can/do you use that information in your own life?
3. What information in this chapter was totally new to you?
4. How can you use that new information in your own life?
5. What information in this chapter was different from what you previously believed?
6. How was this information different?
7. How do you account for the differences between what you believed and what you learned in the chapter?
8. What is the most important thing you learned from reading this chapter?

Personal Application Project 2: Engaging in a Life Review

Refer to the discussion in Chapter 21 of Life Reviews then, using the chart below, conduct your own life review (even if you have not reached middle age). You may also wish to interview an older adult using the same questions that you ask yourself. Consider every aspect of your life using questions such as, "What was most important about your childhood?" "What major events have changed your family?" "What aspects of your family life are you most and least satisfied with right now?" "How would you like to see your family life in the future, and what can you do to bring it there?" "How did you get into the work you are currently in?" (Or, if retired, "How did you get into the work you did over your lifetime?") "How far along have you progressed with respect to your personal goals?" "What can you do to progress along as you have wished?" "Do you need to adjust your goals for the future?" Add other questions concerning your education plans, travel, financial security, religious/spiritual side, and don't forget about the fun stuff.

Life Review Chart				
Aspects of Life	**Past**	**Present**	**Future**	**What I Need to Change**
Family				
Friends				
Education				
Career				
Travel				
Financial Security				
Religious/Spiritual				
Fun & Leisure				
Other				

1. What have you learned about yourself, your goals, and how you have been achieving your goals from reviewing your life so far?
2. How can looking at your life help you understand how things are going, how they got there, and how you can get where you want to go?
3. Is there another method that would be more helpful to you in looking at who you are, where you've been, where you're at right now, and where you want to be in the future? Explain, then use that approach.
4. What has been the most useful outcome of doing a life review?
5. If you interviewed an older adult, what did you learn about that person's goals and whether those goals have been achieved?
6. What might you conclude about development in late adulthood based on your interview and the life review of the older adult? How consistent is this information with what you have learned from the text?

Internet Projects

Check out the McGraw-Hill web site for this text (http://www.mhhe.com/santrockld8). You'll find numerous activities there, in particular various quizzes, flash cards of key terms, and a challenging and fun crossword puzzle. Please note that all website addresses in this Study Guide have been checked and are correct at the time of publication, however, websites may be discontinued or addresses may change so when you search a given site it may no longer be viable. If that occurs, I apologize for the inconvenience, and would appreciate you notifying me so I could make appropriate revisions in future editions of this Study Guide.

Internet Project 1: Theories of Aging

Go to the APA site at http://www.apa.org, then click on the "Public" section and, in the "Search APA & other sites (full text)" box do a search for "Theories of aging." How many entries are there? Are they all specific to the theories of aging discussed in Chapter 20? How many of the articles deal directly with older adults (no, you don't really have to go through **all** of them–when I checked this out there were over 800!)? What types of papers are included (e.g., journal articles dealing with research, reports at symposia, policy papers)? What are the different topics that are covered? As you browse through the different titles (and, hopefully, some of the articles), did you come away with a more positive or more negative view of what it is to be growing older? How did this search add to what you had already learned from reading the chapter?

Internet Project 2: Affecting Social Policy — American Association for Retired Persons (AARP)

The AARP (American Association for Retired Persons) is probably the strongest political voice for older adults in the United States. The website, located at http://www.aarp.com offers such an extensively wide range of information for and about persons over 50 that it is difficult to focus on just one—but let's try. Type "successful aging" into the search box. How many documents came up (when I did this, there were 1133 that matched my query). What is the first document you see (in my search it dealt with volunteering, something I found extremely interesting in terms of successful aging)? As you browse through the document titles, what types of articles do you notice and how do you think they relate to the material in our text? What questions come to mind as you consider these articles in the context of successful aging? Based on what you read in this array of documents, what do you conclude about successful aging in general, and your own plan for ensuring the best possible later years you can have?

Note that there are many options to explore at this site. Please sample at least some of them (e.g., computers & technology, health & wellness, legislative issues, leisure & fun, life transitions, money & work, research & reference, and the volunteer experience). Doing so can help you in terms of your studies, your future career plans, and your own well-being in the later years.

Other Relevant Sites on the Internet

APS site
http://www.psychologicalscience.org/

CBS Healthwatch
http://healthwatch.medscape.com/medscape/p/gcommunity/ghome.asp provides information on a wide range of health topics, as well as many other resources, such as a drug directory, self-care and first aid tips, and a medical dictionary.

Cooper Wellness

http://www.cooperwellness.com is the website of Dr. Kenneth Cooper, who notes "It is easier to maintain good health through proper exercise, diet, and emotional balance than to regain it once it is lost."

Intelihealth

http://www.intelihealth.com/IH/ihtIH offers health information from a variety of sources, including Harvard Medical School. Feel free to search the site for any of the topics covered in this chapter (and others).

The Mayo Clinic

http://www.mayoclinic.com offers information (research, news articles, answers to your questions, etc.) on diseases as well as on healthy living. An important section is "Take Charge of Your Health," which provides several links to pages aimed at promoting personal responsibility for our own healthy lives.

ThirdAge

http://www.thirdage.com is a forum for adults that presents a wide range of topics for the lay person.

Web MD

http://www.webmd.com offers a wide variety of information for the medical profession and for consumers.

Chapter 21: Death and Grieving

Learning Objectives

1. Discuss the definition of death and how it has changed.
2. Explain the living will and the advanced directive.
3. Distinguish between the different types of euthanasia.
4. Discuss current available care for the dying, and why better care is needed.
5. Elaborate on the changing historical circumstances regarding death.
6. Discuss how death is viewed in other cultures compared to the United States.
7. Describe the common causes of and expectations about death at different points in the life span.
8. Discuss the attitudes toward death that children, adolescents, and adults have.
9. Describe Kübler-Ross' five-stage theory of dying, and its criticisms.
10. Explain how perceived control and denial play a role for those who face death.
11. Discuss the contexts in which people die.
12. Describe ways to communicate with a dying person.
13. Explain the dimensions of grieving, elaborating on how different cultures grieve and how grieving can be used to make sense of the world.
14. Discuss how losing a partner impacts the individual.
15. Elaborate on forms of mourning and the meaning of the funeral.
16. Identify the mourning traditions of the Amish and the traditional Jews.

Chapter Outline

DEFINING DEATH AND LIFE/DEATH ISSUES
    Issues in Determining Death
    Decisions Regarding Life, Death, and Health Care
        Natural Death Act and Advanced Directive
        Euthanasia
        Better Care for Dying Individuals
DEATH AND SOCIOHISTORICAL, CULTURAL CONTEXTS
    Changing Historical Circumstances
    Death in Different Cultures
A DEVELOPMENTAL PERSPECTIVE ON DEATH
    Causes of Death and Expectations about Death
    Attitudes Toward Death at Different Points in the Life Span
        Childhood
        Adolescence
        Adulthood
FACING ONE'S OWN DEATH
    Kübler-Ross' Stages of Dying
    Perceived Control and Denial
    The Contexts in Which People Die
COPING WITH THE DEATH OF SOMEONE ELSE
    Communicating with a Dying Person
    Grieving
        Dimensions
        Cultural Diversity

Making Sense of the World
Losing a Life Partner
Forms of Mourning and the Funeral

Self-Test A: Multiple Choice

1. Twenty-five years ago, all of the following were clear signs of death EXCEPT:
   a. lack of breathing.
   b. rigor mortis.
   c. brain death.
   d. nonexistent blood pressure.

2. Elvira was brought into the hospital after a car accident. She has had a flat EEG for over 20 minutes and the doctors have informed her parents that there is no longer any electrical activity in her brain, and that she is brain dead. The doctors have given a(n)_____ definition of death.
   a. psychological
   b. philosophical
   c. neurological
   d. anatomical

3. Dylan watched his father suffer for a year before dying of cancer. Now Dylan wants to be sure that he retains control over any decisions made concerning how, when, and under what circumstances life-sustaining treatments will be used or withheld in the case of his own final illness. To ensure this, Dylan should prepare a:
   a. living trust.
   b. living will.
   c. last will and testament.
   d. power of attorney.

4. Currently, _____ states in the United States have accepted advanced directives reflecting an individual's wishes concerning life-sustaining procedures when death is imminent.
   a. no
   b. 25
   c. 48
   d. 50

5. Active euthanasia is:
   a. allowing the patients, if they so choose, to self-administer a lethal dose of drug.
   b. letting the patient die naturally.
   c. the intentional administration of a lethal drug dose by medical personnel to the dying patient.
   d. allowing the dying patient to decide when painkilling drugs should be administered.

6. Most people tend to find fewer ethical problems with _____ euthanasia, especially where it involves older, terminally ill individuals.
   a. involuntary
   b. active
   c. passive
   d. assisted

7. The Institute of Medicine (1997) reported that death in America is:
   a. most often an easy process.
   b. often lonely, prolonged, and painful.
   c. usually made much easier through use of medication.
   d. increasingly a family-based event.

8. Which of the following is NOT typical of hospice care?
   a. make every effort to prolong life.
   b. bring pain under control.
   c. help dying patients face death in a psychologically healthy way.
   d. include the dying individual's family.

9. In the United States, about _____ percent of all deaths occur in institutions or hospitals.
   a. 20
   b. 50
   c. 80
   d. 90

10. The view of most societies is that death is:
   a. the end of existence.
   b. a biological end to the body, but the spirit lives on.
   c. a time to celebrate the person's life.
   d. a terrifying experience.

11. Denial of death in the United States takes all of the following forms EXCEPT:
   a. use of phrases like "passing on."
   b. the never-ending search for a fountain of youth.
   c. the emphasis on human suffering rather than on prolonging life.
   d. rejection of the elderly.

12. One day Jennifer gets a call from her sister who informs Jennifer that her niece has died from sudden infant death syndrome (SIDS). As a physician, Jennifer realizes that while the cause of SIDS remains unknown, her niece actually died because:
   a. she had a heart attack
   b. she stopped breathing.
   c. she had a massive cerebrovascular accident.
   d. her immune system failed.

13. Death in childhood is most often the result of:
   a. accidents or illness.
   b. SIDS.
   c. childhood diseases.
   d. cancer.

14. Death in adolescence is most likely to occur from any of the following EXCEPT:
   a. suicide.
   b. motor vehicle accidents.
   c. homicide.
   d. cancer.

15. Older adults are more likely to die of:
   a. chronic disease.
   b. accidents.
   c. suicide.
   d. homicide.

16. Most preschool-aged children are not upset by seeing a dead animal. The most likely reason is that:
   a. the dead animal is not a pet and therefore they have not become attached to it.
   b. they have often seen dead animals and heard of death in stories and on TV.
   c. they have had little experience with death; therefore they have not learned to fear it.
   d. they believe the dead can be made alive again.

17. An individual who believes that people die because they were bad or because they wanted to die is most likely in the _____ period of development.
   a. infancy
   b. early childhood
   c. middle or late childhood
   d. adolescent

18. The individual who glosses over death and kids about it, but can also describe it in terms of darkness and nothingness, is most likely in the _____ period of development.
   a. middle childhood
   b. late childhood
   c. adolescent
   d. early adulthood

19. The order of the stages of dying as proposed by Elisabeth Kübler-Ross are:
   a. denial, anger, bargaining, acceptance, depression.
   b. anger, denial, bargaining, depression, acceptance.
   c. denial, anger, bargaining, depression, acceptance.
   d. anger, bargaining, acceptance, depression, denial.

20. Denial of death comes in all of the following forms EXCEPT:
    a. denying the facts.
    b. denying the implications of disease.
    c. denying the finality of death.
    d. denying the inevitability of death.

21. During which stage of death is a person most likely to request to be alone?
    a. denial
    b. bargaining
    c. depression
    d. acceptance

22. When a terminally ill patient becomes depressed, others should:
    a. attempt to cheer up the patient.
    b. talk about anything other than death.
    c. tell the medical staff about it.
    d. accept the depression as normal.

23. A major criticism of Kübler-Ross' stages of dying is that they:
    a. don't actually form an invariant sequence.
    b. only apply to females.
    c. last much longer than she thought.
    d. only explain the pattern found in older adults.

24. After learning she has terminal cancer, Ivana joins a wellness group and begins taking control of as many aspects of her life as she can, believing this will cause her cancer to go into remission. Based on the research, we might expect that Ivana will:
    a. die more quickly.
    b. become more alert and cheerful.
    c. become depressed if this does not work.
    d. become more serious and compulsive.

25. John's mother recently died. He is experiencing emotional blunting, numbness, disbelief, and outbursts of panic. He is exhibiting which dimension of grief?
    a. immediate reaction
    b. pining
    c. separation anxiety
    d. despair and sadness

26. A major problem with long-term grief is the potential for:
    a. depression and suicide.
    b. keeping one's feelings locked away.
    c. sadness turning to uncontrollable rage.
    d. internalization of feelings that leads to the breakdown of the immune system.

27. Cross-cultural research suggests that healthy grieving involves:
    a. breaking bonds with the deceased.
    b. survivors returning to their autonomous lifestyles.
    c. forgetting the deceased as quickly as possible.
    d. a wide range of patterns, with no one ideal way to grieve.

28. In Bali, the bereaved are encouraged to:
    a. dwell at length on their grief.
    b. carry on much as before the death of the loved one.
    c. laugh and be joyful.
    d. maintain ties with the deceased.

29. When mourners repeatedly go over all of the events that led up to the death, they are:
    a. trying to make sense of their world.
    b. creating a potentially harmful situation for their recovery.
    c. setting themselves up for continuing depression.
    d. trying to escape blame for the loved one's death.

30. Research has found all of the following traits to be common for widowed women EXCEPT being:
    a. lonely.
    b. likely to remarry.
    c. poor.
    d. at risk for health problems.

31. Approximately _____ percent of corpses around the world are disposed of by burial.
    a. 20
    b. 40
    c. 60
    d. 80

32. One way to avoid the potential exploitation that may occur in connection with the high cost of funeral expenses is to:
    a. purchase your own funeral arrangements in advance.
    b. put more legal restrictions on the funeral directors and funeral homes.
    c. establish state-run funeral parlors.
    d. prohibit embalming and place limits on funeral costs.

33. Which practice is NOT commonly associated with Amish mourning?
    a. holding the funeral ceremony in a barn in warmer months
    b. a horse and buggy "hearse"
    c. a deceased body dressed in white
    d. support for bereaved family members

34. Chanah and her family are home mourning the death of Chanah's father, Moshe, who has just been buried. During this 7-day period, visitors will come join Chanah and her family to help them deal with feelings of guilt. This period of mourning is referred to as:
    a. aninut.
    b. avelut.
    c. shivah.
    d. sheloshim.

Self-Test B: Matching

Match the following persons with the statement or theory that most closely reflects their perspective:

1. Jack Kevorkian
2. Robert Kastenbaum
3. Elisabeth Kübler-Ross
4. Sarah Wheeler

a. Proposed a five-stage process of death and dying
b. Concerned with strategies nurses can use to help families cope with loss
c. The "suicide doctor" who assists terminally ill patients in ending their lives
d. Hospice care provides important context for humanizing a dying person's life

Essay Questions

1. A good friend has approached you with a difficult decision—his father is in the last stages of a terminal illness and the medication he is on is not controlling the excruciating pain he experiences. Your friend tells you that his father has asked for help in dying, and your friend is torn between the anguish of watching his father suffer and his own moral reluctance to help his father die. He asks for your help in deciding what he should do. Take a totally objective perspective on this, based on what you have read in the chapter on euthanasia—discuss under what circumstances a person in the medical profession might consider terminating a patient's life, and when it would not be appropriate to do so. Include in your answer a discussion of when a person is considered "dead" from a clinical perspective, and how you might advise your friend under those circumstances. Finally, take a stand on the issue of euthanasia and support your position.

2. You have just learned from your mother that your favorite aunt is dying. Having no children of her own she has always been extremely close to you, even more so than any of her other nieces or nephews, although she considers all of you to be like her own children. Your mother says the doctor, a young oncologist, has not yet told your aunt of her diagnosis, wanting to discuss it with the family first. To achieve the best possible outcome for your aunt and for the family who love her, what should be done? Should she be told? If so, why; if not, why not? How should the rest of the family be told? How should family members deal with her and with each other? How would you expect your aunt and other members

of the family to react during and after her death? Would you recommend hospice care? Explain the reasons for your answer.

Scramblers

Unscramble the following people or terms, then describe what they are known for (people) or define them (terms):

1. CAJK NKAEIVKOR

_____

2. ERBOTR NEBTASUAMK

_____

3. NBIRA HDTEA

_____

4. AEIUSTAHNA

_____

5. EHCOISP

_____

6. LADEIN NDA NIOSIOTAL

_____

7. GNERA

_____

8. BGANRIGNAI

_____

9. TPEANCCAEC

_____

10. FRIEG

_____

Key to Self-Test A

1.	c	LO 1	13.	a	LO 7	25.	a	LO 13
2.	c	LO 1	14.	d	LO 7	26.	a	LO 13
3.	b	LO 2	15.	a	LO 7	27.	d	LO 13
4.	d	LO 2	16.	d	LO 8	28.	c	LO 13
5.	c	LO 3	17.	b	LO 8	29.	a	LO 13
6.	c	LO 3	18.	c	LO 8	30.	b	LO 14
7.	b	LO 4	19.	c	LO 9	31.	d	LO 15
8.	a	LO 4	20.	c	LO 9	32.	a	LO 15
9.	c	LO 4	21.	c	LO 9	33.	b	LO 16
10.	b	LO 6	22.	d	LO 9	34.	c	LO 16
11.	c	LO 6	23.	a	LO 9			
12.	b	LO 7	24.	b	LO 10			

Key to Self-Test B

1. c
2. d
3. a
4. b

Key to Essay Questions

1. Whatever your personal biases for or against euthanasia, you will need to put them aside to answer this question. Explain the terms "euthanasia," "passive euthanasia," and "active euthanasia," then explain when they are used. Address the issues of assisted suicide and Dr. Kevorkian—looking at such things as the patient's suffering, moral/ethical concerns (both sides of that issue), and legal concerns; also to be considered here is the financial, physical, and emotional drain on the family as well as their feelings about the dying patient. Then it is important to look at exactly what constitutes death—is it the cessation of breathing, brain function, etc., and discuss the issues involved in brain death. After addressing all of these issues, you may explore your own personal feelings on the subject.

2. Here it would be important to discuss the reasons psychologists suggest it is best to tell a terminal patient of his or her impending death (e.g., putting affairs in order, making decisions such as advanced directives regarding his or her own life and death, etc.); it is also important to be honest with other family members, taking their age into account in terms of how they are told. Family members should be encouraged to talk to each other and to the dying person, noting the many suggestions throughout the chapter on how to communicate with someone who is dying. Then, to predict how your aunt and other family members will react, you will need to discuss Kübler-Ross' stages of dying, noting the limitations of that theory and that there is no one right way to die. Explore the notion of hospice care—what it does and does not offer—taking into consideration your aunt's own wishes. It would also be important to discuss the issue of a living will and preparing a durable power of attorney to ensure that your aunt's wishes will be carried out.

Key to Scramblers

1. Jack Kevorkian: The "suicide doctor" who assists terminally ill patients end their lives
2. Robert Kastenbaum: Hospice care provides an important context for humanizing a dying person's life
3. Brain death: Neurological definition of death; all electrical activity of brain has ceased for a period of time
4. Euthanasia: Painlessly ending the lives of persons suffering from incurable diseases or severe disabilities
5. Hospice: Program committed to making the end of life as free from pain, anxiety, depression as possible
6. Denial and isolation: Stage of dying in which the dying person denies that he/she is really going to die
7. Anger: Stage of dying in which the dying person's denial gives way to anger, rage, resentment, envy
8. Bargaining: Stage of dying in which the dying person develops the hope that death can be postponed
9. Acceptance: Stage in which dying person comes to accept the certainty of his/her death
10. Grief: Emotional numbness, disbelief, despair, sadness, loneliness accompanying loss of a loved one

Research Project 1: Observing Developmental Periods

Contact a local hospital, senior citizen center, community center, hospice, or other facility that sponsors support groups for terminally ill patients and their families to find one that will allow you to sit in on a group meeting and talk to group members (some will, some won't—you'll have to check them out). Learn about their experiences and observe their patterns of dealing with their potential or actual loss; more importantly, observe how they have come to deal with and accept the loss—the strategies they use, the types of support systems they have, etc.

On the basis of your participation and observations, answer the following questions:

1. What similarities did you notice between the terminally ill and their loved ones?
2. What differences did you notice between the terminally ill and their loved ones?
3. Were there differences in the way people dealt with these issues based on gender, age, ethnic or cultural background, marital status, support system, or religious orientation? Explain these differences and what you conclude about how each of these variables affected the individuals' ability to cope with loss.
4. What patterns did you notice for dealing with loss in terms of the material discussed in this chapter?
5. Were your observations consistent with what you might expect from the research described? Explain your response.
6. What might you conclude about coping with one's own death or the death of a loved one based on your observations?

Research Project 2: Helping Others Deal with Death, Dying, and Grief

Dying is a personal experience not only for the terminally ill individual, but for surviving family and friends. Taking account of individual differences (whether based on personality/temperament, cultural background, gender, age of the dying person, age of mourners, etc.), and drawing on the material presented in this chapter, design an intervention that will help the person who is dying as well as family and friends to deal with the impending death and, afterwards, for the survivors to deal with their grief. Be sure to remember that even people from the same family may deal with their grief differently—there is no one "right way" to do it. When you have designed your program, present it to a local hospice, hospital, religious center, or other appropriate organization for feedback and implementation. What types of interventions would you use? How do your strategies differ, depending on the different variable involved? Report what you learn about using such a program—did you get constructive feedback on how to improve it? Was your intervention well received? If it was utilized, what types of comments did you get in terms of how helpful it was for those involved? How did you feel about creating the program and implementing it?

A variation on this project might be specifically to target children—both in terms of children who are terminally ill as well as children who have experienced the loss of a loved one. How would your intervention differ for them, as opposed to dealing with adults? What types of strategies would you use for children that you might not use for adults? Would it be easier or more difficult to work with children? Explain.

Having designed and implemented (or attempted to implement) your death and dying/grief intervention(s), answer the following questions:

1. What similarities did you notice between the terminally ill and their loved ones in the way they responded to the intervention?
2. What differences did you notice between the terminally ill and their loved ones in the way they responded to the intervention?
3. Were there differences in the way people dealt with these issues based on gender, age, ethnic or cultural background, marital status, support system, or religious orientation? Explain these differences and what you conclude about how each of these variables affected the individuals' ability to cope with loss.
4. What patterns did you notice for dealing with loss in terms of the material discussed in this chapter?
5. Were your observations consistent with what you might expect from the research described in the text? Explain.
6. What might you conclude about coping with one's own death or the death of a loved one based on your observations?

Personal Application Project 1: Reflecting on What You Learned

Consider what you read in Chapter 21, then answer the following questions:

1. What information in this chapter did you already know?
2. How can/do you use that information in your own life?
3. What information in this chapter was totally new to you?
4. How can you use that new information in your own life?
5. What information in this chapter was different from what you previously believed?
6. How was this information different?
7. How do you account for the differences between what you believed and what you learned in the chapter?
8. What is the most important thing you learned from reading this chapter?

Personal Application Project 2: Pictorial Life Review

In Chapter 20 of this Study Guide, a Research Project addressed the topic of life reviews. That project is repeated here with some revisions. Think about your own life and ask yourself about your life using the questions suggested, e.g., "What was most important about your childhood?" "What major events have changed your family?" "What aspects of your family life are you most and least satisfied with right now?" "How would you like to see your family life in the future, and what can you do to bring it there?" "How did you get into the work you are currently in?" "How far along have you progressed with respect to your personal goals?" "What can you do to progress along as you have wished?" "Do you need to adjust your goals for the future?" Add any other questions concerning education, travel, financial security, personal relationships, your religious/spiritual side, leisure, or other topics that you consider important or relevant.

After considering all of the issues that you feel are relevant to your life review, present those ideas pictorially. You may draw or paint your life or a self-portrait containing the answers to your questions, put together a collage, or do any other type of visual project that will assist you in seeing your own life in answer to the questions you have asked. After completing the visual project, answer the questions that follow:

1. What did you learn about your goals and whether those goals have been achieved?
2. How can looking at your life help you to understand how things are going, how you got there, and how you can get where you want to go?
3. Is there another method that would be more helpful for looking at these issues? Explain; then use that approach.
4. What has been the most useful outcome for you in doing a life review?
5. What has been the most harmful outcome for you in doing a life review?
6. Butler (1996) noted that "as the past marches in review, the older adult surveys it, observes it, and reflects on it." Did you find this to be so in evaluating your life review? Explain.
7. Butler (1996) also noted that "this reorganization of the past may provide a more valid picture for the individual, providing new and significant meaning to . . . life. It may also help prepare the individual for death, in the process, reducing fear." Did you find this to be so in evaluating your life review? Explain.
8. What might you conclude about development in late adulthood based on your life review?

Internet Projects

Check out the McGraw-Hill web site for this text (http://www.mhhe.com/santrockld8). You'll find numerous activities there, in particular various quizzes, flash cards of key terms, and a challenging and fun crossword puzzle. Please note that all website addresses in this Study Guide have been checked and are correct at the time of publication, however, websites may be discontinued or addresses may change so when you search a given site it may no longer be viable. If that occurs, I apologize for the inconvenience, and would appreciate you notifying me so I could make appropriate revisions in future editions of this Study Guide.

Internet Project 1: Advanced Directives

There are many sites on the Internet where you can find information about advanced directives. Perhaps two of the best resources are the American Bar Association (ABA) and the American Medical Association (AMA). The ABA's web address is: http://www.abanet.org, and I'll "warn" you up front that to get the in-depth advice may take several steps. Try starting with http://www.abanet.org/publiced/practical/healthcare_directives.html. If you don't get a page that says "Division for Public Education—Health Care Advance Directives," it's worth going the longer route: Go to the ABA home page (http://www.abanet.org), then from the menu on the left select "General Public Resources," which will produce a drop-down menu. Select "Public Education." When you get to that page, click on the "Practical Law" link in the "Highlights for consumers" section, which will take you to another page where you will link to "Law for Older Americans"; clicking on that link will take you to "Health Care Advance Directives." Finally, click on that link and it will provide you with a treasure chest of links explaining what advanced directives are, how to draft one, the laws concerning advance directives, etc.

The ABA also has another section with information about advanced directives—a series of articles written about them. You can find these by clicking on the search function at their home page and typing in "advance directives." That will take you to the list of articles.

The other exceptionally good source of information is an article at the AMA's website. You can find it by going to http://www.ama-assn.org/public/booklets/livgwill.htm. This is a booklet on advanced directives that you may print out.

One other good site is the AARP's website. Go to their home page (http://www.aarp.org) and do a search for "advance directives." My search turned up 181 matches for my query.

276

1. Before reviewing the information at these sites, had you prepared any advanced directives (note that you do not need to be elderly to do this—many young people unfortunately find themselves in this predicament)?
2. Has reviewing the information at these sites caused you to consider preparing such a document?
3. If you have chosen not to prepare advanced directives, what do you think is keeping you from doing so?

Internet Project 2: Grieving

The Association for Death Education and Counseling (http://www.adec.org) provides information about death education, bereavement counseling, and care of the dying, although much of the information is limited to members. There are many bulletin boards for special interest groups that cover a wide range of topics in this area (including the loss of pets). Especially helpful, though, is their list of web resources (http://www.adec.org/links/index.htm), which gives six pages worth of web addresses that provide helpful information for dealing with grief and bereavement. Of particular interest to me in my search were two articles in the "Electronic Forum" section that seemed to complement the Sociocultural Worlds of Development box in Chapter 21. One of the articles at the time of my search (which may still be available when you access the site) dealt with Jewish Burial and the Sudden Death of a Student in Zimbabwe. Review these articles, then compare grieving practices in both cultures.

1. How similar was the information about Jewish burial at the ADEC site with what you read in the text? Were there differences?
2. What similarities did you notice between the Jewish customs for grieving and those described in Zimbabwe?
3. What differences did you notice between the Jewish customs for grieving and those described in Zimbabwe?
4. What have you learned about grieving practices around the world that could help you deal with loss on a personal level?
5. What have you learned about grieving practices around the world that could help you as a health professional?
6. If you were to provide counseling to someone who is grieving the loss of a loved one, what aspects of these articles (and any information from the text) would you find most helpful?
7. From reading about grieving and helping individuals with the loss of a loved one, what have you learned specifically to avoid?
8. How can this information help you in your own personal life and in your professional life?

Other Relevant Sites on the Internet

APA site
http://www.apa.org

APS site
http://www.psychologicalscience.org/

American Association for Retired Persons (AARP)
http://www.aarp.org is the web site for AARP, an especially powerful organization that educates, lobbies, and provides services about and for persons age 50 and above.

Intelihealth

http://www.intelihealth.com/IH/ihtIH offers health information from a variety of sources, including Harvard Medical School. Feel free to search the site for any of the topics covered in this chapter (and others).

Medline Plus Health Information

http://medlineplus.nlm.nih.gov/medlineplus/bereavement.html offers many links to articles and organizations that deal with grief and bereavement for all age groups.

Web MD

http://www.webmd.com offers a wide variety of information for the medical profession and for consumers.